MEXICO PAPERS

VOLUME TWO

J.D. GILL, PH.D.

Create Space
2016

BOOKS BY J.D. GILL

FORMS OF LIFE and other essays
LETTERS TO JIM
FINDING HUMAN
LETTERS OF JULIET to the Knight in Rusty Armor
ONE HUNDRED REASONS WHY I LOVE YOU
THE MISERY OF THE GOOD CHILD
CIRCUMFERENCE a memoir
IN BETWEEN poems 1964 - 1996
RECURRING THEMES IN THE TAROT AND THE SELF

CONTENTS

VOLUME ONE

Contents 7
Forward 13

MEXICO ONE

1. Overview 15

MEXICO TWO

1. Initiation and the Path to Higher Forms . . 17
2. The Greek Diagnostic Manual 41
3. The Return to the Darkness 71
4. The Higher Forms 101
5. Attaining the Complete Self 125

MEXICO FOUR

1. Introduction 133
2. Basic Concepts 141
3. The Mother/Child Archetype 181
4. Feminine Development 215
5. Group Structures 231
6. The Fear of the Feminine 245
7. The Center 263
8. Closing Comments 269

MEXICO FIVE

1. Introductory Remarks 273
2. Developmental Family Dynamics/Seeing the
   Self 277
3. Dysfunctional Family Dynamics 305
4. Connections and the Self, The Unconscious,
   Object Connections, and Attachment Patterns 329
5. The Wound of the Father 347
6. The Significance of Symbols 391
7. Note on Psychotherapy and Managed Care . 411
8. Treating the Self 421
9. How to Treat the Self, Summary 439

MEXICO SIX

1. Introduction: Getting Unstuck/Getting Oriented 445
2. The Problem of Polarized Opposites and the
   Reintegration of the Self 475

References 499
About the Author 525

VOLUME TWO

Contents 7
Forward 13

MEXICO SIX (Continued)

3. The Eleusinian Mysteries 15
4. Treatment Strategies 43

MEXICO SEVEN

1. Introduction 68
2. Relationship Problems and the Greater and
   Lesser Past 70
3. Context Dilemmas 92
4. Dionysos and the Bacchae 103

MEXICO EIGHT

1. Psychotherapy, The Entire Context . . . 128
2. Alchemy and the Unconscious . . . 172
3. Alchemy and the Unconscious Two . . 213
4. An Analysis of the Coniunctio of Alchemy . 236
5 The Androgyne 267
6. Bringing it all Together: Treatment Options 270

MEXICO TEN

1. Introductory Remarks 296
2. Kohut 299
3. Disorders of the Self 310
4. Development and the Treatment of the False
Self 350
5. The Self and Its Wounds 366
6. Developmental Levels 376

References 381
About the Author 407

VOLUME THREE

Contents 7
Forward 13

MEXICO ELEVEN

1. Resistance and Transformation 15
2. The Weight of Love 75
3. Basics of Object Relations according to
   Thomas Ogden 91
4. Foundations of Perversion 130
5. Externalization and "Reality" 159

MEXICO TWELVE

1. Intro: Two Points 194
2. Psychoanalytic Principles 200
3. Defense Systems 271
4. Elements of Psychodynamic Assessment 309
5. Borderline Personality Issues . . . 323
6. Two Person Theory 359
7. Countertransference Issues 378
8. A Note on Reality Testing 393

MEXICO THIRTEEN

1. Feminism and "Recognition:" How it
   Changes Everything 395
2. Feminism and "Recognition:" Master and
   Slave 414
3. Feminism and "Recognition:" Women's

Desire 433
4. Feminism and "Recognition:" The Oedipal
   Riddle 439
5. Feminism and Recognition: Gender
   Concepts and Domination 460

References 475
About the Author 501

The Tree of Life

FORWARD

These lectures were given during an annual Study/Play Tour to Mexico which was sponsored by the University of Utah Neuropsychiatric Institute beginning in 1993 and continuing for the following twelve years.

The goal of the project was to provide information to mental health workers that was likely new to them and also humane.

The idea was originally hatched in my supervision group at the hospital and was initially aided by Mary Talboys, LCSW, assistant administrator. The trip quickly became very popular and was full each year. Cities visited included Cancun, Cabo San Lucas, Puerto Vallarta, Mazatlan, and Isle Mujeres.

After the fourth year the trip was managed by Tom Woolf, LCSW who was also an instructor in philosophy at the University of Utah.

Lectures began with concepts of abuse, dysfunctional living, mythology, and Jungian psychology. From this the direction moved to more main-line psychotherapy and psychoanalysis, and always included a cultural component.

The group met from nine A.M. until noon each day except one which was set aside for a trip to neighboring attractions. Discussion and participation were encouraged.

Lectures were not written for the first year's trip. Years three and nine are omitted here as the material for these years was used to create the stand alone volume *Recurring Themes in the Tarot and the Self.* Preparations for the thirteenth year which did not materialize are included.

The treatment of Eros and Psyche from Mexico Eleven was omitted, as this appears in the volume *Finding Human.*

Also not included here is the almost magical atmosphere that was generated during these trips. Sessions tended to be intense and transformative. Rarely were they missed for other activities. The camaraderie that was developed persisted long after the series had ended.

Of course it did not hurt sessions were held in Mexico in the middle of the Utah winter when everyone was desperate for a break. To truly recapture the essence of these lectures they should be read when the reader has retreated to a tropical white sand beach with sun screen and an ample supply of beer.

MEXICO SIX (CONTINUED)

3. THE ELEUSINIAN MYSTERIES

It would be hard to find a more meaningful example of how life extends beyond the present than the ancient rites practiced at Eleusus in Greece.

I have been fascinated, if not obsessed, by this topic for years.

In fact, it is difficult to write about the mysteries--as many who have also tried this project have noted.

Earlier in the spring of this year I traveled to Eleusis with my son Anthony to visit the original site. It was for me a profound experience indeed.

The mysteries held at Eleusis were widely considered to be the most sacred of the rites in ancient Greece.

There, yearly, the proceedings in honor of the goddess Demeter were held. Contrary to popular modern re- constructionist views, these were *central* to Greek life.

Why were they so tremendously important? And-- what can we learn from them that might apply to our own lives?

First, it will help to get a brief overview of the climate in which these rites arose.

As I stated in Chapter One, due to vigorous efforts to counter the tremendous debt they owed to Gnosticism and other Greek influences, the Christian church tried very hard to distance itself from Greek sources. The main tool used in doing this was to focus not on the sa- cred--as the Greeks were obsessed with doing, but rather on the historical or profane. Thus the Christians stressed their historical character, supporting documents, and out- look.

In fact this focus makes the Judeo-Christian develop- ment almost unique among the religious developments of the high-culture systems.

Despite these efforts, it nevertheless remains quite ob- vious that Greek philosophy, myths, and symbols were a *major* influence on Christian developments--if not active- ly used, though disguised (Hatch, 1957).

For us, due to our life-long submergence in the Christ- ian culture of the West, it is a bit tricky to understand the Greeks of the pre-Christian era. This is true, because we tend to be biased by mind-body dualism and our notions of a *personal* connection to a deity.

To begin with, the Greek world was a highly educated world. As the society matured toward the Christian Era, the educational level gradually grew to the point it broke down the old aristocracy as learning became more public. Also at this time philosophy lost much of its creativity, became a discipline, and began to deteriorate. This was the time of the Greek school known as the Sophists.

Even so, it was difficult for the Greeks to accept Christianity which was by their standards conceptually very crude. In the place of ancient revealing, prophesying, and predicting/disclosing, the Christians instead stressed a dogmatic sort of preaching. Hatch (1957) said, "Prophesy died when the Catholic Church was born...In place of prophesying came preaching...[further, the church] preached conquest at the price of reality (pp. 107, 114)."

Greek learning, by contrast, centered around Homer. Homer was read not simply for the stories involved but for the truths revealed by them. And while such writing cannot strictly be called "allegory," it did function for the Greeks in a symbolic fashion (i.e., it "opened" to elements beyond the literal meaning of the tales themselves).

If the Christian Testaments are read in this fashion, they tend to be interpreted as allegories or symbolic carriers of meaning as well beyond exactly *what* is said.

The mysteries at Eleusis were highly symbolic.

In Greece, knowledge (i.e., "important" knowledge) came to be regarded as a secret. The gods only intended the wise to get it--that is, those properly prepared. Significant insights would thus be denied those who were incapable of grasping and honoring them.

Hatch said, "Difficulties and impossibilities were introduced in order to prevent men from being drawn into adherence with the literal meaning (Ibid, p. 78)." (How far we have come!) (See also Kermode, 1979.)

Eliade (1963) pointed out in this light that throughout ancient societies the word "myth" meant "true story." It was "a most precious possession because it [was] sacred, exemplary, significant (p. 1)."

Because of this, the myths were not recited before the uninitiated.

A main theme expressed over and over was "the fall from the order of being, and the return to it (Ibid., p. 50)." This theme has, of course, been a fundamental pattern in human existence.

In fact, the rise of psychoanalysis can be accounted for by the same ancient longing to be able to return to the origins--in order to begin anew.

In this light, it was the ancient view that a "true new beginning [could] come only after a real end (Ibid., p. 74)."

Thus the self was considered to be only apparently enslaved. Liberation "is simply *becoming conscious* of its eternal freedom (Ibid, p. 118)." For this reason, ignorance is really ignorance of the self.

Forgetting, induced by the river Lethe, was an essential part of the realm of death in the Greek view.

In Greece there were thus two kinds of memory: primordial or "essential" and personal.

This is why in Plato's dialogue The Meno, learning is equated with remembering. In focusing on earthly life, he held, the soul forgets the Ideas, that is the eternal forms. (The word "religio" means "linking back.")

The conscious mind excludes. This is how consciousness works, as opposed to the more immediate primitive "openness."

Thus "behind" every worldly event exists a significant transcendent element--as a metaphor.

If the study of mythology, ancient rites, and themes are pushed back far enough, clear conceptualizations begin to fail, and one finds oneself picking between shards of ideas, that is attempts to render simple human impulses into conceptual terms, &c.--what Kerenyi calls "mythologem." (The German word is "begrundung."). (See also Foucault, 1994.)

Over time, out of these crude, pre-conceptual, elements more or less clear themes begin to be developed.

These begin to be graspable and hence more or less widely known. Later, clear themes developed that found their way into ancient rites and eventually even into developed myths

The mysteries were a method of access to such fundamental or transcendent truths, the "greater ground" if you will.

At Eleusis a code of silence was enforced, which interestingly enough was never significantly broken (this is why we have no written or public record of the content of the rites). The code of silence was not designed to prevent the *betrayal* of the mysteries so much as to prevent the *conceptual dissolution and distortion* of them.

According to Kerenyi (1976), the divine child embraces the miracle of birth as well as the notion of life's promise and potency.

The childhood of Hermes was considered to be the ideal story of the divine child. Dionysos was also closely related, as were many gods.

The early mythologem or primal theme of femininity was called "Kore." Kore was the goddess maiden.

The figure of Kore represented woman's capacity

Actually, throughout ancient cultures the maiden goddess was more common than male gods. This is, in part, why shrines to Athena occupy a central place in most Greek cities. Athena's essence is Kore.

"Parthenos" is another Greek name for virgin.

Persephone came to be regarded as the ideal embodiment of Kore.

In an important sense, Demeter the mother and Persephone the daughter are each aspects of the other. Often included also is Hecate who is representative of the dark side.

These three aspects of the figure suggest such three aspects exist in all persons.

Let's see, where has this idea appeared again, namely "three beings in one form?" Not to mention the eternal progression involved and the notion of life's (eternal) continuation?

Demeter, Persephone's mother, was associated with the earth and hence the grain. Her name in Rome is Ceres, from which we get the word "cereal." This dimension may be regarded as "food for the body."

She was also associated with the mystery rites at Eleusis. This dimension may be regarded as "food for the soul."

Thus both the lower and higher regions have a primordial mother figure.

Persephone, who was the daughter of Demeter, differed from Athena, Artemis, Hecate and others in that she was "completely passive." Persephone was worshiped as "Queen of the dead." Thus, her fate was considered an embodiment of the fulfillment and dominion of death.

Every September initiates came to the Sanctuary at Eleusis from all over the world to experience the sacred rites.

The rites at Eleusis were called the "greater mysteries." "Lesser mysteries" were performed at Agra. Eleusis was an establishment fourteen miles southwest of Athens. It was settled between 1900-1600 BCE.

The meaning of the name Eleusis is "the place of happy arrival."

The first temple to Demeter was likely constructed in 1500-1425 BCE. In 800 BCE the Mysteries were made a part of the Athenian sacred festivals by law.

Later, during the Roman period, the emperors Hadrian, Antonius Pius, and Marcus Aurelius gave the final form to the constructions at Eleusis.

The Mysteries flourished until the decree of Theodosius I in 379 that formally forbad them. This was done to cut down the considerable competition exerted by the mysteries on the now-official Roman state religion: Christianity.

Built in one form or another over a period of about 2,000 years, the Telesterion, or main temple, at Eleusis was destroyed for the final time in 396 CE by Alaric, king of the Visigoths, during one of the frequent invasions of Greece that took place in the ancient world.

It was said that when the temple was destroyed, *all Greece died*, that is its very essence had been destroyed. So central were the rites to the lives of the Greeks that the "core," if you will, of the ancient world finally expired at that point.

The mysteries were conducted at Eleusis for about 2,000 years.

In the account that follows, I shall primarily rely, among many other sources, on the work of Kerenyi (1976), the Hungarian mythologist and classical scholar, who devoted significant portions of his life to the study of the mysteries--and, in fact, lived at Eleusis for considerable period while compiling his materials.

The rites were based on the myth of the Goddess Demeter and her struggles to be reunified with her daughter Kore (Perephone) after she had been ravished and taken off by Hades, god of the underworld--thus to the regions of death.

The story is recounted in the Homeric Hymns and follows below. It may be seen the Homeric Hymn to Demeter concerns mostly the mother's pain and grief over being separated from her daughter.

Persephone, who was a mature adolescent, was playing with her friends in a meadow when she spotted and picked a Narcissus blossom. At this point the earth opened and Persephone was suddenly taken off by Hades on his great chariot to his kingdom in the underworld (Hades was a brother of Zeus and thus a major deity).

Thus Demeter was bereft of Persephone. Demeter in her grief could get no one to intercede for her, not Helios, not Hyperion, not even Zeus. She therefore donned peasant clothes and went about wandering and mourning her loss. She eventually sat by a well at Eleusis called the well of the Maiden and was discovered by the daughters of Celios. She was taken to their house at Eleusis where she became a nurse to the youngest child, a son. At night she placed him in the fire--in order to make him immortal--but was discovered and abruptly dismissed.

She had a temple built to her at Eleusis in which she might teach her rites. In her grief she blighted the earth so nothing would grow (as a symbol of her grief). This resulted in a famine that would have destroyed the whole race. She was called before Zeus and ordered to yield, but she stubbornly refused, demanding the return of her daughter. Zeus relented and got Hermes to go to Hades and bring her back. But before Persephone left Hades, she unwittingly ate a pomegranate seed, which according to the Greek notion, meant she had to return to him.

Mother and daughter were reunited, but Persephone could only stay with her mother two thirds of the year (i.e., summer and the growing season) and then was required to return to Hades for one third of the year (i.e., winter). Thus the miseries of winter may be seen as duplicating the grief in Demeter's heart at losing Persephone.

To fulfill her obligation to Zeus, Demeter gave seeds to Triptolemos to distribute and make the earth flower again. Along with Persephone she taught her rites. Again, Demeter is considered to have brought two gifts to the human race. First is the grain which is often called the "lesser gift" and second are the mysteries which are often called the "greater gift." (The lesser gift is survival and life in the physical sense; the greater gift is eternal life or survival in the "higher" sense.)

It is important to notice that the mother never quite succeeds in getting the daughter back entirely.

The point of the Hymn is that good concealed in evil is a symbol of immortality (i.e., the eternal transmutation of one substance or form into another).

The well in Eleusis to which Demeter came in her grief, today exists within the sanctuary. It is called the "Kasllichoron" which means the well of the beautiful dances.

One account of the meeting between the daughters of Celios and the grieving and disguised Demeter is that one of the daughters in an effort to cheer up the mournful stranger performed a crude gesture: she flashed her genitals. The incongruence of this irreverence made Demeter finally laugh.

The myth of Demeter and Persephone is archetypal, and closely related elements or "mythologems" predate developed Greek culture. There exists, for example, the interior of a cup that is Minoan and dates from approximately 2,000 BCE that depicts Persephone rising out of the ground. Also there are shards of this myth in the Egyptian rites of Isis, which date from an even earlier period.

Clearly, the Kore figure did not begin with Olympian mythology.

It is actually quite generally accepted that the notions of Demeter and Persephone that figured in developed Hellenic mythology originally came to Greece through Crete.

The Demetrian idea essentially has to do with grain and motherhood. In fact at the apex of the mysteries, a single ear of corn was held aloft by the Hierophant to symbolize this idea.

The ear of corn is dead, having been harvested. Yet at the same time it contains within itself the seeds of its own regeneration and survival. Demeter bestowed immortality on souls, which was akin to the renewing quality of the grain.

Kerenyi (1949) said:

> The grain figure is essentially the figure
> of both origin and end of mother and daugh-
> ter; and just because of that it points beyond
> the individual to the universal and eternal. It
> is always *the grain* that sinks to earth and

returns, always the grain that is mown down in golden fullness and yet, as fat and healthy seed, remains whole, mother and daughter in one (p. 117)."

It is no accident the rites at Eleusis were held at the traditional time of sowing in Greece: autumn. It was the sowing of the grain that reminded the Greeks of Kore's rape. (Rape here is thought of in the sense of the breaking of the sacred mother-daughter bond by the sexual male.)

Just as fire is the fate of the mature grain (it is baked to perfection to become food), the seed metaphor has long been central to symbolism. The seed decays under the earth which is a fruitful death.

The fact that Persephone could only appear part of the year reflects the Greek notion that only one aspect of the goddess could appear at any one time. Kerenyi pointed out that as Persephone, she exemplifies the Greek idea of "non-being." As Demeter, she is the Hellenic idea of "all-mother."

To Greeks, of course, non-being is the root-aspect of being.

At Eleusis the notion which was achieved was the *identity* of mother and daughter--hence eternal continuation.

Neumann (1962) pointed out that in depictions where Demeter and Persephone are seen together, it is difficult to tell them apart. Persephone is often holding a flower, and Demeter is holding a fruit.

Kerenyi (1949) said:

> The idea of the original mother-daughter goddess, at root a single entity, is at the same time the idea of *rebirth*...to enter into the figure of Demeter means to be pursued, to be robbed, raped, to fail to understand, to rage and grieve, but then to get everything back and be born again (p. 123)."

This then was the universal principle of life and the fate of everything mortal.

The answer, in other words, was to enter into "divine motherhood." This was the *route* through which the initiations proceeded.

Since the eternal self cannot be one thing in men and something else in women, masculinity and femininity might be considered *inflections* of a complete self.

Kerenyi (1967) argued that "feminine destiny" thus cannot be the self, but is, on the other hand, a *step* on the way to the self.

It must be stressed, as opposed to Jung's suggestions concerning conceptual notions that function as archetypes, Kerenyi spoke of "archetypal facts of human existence." These are *not* conceptual entities in origin, but "realities which cannot be mere realities of the psyche and which, of course, are also not concrete in the manner of tangible objects (Ibid, p. xxxii)."

Only later, after considerable development, do such fragments and themes become conceptualized in such a way they are able to form clear concepts, such as archetypes as described by Jung.

For example, in the Greek view each life has a masculine and feminine origin. Hermes embodied the masculine source, and Demeter (or Aphrodite) embodied the feminine source.)

Thus at the mysteries both men and women were able to participate directly in the mysteries, but clearly NOT in an intellectual (i.e., conceptual) way.

Both *did* identify with (i.e., symbolically become) the goddess. It was through this route that the rites unfolded.

Thus the process was distinctly *feminine*; it was not masculine. That is, one surrendered to the mysteries; one did not "grasp the concept" or "get on top of and master the notions."

The mysteries, in other words, pushed beyond the conceptual, or "dualistic" region to attain a more primitive or "deeper" ground.

For example, water played an important role as well as darkness. Surrender was the mode required.

At Eleusis the initiates fasted for nine days and drank the "kykeon" which was the drink of Demeter and consisted of barley, water, and pennyroyal or mint. It was slightly alcoholic. These outward preparations helped the initiates attain the inner light. (On top of significant hunger even a minor amount of alcohol would have an effect.)

If you travel to Eleusis, you will find that the modern world and its development has not been at all kind to Eleusis--as it has been kind to many other sites.

The sacred way along which the initiates traveled from the Acropolis in Athens to Eleusis is now the precise path of the main Athens-Corinth superhighway. It must have been some sight when it was simply a pathway through low rolling hills and blowing grass.

Also the modern city of Eleusis, which is now called Elefsena, is a major Greek petroleum processing and shipping center. The azure bay of Eleusis is filled with huge tankers, container ships, and much of the traffic you would routinely find in a significant port. The air pollution is terrible. Needless to say, this is now not a blissful spot.

Further, the Sanctuary there is NOT a major tourist destination. It is not marked. There is no clearly-identified, convenient transportation to take visitors there, no tour-bus. The closest bus-stop is about one-third of a mile away. You are very much on your own--and must know what you are doing.

There is a positive side to this, however. The day I was there, there were only three other people who visited the rather large excavations. One left just as we came, and two others came about ninety minutes before we left. Due to the size of the space, however, we literally had the place to ourselves.

This is a dramatic contrast to popular destinations such as Delphi. It would not surprise me to learn that over 2,000 people per day visit the ruins at Delphi--and this is a three hour bus ride from Athens, each way! (We, therefore, went to Delphi on our own and arranged to get there about thirty minutes before the last tour-bus left. We then could explore the site without the majority of distractions and the--typically brainless--distraction of the crowds.)

I won't even mention the tourist pressure and traffic at the easily accessible Acropolis at Athens!

The Greeks held two levels of initiation. The "myesis" was held in early spring at Agra, a suburb of Athens by the river Ilissos. The "epopteia" was held in autumn at Eleusis. These were the so-called lesser and greater mysteries.

The word for to-initiate, "telos," means to close, as of the eyes and mouth. Thus in the initiation the eyes were occluded from the irrelevant (i.e., the external or the so-called "lower forms.").

"Myesis" was derived from the verb for action; "epopteia" was the state of "having seen."

The initiates were called the "mystai."

The lesser mysteries were held in the month of February or early March (Authesterion). Initiates participated in the lesser mysteries and were then allowed to attend the rites at Eleusis one year later.

The Hierophant, or high priest of the rites, when at Agra was dressed as Dionysos. There a ram, animal of Dionysos, was slaughtered and also pigs, animals associated with Demeter.

Hierophant means priestly demonstrator.

The rites themselves included placing the initiates in giant winnowing baskets. Thus they were considered the seeds of what was to come. Also, according to some accounts, the story of Demeter and Persephone was acted out. Thus, these were the outward manifestation of the rites.

The mystery rites that were later held at Eleusis began on the 14th of Boedromion which was the 26th or 27th of September. Here, the initiates first made appropriate sacrifices at the altars of the goddesses at the eschara, in the court of the precinct proper. This was done in order to be considered worthy to take the goddess' grief upon themselves. They also had prepared themselves by fasting. Demeter led the procession with sacred symbols in a casket that she carried along the Sacred Way to the Stoa Poikile in the Agora, just beneath the Acropolis at Athens (see Preka-Alexandri, pp. 14ff.).

The next day (the 15th of Boedromion), the Heirophant made the "prorrhesis," the official proclamation of the beginning of the festival.

On the next day, the purification ceremony of the initiates took place in the sea at Phaleron along with the sacrifice of young pigs. The call rang out, "Initiates to the sea." This re-unification with the sea was a re-unification with the primal waters, where even the mysteries came from.

The next day (the 17th) sacrifices were made at the Eleusinian sanctuary in the Agora. During this ritual, a sow was offered up to Demeter. This was sacrificed and initiates sat upon its skin as an act of purification and identity.

On the third day important personalities of the day were able to able to begin the initiation.

On the 19th of the month the procession of initiates carried the symbols used in the rites along the Sacred Way to Eleusis. At altars and shrines along the way the initiates offered sacrifices and chanted hymns. The procession ended at the courtyard of the sanctuary at Eleusis where the group was met by the priests and where dances were performed throughout the night in honor of the goddess.

During the procession the mystai bore torches and wore myrtle leaves in their hair. The symbolism of the torches concerns the masculine fire igniting in the feminine wood. Myrtle was a plant sacred to Dionysos. The path was a re-tracement of that of the grieving goddess.

The women bore kykeon vessels securely bound to their heads. The men carried little pitchers.

This festival proper which began on the 19th at Eleusis was called the "Mysteria."

The 20th began in that evening and holy night. The rule of secrecy was in place from the moment of gathering.

When they reached the sanctuary, the mystai entered the Propylaia or outer court which is bounded by Roman arches. They passed the sacred well, but were forbidden to sit here.

At the head of the procession was the mystagogos who was the priest leading the initiates.

Demeter received the arriving mystai near an omphallos that was likely positioned before the Ploutonion which was the cave from which Persephone arrived and from which she also departed.

The mystai then proceeded up a little hill to the Teleristron or temple in which the rites proper took place. The Teleristron was an enormous building, rebuilt over a period of greater than a thousand years. It measured 59 x

59 yards in final form, and was the largest building in classical Greece.

The remains of this enormous building indicate interior steps on three sides. These were apparently used for standing rather than for sitting.

Even with its enormous size, the Telesterion was not large enough to hold the entire procession. Only those who had fasted for nine days were allowed to march on the tenth day and drink the kykeon.

The phrase that was uttered at the door of the Telesterion in order to gain admittance was, "I have fasted, I have drunk the kykeon."

Close to the center of this structure there was a smaller interior temple called the Anaktoron. This structure was strictly off limits to the mystai and had one door that could be opened to allow the Hierophant to obtain sacred objects. A green light emanated from the interior of this structure.

Facing this door, the Hierophant had a covered throne.

The mysteries consisted of doing, saying, and showing. The dance, and not the story, was the sacred secret. At the proper moment the Hierophant "revealed" specific sacred objects whose symbolic significance would be clear at such points by the initiates.

On the 21st the "epopteia" was performed, which was the highest stage of initiation.

At the precise moment in the rites when the Kore was called, the Hierophant beat the "echeion," which was a large gong that had a shattering effect. Such a device was also used in the theater to simulate thunder (thunder, according to the Greeks came from the underworld).

When the Hierophant gave the word, a great fire rose —that was visible to ships at sea. He said, "The Mistress has given birth to a holy boy. "Brimo has given birth to Brimos!" This implied the "strong one" to the "strong one."

Brimo means the queen of the dead (Persephone), and Brimos means divine child (Dionysos).

(Though, remember, due to the fundamental identity between them, Brimo implies mother plus daughter-- hence all human continuity.)

Thus the sense of the birth of Brimos implied the continuation of all of life.

"The queen of the dead herself had given birth in fire to a mighty son," said Kerenyi (1967, p. 93).

The implications of this were apparent to the mystai. *a birth in death* was possible! By analogy this was also possible for all human beings who had faith in the goddess.

The fire symbolism that announced a beatific event, was later taken into Christianity.

When the echeion was beaten, the epopteia began. Ineffable items were observed. Later, the Hierophant held up a single ear of mown corn (grain).

This act is surprisingly similar to the "flower sermon" of the Buddha. Here, to express the meaning of life, the Buddha held up a single flower and said nothing. That was the sermon. Either you grasped the principle, or you did not. (The flower--as the ear of corn--WAS life, in the case of the flower, in its season of youthful promise.)

The ear of corn is symbolic of death and birth, thus the fate of all living things. That is the harvested ear of corn is dead, but by planting its kernels, new life is able to come forth. Thus new life is contained in death.

"Every grain of wheat and every maiden contains, as it were, all its descendants and all her descendants--an infinite series of mothers and daughters in one (Ibid, p. 153)."

It is likely the mystai were able to find themselves equated in identity with each element of this ritual, including the ear of corn. Such equation depended on the capacity for a special sort of seeing, a kind of "metaphorical seeing" if you will. Here, distinctness was broken down and the fundamental unity was directly experienced.

No distinction was made between the great light of the mysteries and the light of the sun.

On the 22nd the initiates poured great quantities of libations into the depth of the earth at the Plouteonion. This was accompanied by the cries of "Hye, Kye." The cry was first uttered toward the heavens and secondly toward the earth (the paternal and maternal regions). Hye means flow (rain), and Kye means conceive.

The following day, on the 23rd, the initiates returned to their homes, in a much heightened state.

From the time of their gathering the initiates were placed under an oath of silence. The punishment for betraying this was severe: banishment or death.

Participation in the rites offered a guarantee of life without the fear of death, of confidence in the face of life's tragedies.

At Eleusis initiates came into contact with the "arrheton" which is the "ineffable secret." (The "aporrheton" is a secret kept under a law of silence.)

The Arrheton at Eleusis concerned Persephone. She was "Arrhetos Koura" or the ineffable maiden. She WAS the secret. Mythology containing and illuminating this tale was simply preparation for the mystery.

There is absolutely no public thing that is traceable to the mystery rites. Whatever was known was not in the mysteries.

Also the pomegranate is associated with Dionysos. It is an expression of the desire for fertility (i.e., it has an abundance of seeds). Further the pomegranate is closely associated with the vine to the Greeks.

Pomegranates were banned at Eleusis.

The word "theos" was equivalent to the Greek name for Dionysos. ("Thea" is another name for Persephone-- both are divine, archetypal children.)

Success at Eleusis required one to develop a transcendent sort of capacity, that is, this region was now immediately available to one. Such a capacity was in the nature of a psychic and emotional reality.

It is interesting that Aristotle in his work On Philosophy realized the awareness gained at Eleusis was different from "ordinary" learning especially in that at Eleusis one has not to expend effort to grasp a concept but rather must learn to be passive and allow him or herself to be put into a state.

This actually emphasizes the preparations without which the epopteia could not succeed. A state of complete passivity and receptivity (i.e., surrender) was required without which the epopteia was impossible.

Often, in fact, initiates had to return to Eleusis more than once to attain the breakthrough.

It was the notion of the Greeks that if one took death upon oneself in a ceremony, this meant immortality. As the mysteries had demonstrated, life eternally comes from death.

The initiates had entered into the role of the goddess searching for her daughter. They were prepared the same way as Demeter was. They also experienced the miracle of reunion and the ultimate result of this which was the divine child/divine sight.

The divine child is, of course, the birth of the self. This is a transcendent truth that exists, if you will, beyond the physical sector though it is related to it in metaphorical character.

Clearly the feminine source of life is the same for men and for women alike.

The rites at Eleusis were, thus, the Greek way of moving beyond the factual world of conscious thought to directly encounter an experience of the unconscious dimensions, that is the "greater life" which always exists beyond, as well as surrounds, the "lesser life."

Actually such duality extended to the person of Persephone herself who was absent from the underworld and yet somehow able to execute her role as queen at the same time. Also similarly, after she returned to the underworld, she was nevertheless present with Demeter at the sending out of the grain with Triptolomos--as is depicted in the famous sculptural panel.

In an analogous way the initiates experienced their unity with all of life. The fate of each thing was their own fate.

This was a breakthrough to a kind of wordless knowledge that placed the perceiver on the same plane as the subject known and visa versa. The unity of all things, in other words, was not a conceptual truth but an intimately experienced reality of great force.

Very often people behave quite well in utter "inner" misery. And many people have found a degree of external success only to live at the same time rather meaningless lives.

To more fully understand ourselves and others requires moving beyond the conceptual level to encounter the greater regions which lie beyond this sector--call them what you will: the unconscious, the spiritual dimension, pipe-dreams, &c. I call them the "metaphorical regions."

This is precisely the distinction Eliade had in mind when he described the sacred and the profane.

Further, perhaps the most profound experiences in life are to be had in relation to this "sacred," not to the empirical zone.

Modern life--especially in the West, has tended to emphasize the factual and external at the expense of the symbolic and "internal." This is especially true in our culture which is perhaps the most factually externalized culture the world has ever known.

To attain a meaningful life is to attain access to the entire self, not part of the self. This allows persons to come to awareness of who they really are, not just the portions of themselves that were allowed in their upbringing or culture.

The real self is not a partial entity. In fact, if the notions at Eleusis, which characterized the Greek culture in an ideal way--if these notions are correct, we are not even individual in the higher sense.

Thus, for the mystai, Eleusis was, profoundly, the place of true birth. The real life began there.

4. TREATMENT STRATEGIES

So look where we are left!

We have learned that who we have been required to be is not who we are.

Through the interactions we routinely create with others, we continue to find ways to live in unreality.

And if this weren't bad enough--we even claim we like it!

What a mess!

Earlier this week, I related that in Greek Mythology, sleep and death, Hypnos and Thanatos, were considered to be brothers. That is, being awake allows for awareness which is equated with life. Unawareness is death.

In its best form, psychotherapy is a method whereby we might be aided to become more awake--and thus in a position to resolve some of the roadblocks in our lives.

Somehow, we must find a way beyond who we have been taught to be, beyond who others are routinely taking us to be (at least SEEM to be taking us to be), beyond who we experience ourselves to be--all of this so that we might have a few moments of genuine life instead of the distorted life we know all too well and which doesn't really allow us to come to a genuine peace with ourselves, with others, or with the world.

So, what, specifically, is in the way?

First are the consequences of our developmental backgrounds. Thus, due to their own developmental "incompleteness" and other problems, our parents couldn't be their own real selves either--and as a result, they were unable to allow, or encourage, us to be our real selves.

The result was approximate development.

Secondly the problems we encounter are furthered when we are "required" to think of ourselves and everything else in dualistic terms--rather then allowing for a unified view that would heal opposites. Personal results of this include "unknown" and unowned facets of the self, huge energy expenditures in the service of repression and projection, as well as endlessly "artificial" interactions with whomever and whatever is around us.

Finally, are problems--significantly based on the above two areas--that are related to living *primarily* within the profane sector of life rather than allowing for or attaining access to the sacred sector in addition (to use Eliad's language).

Thus, as well as being raised in such a way that we are deprived of a more-or-less genuine sense of identity, we are also denied access to the larger world of significant meaning--and, ultimately, belonging.

How might one aid--rather than unwittingly hinder--the healing process?

From what "positions" should we practice as therapists?

Strupp (1960, 1991) found in his research into the psychotherapeutic process that: (1) therapists rapidly developed--often within the first few minutes of the very first session--a generally positive or negative attitude toward the patient. This initial attitude tends, he found, to persist, and (2) this attitude on the part of the therapist has a profound effect on the therapist's diagnostic and prognostic judgements about the patient, treatment plans, as well as the empathic quality the therapist is able to bring to the interaction.

In short, the therapist was found to be in a similar position to the one that has been described as pertaining to the parents (i.e., the therapist's views must rise only *within* the therapist's capacities--consequently, it is only within these capacities that the patient will be allowed to advance and flourish).

As psychoanalysis in its many forms has LONG realized, therapist's attitudes--especially empathic qualities--are readily communicated to the patient, "who will react reciprocally (Strupp, p. 135)."

Thus, in precisely this way the therapy situation tends to unwittingly *duplicate* the background of *both* the patient and the therapist--so they can each work very hard and confidently know they will get to the same place.

This also, more importantly, suggests that the quality of the *relationship* with the therapist is by far the most important component of psychotherapy. Specific technique plays a significantly smaller role.

That is, psychological problems which may be helped by psychotherapy, are by nature *relational*.

Further, empathetic listening is critical. This especially concerns negative or critical comments on the part of the therapist--which are *always* harmful. (Such views are likely projective on the part of the therapist as well as duplicating of the formative experiences of the patient.)

The immediate implications of these views are that a complete or adequate therapist is actually a complete or adequate human being. Approximations, facades, "professional demeanors," or worse "outright falsehoods" conveyed to patients cannot be very helpful.

This is also why, in study after study, the specific technique employed by the therapist is rated as less important in contributing to patient progress than is the quality of the patient-therapist interaction itself.

In fact a study published just two months ago (12-96 Journal of Consulting and Clinical Psychology) reported the results of a far-reaching study conducted by Blatt at Yale University School of Medicine and funded by NIMH. Blatt's group found that therapists who facilitated the greatest improvement in depressed people (1) focused on psychological as opposed to biological factors, (2) generally used psychotherapy alone rather than in combination with psychoactive drugs, and (3) expected treatment to take longer than less effective therapists.

Blatt et. al. reported:

Clinicians who created a strong therapeutic alliance, a measure of the collaborative bond between therapist and client, were most successful...Moreover, clients who perceived their therapists as empathic and caring responded best to antidepressant drugs (Science News, 151, 1-11-97, p. 21).

Of the above results, Stupp said:

The NIMH study indicates that the therapeutic alliance is more critical than the techniques a therapist employs or the drugs that may be prescribed...This is currently not a popular view among many researchers, and it isn't what health care insurer want to hear either (Ibid.).

Strupp elsewhere quoted Kottler (1990) as suggesting "through training, practice, and dedication, *therapeutic skills become part of the therapist's very being* (Strupp, p. 138)."

Wells, et. al., 1995, argued therapists by and large encounter patients who have been raised in a climate in which they were typically forced to internalize their parent's pathology. Children are, after all, dependent and must find a way to survive.

The result of being raised in a home with chronic maladaptive adjustment patterns--as most children are to one degree or another--is that the child was placed in a position in which he or she internalized more or less terrifying and impinging (i.e., intrusive) object relations (interaction "expectations").

These patterns, of course, tend to be *re-duplicated* again and again in patient's primary relationships, most commonly through the mechanisms of projective and introjective identification.

Wells, et. al. went on to argue that most trauma associated with past interactions tends to be hidden and associated with shame. This is done as the patient is seen as trying to avoid vulnerability in interactions that he or she can only imagine will be similar in character to those experienced before.

Patients, thus, tend to "choose" the compensatory illusions of: security, power, and externalizing of threats (paranoid style); the over-use of control and the need to always be right (obsessive style); grandiose entitlements (narcissistic style); or making oneself needed through excessive self-sacrifice and unilateral care taking (masochistic style, "co-dependency"), &c.

It is of course in just such over learned patterns patients tend to interact with therapists. The therapeutic challenge is, of course, for the therapist NOT to unwittingly fall into such patterns and duplicate the experiences patients have always known.

It cannot be overstressed: the result of compromised developmental histories is necessarily a significant sense of shame.

Alice Miller (1981), for example argued that the mother of a child in such a context is one who loves her child "as her self-object, excessively, though not in the manner that he [or she] needs, and always on the condition that he presents his false self (p. 14)."

As a result of such treatment, one simply cannot imagine a situation in which the real or entire self might be acceptable. Though such a situation is longed for, *in the presence of others*, one will tend to duplicate the interaction patterns that have "worked" in the past, that is one will continue to think his or her real self is defective and will tend to remain "cloaked."

The problem with this is that significant shame is typically hidden. Thus attempts to escape shame tend to be manifest in treatment in disguised ways. For example, common manifestations include somatization, dissociation, anxiety and depression, over and under-valuations, grandiose ambition or fantasies, chronic feelings of emptiness and boredom, a passion for external acclaim, brilliance, or wealth, suicide talk or attempts, substance abuse, and various forms of masochism, as well as appearance of "resistance" in treatment, among others.

It has, additionally, been argued (e.g., Pearson, 1966, et al) that the devaluing so commonly seen both within and outside therapy is a "main defense" that is used to protect a vulnerable and impaired self by projecting aggression and persecutory internalizations that are actually internally directed toward a hungry and envious self.

Such "approximate" people will have great deficiencies in their capacity to love and be genuinely concerned about others. Thus partners of such patients tend themselves to be unhappy as they too are likely unwittingly drawn into reenactments of prior experiences with patients.

Obviously, there is a significant relationship between shame and denial.

Such symptoms may in effect be attempts on the part of patients to escape from aversive self awareness as well as expected aversive external treatment.

Shapiro (1966) summarized such views by saying that "The self-estrangement present in psychopathology is of a broad kind...[which] forestall[s] anxiety but distort[s] self-awareness and cut[s] the individual off from whole aspects of his [or her] own subjective life (p. 3)."

This phenomenon will be coupled with an intense desire on the part of patients to be mirrored by the therapist--as a kind of cooperative and supportive partner in the world of the patient rather than the therapist being a separate person in his or her own right.

The point is that a central task of treatment is for the therapist to provide the sorts of genuine acceptance and shame mitigating experiences the child did not receive in his or her "original" upbringing.

What makes all of this so tricky is that as a rule shame is only tolerable in small doses.

Any experience of empathetic failure on the part of the therapist will likely result in renewed efforts on the part of patients to hide their shame--with the disguised effect of anger, sadness, &c.

That is, as Kohut (1977) argued, normal development allows the child to experience defeat *in small doses and in the presence of empathic support* so the experience of being overwhelmed and consequent wounds to self esteem are minimized. The pathogenic situation, on the other hand, is one in which the child is bereft of such support and is thus routinely overwhelmed by experiences he or she is not yet equipped to handle. The inevitable result is a sense of worthlessness and vulnerability.

It is precisely this gradual (adequately empathetic) context the therapist must provide.

Therapists treating such conditions must thus be on high alert to avoid unwitting countertransference shame. In additional to the above considerations, such responses are common in therapist's ignoring of patient shame as it is too taxing for the therapist to address. Even worse is the countertransference use of *denial* in an attempt to cover up therapists' painful feelings or their own incomplete and damaged selves.

Additionally, therapists must be careful not to unwittingly perpetuate dualistic stereotypes of patients.

That is, excessively categorizing patients (as they routinely seem to tend to do in idle chatter or even (with patient names omitted) in the lunch-room).

Thus when, for example, one sees a patient as "weak," it is helpful to realize this and wonder where the patient's strength is. The same goes for broader areas such as being successful or unsuccessful, happy or unhappy, male or female, making or not making progress, likable or not-likable, &c.

Where are the parts not allowed to be? Why aren't they clearly on view?

Thus in this sense it is important to remember the "good kid" is *never* the real kid, nor is the "bad kid," &c.

Genuinely accepting and welcoming views on the part of therapists, on the other hand, tend to provide powerful counterbalancing contexts for patients' own internalized powerful and fiercely demanding views.

So, let us assume, just for a moment, the therapist is relatively adequate in most of these areas. What must the patient do?

If all has gone tolerably well, the patient will have discovered that he or she has survived childhood with a "multitude of battle scars and wounds, all received in the name of primal trust.

After all, if you can't trust your own mother, who can you trust?

Answer: *nobody.*

This goes especially for the therapist, who aside from being mother's (or father's) own secret "undercover" servant, is a complete stranger.

All of us know we are not to trust strangers.

Again, Hillman (1975) presented a phenomenal account of trust issues as well as our routine experience of betrayal as seen in the treatment process.

The problem is we have each developed an unwitting dependence on our notions of basic trust as a primary basis for adult relationships. The effect of this, aside from our endless frustrations at somehow being constantly able to set up our own idiosyncratic pasts in the future, is the fact we tend to remain forever trapped in infancy.

Weinhold (1991), for example, said:

> Under the spell of primal trust, first experienced as part of the bonding process with your mother, you tend to maintain a fairly ego-centered, limited view of your relationships. In this view, everyone behaves according to the way you would like them to behave. As a young child, you believed in this make-believe condition where you saw the world and other significant people in your life as always fair and just and existing to serve all your needs (p. 105).

Winnicott (1965) suggested the (good) mother actually actively distorts the world for her child. That is, she deliberately creates an environment in which the infant's stress is *minimized*. Thus if the infant is hungry, everything else is dropped, and the infant is fed. If the infant wakes in the night, help comes. In other words, the infant's "environment" including significant others simply exist to do the bidding of the infant. This is done so the infant will not be overwhelmed by the new (i.e., "external") environment and may maximize development during this initial period of symbiotic fusion.

As Joseph Campbell (1988), among others, has pointed out, it is precisely this experience that is typically responsible for our concept of Eden (which we as recipients of the cultural training common in the West usually then project).

Thus, without realizing it, we as people want to try to return to this blissful--and artificial--state of "oneness and perfection" we experienced so briefly in the earliest part of our childhoods.

The problem is, the people we choose as lovers are forever, sadly, letting us down. Their own needs keep getting in our way! What the hell kind of parent--even pseudo-parent--are they anyway?

We, of course, also unwittingly want the therapist to respond as an "ideal" servant. This is why mirroring as well as an adequate working sense of empathy on the part of the therapist is so essential. When the therapist cannot see beyond his or her own needs as regards the patient, or when there can be no consideration over and above the "treatment goals" dictated by the treatment plan (to be successfully accomplished, of course, within the "proper" time frame or number of sessions), the patient will feel a duplication of this original wounding.

The point is that betrayals, failures, and let downs--especially of a significant nature--in fact provide an unparalleled sort of opportunity for growth. In fact, it is precisely the option of moving forward at such points that allows for a moving beyond the prison cells of childhood as well as an endlessly frustrating and futile adjustment pattern, which can only fail.

That is, either I am able to learn that my unconscious "expectations" and longings for a re-fusion and an "eternal, blissful, state of stress-free happiness, perfection, satisfaction, and well being" cannot possibly be reconstructed in the ordinary flow of reality" and therefore are forever doomed to the regions of fantasy (i.e., moving backward in a sort of loyal obedience to my past "grounding")--or I am able to move in the opposite direction toward a discovery of the new, what is really there, and a life and set of interactions that *are* possible at last.

Thus, one constantly and primarily either moves forward or backward. It is of course a lot more common to find people moving, or attempting to move, backward rather than forward.

Hillman's account of the "moving backward" option is a movement back into what he calls the "sterile choices." These are revenge, denial, cynicism, paranoia (i.e., pervasive lack of trust), and self-betrayal. None of these ever truly work.

Revenge is based on the Mosaic code and is based on a natural impulse to hurt back as a response to being hurt. The problem with such an approach, whether directed to the self, others, or situations is that in reality it tends to lead to cruelty as it inevitably breeds more of the same pattern and as a result tends to become all-consuming.

Denial functions are employed to hide and therefore distort the nature of both the self and others. Thus, for example, I may respond to the betraying self, others, or situation by denying the value each has and only seeing my, their, or its evil ways. I may say, "This job sucks," "All men/women are jerks," "I am an idiot," &c.

Cynicism results in my decision I will never trust anyone ever again and will just "play it cool." This may tend to make me feel safe (i.e., within my own "fortress walls"), but it positions me in a place where I cannot see any of the truly positive elements in life (Weinhold, p. 107).

Perhaps the most problematical result of cynicism, however, is self-betrayal. Here as a result of the failure of basic trust in the self, others, or situation, I begin to devalue myself. Thus I hand myself over to the enemy within (i.e., the punitive introject or punitive parent) and brutalize myself in ways that are sadly familiar from my early experiences.

In the paranoid position, I attempt to create only failsafe relationships, complete with guarantees against any possible future lapses in devotion, &c. Without such guarantees, I refuse to move.

It need not be stressed each of these situations may be (re)duplicated in the treatment hour--and by both patient and therapist!

What then might the mature dimension be?

First, following a betrayal, failure, or major let-down, I may use such an experience as an opportunity to learn more about the nature of reality (i.e., as opposed to my "typical" fantasy). In fact, in such a situation, what I have just discovered is that things are not the way I thought they were. Such an outcome is certainly not what my dreams have told me life would be about. This is an opportunity to learn that actually reality is not wrong; in fact, my dream is wrong. To continue to block off the portions of reality that don't fit my dreams in favor of preserving the dream is to forever attempt to set up a life that isn't really here and is, in short, impossible. Such a development allows me to stop specifying how the self, others, and world need to be and to begin to truly learn what these things actually are.

An additional and amazingly powerful alternative is to use the event as an opportunity to become "more conscious of and to integrate [my] own integrated parts that [in fact] have led...to a betrayal (Ibid, p. 108)." In this alternative, I will likely confront the necessity to re-integrate projected as well as denied elements of myself that I have instead wanted (demanded) others or the world to accommodate in me.

Finally, perhaps the most advanced move possible at such a juncture is to move to the transcendent possibility of forgiveness. This "involves no denial, no wishing..., no magical incantations, only an honest accounting of who you are and who the other person really is, including the limitations and failings of yourself and the [other]. It also includes an empathy for the other because of the recognition of your own limitations and failings (Ibid, p. 109)."

Thus we were wounded first by our parents and later by others with whom we attempted to set up close relationships.

It will happen as well within the therapy situation. How this is managed will prove crucial to recovery.

The hope we have is that we can stop trying to live by the blueprints and necessities of our pasts, and move beyond this to a genuine possibility of new discovery.

Breaking out from one's longing for primal trust and a place where dreams held since imprisoned childhoods will come true, is to move beyond the family in an important way and allow for an ability to genuinely discover what one's life could possibly be.

It is also to allow for an end to the unwitting treatment of the self in the same fashion as it was treated in the past during our earliest development.

This is to allow for a moving beyond the hall of mirrors where I have lived, albeit in discontent, for a long time.

Being aware of the necessity of such a transition and helping it along as much as possible is the requirement of an adequate therapist. Obviously, to be adequate in this way the therapist must have tolerably made significant progress on the same journey as well as being able to respond to the patient in as judgment-free a context as possible. In addition, the therapist must be able to genuinely support the patient's becoming who he or she needs to be rather than his or her becoming someone the therapist needs patients to be, &c.

The important therapeutic statements, therefore, are:

(1) "You may do whatever you want to do, but this IS what you are doing now." Such a comment supports liberty of being yet does at the same time provide (hopefully) accurate reality testing.

(2) "Do what you need to do; I will support you." Thus, you will be supported for being who you discover yourself to be, not simply who I need you to be.

In such a climate, the original wound of constriction for the essential purposes of satisfying the parent are largely overcome. Thus the patient is allowed to move beyond prior restrictions--and, in effect, truly break out of the endless house of mirrors at last.

Also, in order to get beyond pervasive feelings such as guilt, resentment, envy, jealousy, and depression, it is necessary to re-discover what the un allowed feelings were that these experiences originally replaced.

According to Alice Miller (1983) staying stuck in infancy is largely due to being:

(1) hurt as a small child, without anyone
noticing your hurt,

(2) told not to be angry at being hurt,

(3) forced to show gratitude toward those who hurt you because they had good intentions,

(4) told to forget everything that happened,

(5) shown how to discharge stored-up anger onto others--or shown how to direct it against yourself (i.e., rather than directing it against parents).

Solving the dilemmas that result from these kinds of experience requires getting in touch with one's basic, human feelings as well as how to accept them--rather than shunting them off into shame-based options.

Basic human emotions include: anger, fear, sexuality, tenderness, sadness, excitement, and happiness or joyfulness.

Often parents cannot stand to see these emotions in their children; it calls up their own unfinished issues related to such dimensions. It is therefore critical that the therapist be able to encourage, receive, and comfortably welcome as well as respond to precisely such emotions, especially the "big three:" anger, sex, and fear.

These are, of course, the dimensions many parents have the most difficulty tolerating.

Actually, in an important way, what we need to be allowed to experience is an opportunity to safely move beyond our defenses to a position of spontaneous surrender to things as they actually are.

Surrender has a masculine and a feminine side.

The feminine side of surrender, especially, has to do with learning to accept what is really there without undue resistance, rather than only being able to accept that which pleases me--or only what I want to accept--or wishing endlessly I could change what is in fact actually there.

The masculine side, especially, has to do with learning how to willingly take control or responsibility without guilt. This means, for example, I can take over my own life without feeling guilty, because in doing such a thing, I am robbing my parents of the job they want.

Of course, we must all learn both sides, in the proportions we discover we need rather than the portions that were assigned to us. We need to learn this instead of seeking such traits in others which will ultimately end in dissatisfaction or futility.

Further, what we try to avoid in others, we tend to continually find in our own lives.

An excellent exercise in helping to address such dimensions is to make a list of questions that will help outline the biases of our parents. One might even make a list of the issues involved. (It is probably better to make a separate list for one's mother and one's father.) We might for example ask:

Were you wanted?

Were you the sex your parent wanted?
Were you treated as a burden?
How were school issues treated?
How were special days and holidays treated?
How--and when--were you disciplined?
How--and when--were you praised?
How were your needs for independence handled?
Were you encouraged to try new things?
How were your fears managed?
How did your parents handle your illnesses?
What were your parents' attitudes about each other?
What did your parents' teach you about women/men?
How did your parents' treat your friends, lovers, &c?
How were information and guidance handled?
How were rules managed?
How was power managed?
Who dominated whom?
Did your parents give you their fears?
How did your parents laugh and have fun?
How did they hurt and express sadness?
How was shame handled?
How was money handled/thought of?
How did they respond to success or failure?
How did they respond to your success or fail ure?
Were there significant secrets? What were they?
What kind of sex education did you receive?
Did your parents try to impose their standards and "values" on you?

What relationship did your parents have toward
the spiritual dimensions?
What sort of spiritual adjustment (i.e., relation
to
metaphorical regions) did your parents allow
or demand for you?   &c., &c.

Such a project helps focus one on the specific dimensions of one's past, rather than requiring one to rely on
vague conceptions and distortions.

Again, a separate accounting for one's mother and father is helpful.

The task following this is to allow oneself to feel angry and outraged at how one was treated.   One might
even allow oneself to become enraged at the parent(s) for
treating one in such ways.

One cannot learn to successfully manage one's anger
until the anger itself is allowed to be expressed and
"spent." That is the anger will remain improperly channeled into compensatory channels or stifled until "freed."

Such a procedure allows one to begin to develop a
new understanding of what really happened.   Also, as
anger gives way, one usually feels sad about what remained dented and unfulfilled about one's own life as
well as one's parents' lives.

This allows for a successful grieving of childhood as
well as the stimulus to move on to establish, through the

process of genuine discovery, one's actual identity and life.

Obviously the answer lies in our own ability to treat ourselves differently from how we were treated in our childhoods--rather than constantly looking for someone else to do this for us.

Also, it allows for a forgiveness of the whole mess. We can forgive ourselves for our own shortcomings. We can also forgive our parents as well as all the people who wounded, hindered us. Again, this may be achieved as it is possible to see at last the parent's own approximations and how they attempted to cope with these in their own rights.

The final step is saying goodbye to the old relationship one had maintained for so long with one's parents. This allows not only for the creation of a new relationship with them--or the memory of them--but also with the self and others as well.

This is also truly to move into the new life, the life one has always sought but never found.

To be helpful to others attempting to resolve such issues and complete such developmental journeys, therapists require the capacities to tolerably resolve such issues and complete such developmental journeys themselves.

The solution to becoming an effective therapist is thus not to master the right sort of technique, but to develop a genuine human ability to treat the patient in significantly more receptive, genuine, and expanded fashion than was encountered by that patient in his or her own childhood.

There simply is no short-cut to this.

Further, if the parents are lacking a developed sense of the spiritual or metaphorical dimensions of life, such dimensions will be damaged in the child as well.

It is highly helpful if the therapist has an effective sense of the regions that lie beyond descriptive dimensions so the patient will be able to recover as well this aspect of his or her life and identity.

Ultimately, of course, there will always be the world we know and the world that lies beyond what we know.

What we do with that which lies beyond is crucial. Do we embrace it, attempt to press into it, worship it, "factualize" it (i.e., think of it as merely an extension of that we know now), fear it, defend as much as possible against it, try to ignore it, &c.

Clearly, how we deal with such regions will also say something about how we deal with anything beyond us-- as well as who we are.

Perhaps this is the ultimate issue, the one for which all others are simply preparation.

Life is a constant process of leaving where we are now in order to arrive at a place beyond that.

Hart Crane (1933/1958) wrote:

> The silver strophe...the canto
> bright with myth...
> Yes, light. And it is always
> always, always the eternal rainbow
> And it is always the day, the day of unkind
> farewell.

Hopefully, as therapists we can help our patients attain the open ability to leave in order to arrive.

MEXICO SEVEN

1. INTRODUCTION

Welcome to Mexico!

Here we are again! I don't know about you, but I don't think I would have dreamed we would keep this going for seven years—especially with the hospital's support.

This year, as usual, I have tried to put together a program that tends to move beyond typical "nuts and bolts" treatment in order to add an—I hope—deeper dimension to both our treatment of others and at the same time hopefully a more expanded sense of what it is to be a human being.

And as usual, I have tried to bring fresh material, different angles, cover new territory, thrill your hearts, and

lift your "morality" (especially since that seems so important to the always-with-us right wing).

I am left hoping this material is interesting, useful, or
directly clinically helpful for you. And, again, thank you
so much for coming along. As usual, it is impossible to
overstate the effort, worry, skill, and general phenomenal
efforts of Tom Woolf in enabling us to be here. It is an
enormous pleasure to work with him, and I have come to
regard him as a good friend, infamous drinking buddy
(along with someone named Ross), and an incredible
support to this event.

We will meet each morning, except Thursday, at 9:00
AM and hold forth—with a break included—until approximately Noon. After this, we will be set free on the
outside area to try to recover enough to withstand the
next morning's presentations. See? Where else could
you get learning and treatment all in one package?

On Thursday, for those interested, Gill's Cheapo Tours
will swing into operation. Further details to be announced.

Finally, if there is anything you need, please let us
know. Your requirements will be considered in depth
over the proper libations until some sort of stunning solution achieved!

Shall we begin?

2. RELATIONSHIP PROBLEMS AND THE GREATER AND LESSER PAST

So, why is it our relationships don't work? Why haven't they ever worked?

The keys to solving this seemingly endless puzzle always manage to elude us somehow, no matter how we try to get our hands on them. Why does happiness mock us? What is life anyway: a series of losses and frustrations—almosts. And then those sweet distorted memories of how it never was.

Is this the true human condition, forever to be denied in public? After all, I've done everything I should, as well as I could—so what's happening, doctor?

To borrow a notion from Lorna Benjamin (who borrowed it from Bowlby) throughout our lives—as well as our relationships—we unwittingly maintain an (primary) unconscious tie to our early attachments. The symptoms or problems we constantly face are, she said, "natural consequences of those underlying loyalties (Lecture, UNI, 1997)."

Obviously present behavioral or conceptual maneuvers are (at least) heavily competed against by these old patterns—if not simply conquered or rendered outright useless by them.

Her word is "copy."

Thus, she said, we copy important people. We:

>Identify with them (act like them)
>Recreate the relationship (recreate old context in terms of present interactions)
>Introject them (treat ourselves as we were treated by them)

Finally, she added that the core self (i.e., my notion of who I am) is based on how I have been treated in these interactions.

How well or poorly we understand this, we can all attest to its significance from our own experience.

I assume the relationship we are all looking for is one that develops from a genuine opening and offering of a real self and a real self. This kind of "depth transformation" is truly life changing.

Yet this implies before I can take part in such an interaction, I need to be able to more or less know something about just who this real self is. Is it who my parents thought it was? Is it the "me" I offer for day to day public interaction? Typically not.

It may be I realize I don't know much about my real self. I am too busy with "external" issues, "things," or survival in the system.

And why after all, place all this emphasis on elements that comprise "the real self" which everyone seems to be talking about endlessly? Why is that so hard to know?

My comments here will be rather heavily based on the work of Mollen (1993), an English theorist who received his psychoanalytic training at the Tavistock Clinic in London, as well as many other writers.

Though much is being said about it, the concept of the self is actually relatively new in (structural) psychotherapy. Freud didn't find a need for it. Further many writers: Winnecott, Kohut, Fairbairn, Shafer, Hartmann, et al. used the terms "ego" and "self" interchangeably (i.e., without a distinct significance of its own).

It was Kohut (1971, 1984) who felt that the experience of (1) shame and (2) self consciousness were basic components of the core-of-self.

(What I am ashamed of is not likely going to be a major component I (openly or knowingly) share in most of my relationships, so just who IS this person I offer for others to know?)

Further, as I'm sure you know, Kohut (ibid.) stressed that any disturbance in the self would be observed as a disturbance in the therapist—that is in a relationship that is presumably important. Thus, the patient tends to unwittingly use the analyst as a "functional part of the self" as he or she inevitably—in addition to any "problems" that may be discussed—seeks the experience of dearly wished healing empathy denied earlier.

Oddly, to clarify the difference between his view and those of the (more common) object-relations "school writers," Kohut specifically focused—at least initially—on the self rather than the self-other dyad. Thus rather than talking about self and objects, he spoke of selfobjects (Ibid.).

Thus, rather than looking at our relationships with that which is outside us, he looked at our "notions," if you will, of what is inside that actually color our connections with what is "actually" outside (whatever that means).

According to this view, the self, thus, essentially experiences itself as both subject and as object. These form the background (subject) and foreground (object) self, as he put it. In the sense of shame, the background self is moved to the foreground ((i.e., how I feel about myself or how I see it becomes (objectively) real)).

The self you see is "me;" the self I see is "I." As I skew more toward me, I tend to get more out of touch with I (objectification).

Thus when the core-self is unstable or minimized in this way, what is outside takes on "exceptional emotional importance." Again, the normally subjective, experiencing self that is usually in the background moves to the foreground.

A common result is that one feels insubstantial—with or without others. This, Kohut argued, is typically due to the defensive projection onto others in fantasy of parts of the self, especially aggressive parts. Such a pattern leaves the self depleted—and in turn frequently results in a withdrawal of resonant emotional investment from the world and significant others.

Greenwald (1980) further suggested the concept of the "totalitarian ego" as the element that distorts (objective) reality in order to maintain its own illusions, including the production of rage when one's illusions are not verified.

Thus if a partner isn't measuring up to my "expectations," that is my notion of how the world and others "should be." Such a conception can override any relationship it seems.

Kohut concluded that it is only when one can give up one's illusions that one can embrace actual reality, i.e., can move to true object-relatedness at that time.

In other words, I must get beyond my own "colorations" of what I experience in order to experience what is genuinely there—uncolored or undistorted by me.

[Kohut, thus, remained in the empirical notions of objective reality and had not moved to post modern views of construction.]

In a similar vein Lacan (1977) stressed the consequences of what he called the "mirror function." His idea was that an infant or very young child is going to have an unclear sense of self. Everything seems so vast and complex. At this point someone shows the child his/her image in a mirror. Well, that sure isn't very diffuse! Quite the opposite, it is coherent, entire, and beautifully formed. Then these others say, "That's you!"

"*That* is me!" Thus "I" am out there and not in here at all.

For this reason Lacan said a sense of self is based on "alienation."

Further, as Mahler (1955, 1975) had suggested, (open) self reflection is only possible upon successful separation from the mother.

To this Kohut (Ibid.) added that failure to separate resulted in a lack of self-reflection and a lack of a sense of self as an "independent center of initiative." In such a situation, one can ONLY experience oneself as an object in relation to other subjects—as was the case with the experience with mother. That is, intersubjectivity is not achieved.

Actually, the father would seem to be crucial and necessary in the task of successful separation from the mother. And thus it appears that capacity for (more or less) accurate self reflection is due in an important sense to the influence of the father. (I will say more about this a little farther on.)

All of these issues are carried into relationships (as Benjamin's "copy processes") where they tend to serve as a very capable prophylaxis against what is really "out there."

Wounds or lack of adequate development in the sense of the self are, further, held to result in a sense of shame. It is actually amazing that the emotion of shame has been so largely neglected in the psychological literature.

According to Kohut (1977) it is shame that actually heightens an awareness of the true self—that is, it targets that which is/was found defective. Thus, shame serves to bring back an awareness of the self at a time when its identity consisted of an identification with someone "external" (typically mother). For this reason, shame is at its height when one is pulling away: e.g. infancy, adolescence, psychotherapy.

"Countershame" (i.e., apparent utter lack of shame) may be seen as actually a reaction-formation against (deeply experienced or profound) shame. And displaced as well as projected shame is also common to the end of avoiding a more accurate view of the self (i.e., in accord with earlier unconscious ties).

Persons with no secure sense of self may thus be seen to be afraid of being evaluated, rejected, or ignored, and tend to display, on the other hand, a strong delight at being applauded.

According to many, many   writers, a weak sense of self is typically due to an over-controlling and engulfing mother.

(As I say this, I can almost hear the groans. Oh sure; here we go—it's always mother!   What about father? Well, I'm coming to that; hold on.)

Thus, just as the mother's punishment of the child's genital play is considered one of the first narcissistic injuries, in her meeting and making sense of the child's spontaneous sense of grandiosity, the mother inevitably substitutes (to some degree or other) her own gesture, which is to be given sense by the compliance of the infant.

Such a situation actually forms the developmental matrix that will function as one's bedrock, what one has available to "share" in one's relationships.

Mollon (1993) said, "In my experience, many patients who are particularly shame-prone seem to have had controlling mothers who devalued the father (p. 50)."

In any case it would seem that from one's own personal point of view, shame occurs when the environment doesn't respond as expected—that is, not as an extension of the self (the "expectations" or blue-prints).

This shame is often hiding behind rage and guilt (on the part of the mother as well).

Winnicott (1976) used the term "false self" to describe the self that is acceptable to a mother who has required the child to play a role of her own (unwitting) requirement rather than getting in touch with the child's real self —which would "emerge" on its own if given the proper environment.

Thus aspects of the child that were not consistent with the mother's expectations were often (obligingly) not recognized. Such a mother reinforced separation only and ultimately in relation to herself, typically applauding only those achievements that confirmed her.

The child was required to collude.

In such a situation, the father is often mocked, devalued, or effectively sidelined and thus cannot function as a meaningful input source for the child. Such a child will tend to display a strong need for approval and attention from others, i.e., a high degree of vulnerability to others' opinions.

Children in this predicament often become "compulsive accommodators."

How many relationships are in fact conducted this precise way?

(In common relationship lingo, this situation is called "co-dependency.")

On the other hand, "Recognition by the parents that the child has a self that unfolds according to its own blueprint seems critical."

For this reason, Kohut emphasized empathy over "guidance." He spoke of the "gleam in the mother's eye."

Of course all these notions apply to lovers and to those in significant relationships as well as to mothers and infants.

A constant pattern of self-monitoring may actually be developed as an attempt to exclude the other in order to ward off what are the others' expected un-empathic responses. Thus, for example, a new environment is quite often experienced as being unknown, unknowing, and un-empathic. Unfortunately, the typical counter-transference response to this is on the part of a therapist (or friend or lover) is: boredom—which is, of course, hardly empathetic.

Kohut stressed the mirroring response required to go beyond this surface image that is presented in order to contact empathetically with the actual experiencing (subjective) self. Again, this is, clearly, what the mother did NOT do.

Actually, in the situation where one has a largely engulfing and over-controlling mother, the typical mother-child situation tends to be simply reversed. That is, the child now tends to become a self-object for the mother and thus cannot respond as who he or she is, but on the other hand is "…captured by a projected image from the mother's psyche."

The father is often ineffectual to intervene.

Of course, it would seem a fairly secure and workable sense of self-worth and efficacy is primarily based on the infant's ability to evoke a "meaningful emotional response in the other"—who is originally the parent, and later often significant friends and lovers.

"Oddly" powerful shame may be seen as a component of narcissistic vulnerability wherein the world does not respond as expected (i.e., as parents responded). The subsequent experience of embarrassment typically stems from a history of experiencing the mother who saw a self object of her own origin rather than seeing the actual (external) child. In this situation, the actual child was usually rejected or humiliated when he or she appeared— rather than the desired self object reflection.

Such treatment and context is introjected by the child and thus constantly expected, especially from lovers and significant friends—if not all "external" people.

That is, these experiences are all I have to comprise my "expectations" and "blue-prints" of life, relationships, and (most tragically) my own children.

Ultimately, the child of such a mother fears actually looking at others too closely as this might result in the dreaded lack of an empathetic response.

It is for these reasons, Kohut (1979) suggested we need empathy as much as we need air.

So—what about fathers?.

Many writers have stated that the development of a coherent sense of self is basically a two part process: the first may be called the "mommy part" and the second the "daddy part."

I have been detailing the mommy part. It must be remembered the mother is the first symbiotic object. The child introjects the mother's attitudes and feelings about the child. This becomes the core sense of the child's self.

Such introjection occurs, in other words, in spite of denial or other "distorting" or "cover-up" moves on the part of such a mother or family context.

When the child arrives at the age of eighteen months or so, and when he or she has learned enough grammatical structure to be able to use words meaningfully (i.e., what many, erroneously, call "learning the names of things"). It is time for the daddy part.

Grammar essentially provides the tool for conceptually separating elements in the surround. With the resulting capacity to sense difference, it is thought critical that I have a strong, warm daddy whom my mother admires and who can provide a different, and distinctly "non-mommy" experience.

Thus I may go off with such a daddy and realize: "This is not the same!" Because of awareness of such experiences, I begin to learn about the world beyond mommy. Further, father (hopefully quite genuinely) loves me. He quite typically allows difference in a profound way my mother may not.

In other words, the interaction with my mother is more typically a kind of "identity connection" (i.e., self to self or self-object) whereas the interaction with my father is more typically a relationship proper (i.e., self to another).

Further, if my daddy is able to function as an effective bulwark against my re-absorption back into the world of the mother, I can begin to learn—by the time-honored "flounder" method—who I am. That is, I can be who I discover myself to be rather than being "forced" to be who I am required to be (as would form the case if I were being pulled back into the "undifferentiated" world of the mother). Typically, a strong, loving father doesn't care if I am separate—which is one of the critical differences he can provide.

Additionally, I can also learn significant elements about my gender identity from my father. This can be effected by identification if I am a son. If I am a daughter, I can have the experience of being treated as a "this" by a "that." Such interactions serve to ground identity as well as sex role. Neither experience is meaningfully possible back in the world of my mother.

Again, interaction with my mother is typically based on "identity" (i.e., same to same)," and my relationship with my father is typically based on "connection" or "relationship" proper (i.e., other to other).

Entry into this "triadic position" through a successful experience with my father and out of the essentially "dyadic position" with my mother typically results in a radical restructuring of the self. This is truly a basic shift from a mirror interaction (i.e., dealing with the "same") to a mediate relationship (i.e., dealing with an "other").

The importance of a strong, warm, connected, and effective father is impossible to overemphasize. If a receptive, responsive, and adequate mother is required for a coherent sense of "core-self," so an adequately individuated father is required as a bridge for the self to venture beyond the domain of the mother and actually connect in an effective way with the larger world outside (i.e., father's region).

Yet, just how many such fathers are there? Many of us in fact lack such an experience—which goes a long way toward explaining several of the difficulties we seem to be having over and over again.

In fact, in the absence of such a father, extension from the world of the mother in one's life is extremely difficult, if even possible.

NARCISSISM

It is possible to see that a child, in order to develop a healthy and coherent sense of self requires the experience of a person who can more or less accurately mirror the child's emerging sense of self –or at least a person the child can truly idealize.

In this same way, a patient will be dependent on the more or less adequate mirroring of the therapist (or the lover or significant friend: apply your own context). What a patient (or lover, &c.) does not need is a therapist (or lover) attempting to impose his or her own view (i.e., self-object) on the patient—which would, of course, be a duplication of the patient's primary experience and yet thus typically be thought normal by such a patient.

When a mother (or therapist) requires the child to collude with her (or his) self-object of the child, the child is placed in the reverse of the healthy position. That is, it becomes the task of such a child to mirror the mother rather than the mother (or therapist or lover, &c.) being able to mirror the child. This kind of situation, of course, derails the child away from his or her own developmental needs in favor of the mother's agenda.

Further, without an effective father to "intervene," escape often becomes a distant wish, perhaps the famous "knight on a white horse" fantasy.

A child in such a situation tends to learn that expressions of the "real self" are devalued and disapproved. The child then internalizes these experiences and (forever) treats his or her own self the same way. In sum, such a child is trained to base the self on collusion rather than grounded on dependable instincts.

Mollen (Ibid.) remarked one patient seemed overwhelmingly to be: "...looking for himself in the picture someone else had of him."

This procedure leads to development of a conditional symbiotic relationship, which requires the child to leave undiscovered or disavow real elements of the self in the service of effective collusion.

Thus, quite plainly, it may be seen the child introjects what the mother projects.

This situation leads to a condition and sense of "possessor" and "possessed."

For this reason, that mirroring which one initially experiences with one's mother in fact determines the scope of mirroring one be able to maintain between one's own ego and self.

Since a person with a more or less pronounced narcissistic illness may be seen to be out of touch with his or her real self, there ensues a failure to live one's true pattern.

In describing what he took to be the essential message of Neitzsche's Also Sprach Zarathustra, Jung (unpublished lecture, quoted in Schwartz-Salant, 1982) said:

If you fulfill the pattern that is peculiar to yourself you have loved yourself, you have accumulated, you have abundance; you borrow virtue then because you have luster, you radiate, from your abundance, something overflows. But if you hate yourself, if you have not accepted your pattern, then there are hungry animals, prowling cats and other beasts in your constitution which get at your neighbors like flies in order to satisfy the appetites which you have failed to satisfy. Therefore Niestzshe says [of] those people who have not ulfilled their individual pattern that the bestowing soul is lacking. There is no radiation, no real warmth; there is hunger and secret stealing (quoted in Schwartz-Salant, 1982).

It may be said fear of the self appears to be based primarily on:

Fear of being overtaken by a force greater
than the ego
Fear of abandonment by others
Fear of envy

For these reasons, in the narcissistic position one tends to be strongly threatened by the notion of the unconscious. It is frightening to depend on anything beyond one's own knowing (which may explain the direction of

American psychology, since American culture is routinely thought of as being narcissistic).

In light of the above, the fear of the feminine is seen as the fear of being engulfed and drawn back into a state where there is no masculine. The fear of the masculine, on the other hand, is seen as the fear of "destructive intrusion."

In this light, a narcissistic position seems to result from a childhood context in which the father is effectively shut out from the mother-child dyad. It is therefore thought that the mother's attitude is critical. That is, without the influence of the father, it is only the mother's attitude that is available for introjection.

Narcissistic pathology may thus be said to directly stem from the non-response of the mother to the real child (she responds out of her own fantasy instead) and the mother's devaluation or distancing of herself and the child from the father. (The successful experience with the father demonstrates that one can have a relationship with the mother and NOT lose individuality and autonomy.)

Narcissism, in this view, actually represents a failure of the child to separate from the mother's image (i.e., failure to move from the dyadic position). The child is discouraged from "linking" with others and required to stay the "same" as the mother.

Further, it is the father who is capable of (adequately) teaching the modulation of aggression. Thus the less father there is, the more aggression there will be. Without the influence of one's father, one remains in danger of responding with rage whenever the world does not respond as wished.

The absence of effective fathers in Kohut's (passim) examples is truly striking (see also Stoller, et. al., passim).

Narcissism consequently may be seen to involve an unwitting collusion between oneself and the mother to deny one's true self as well as excluding the father.

Actually the rage behind this pleasing false self image is immense. This rage, however, must always be repudiated and yet at the same time serves as a major source of shame.

It is amazingly painful to acknowledge the false self in any more or less complete sense. This is the case because according to one's training and range of experience one:

> Needs to always please others (to cover vulnerability).

> "Knows" honest expression leads to internal punishment—which can be severe.

> Has a constant fear others will violate or usurp one's internal sense of autonomy.

TREATMENT

The patient is, according to the present view, thought to be in inevitable conflict with the therapist (and with the process of therapy as a whole), regardless of how "it looks." Such a person both wishes for and fears help.

This is the case as disturbed internal object relations are inevitably externalized in the transference interaction with the therapist. Due to this situation, the therapist WILL tend to be seen as either:

A weak father (who cannot facilitate differentiation), or an engulfing mother (who cannot receive the actual child)

In such a situation, the therapist must at all costs resist the patient's unwitting attempts to form a "collusive false-self alliance" (i.e., duplicate the past). The patient will quite naturally, "firmly" based on his or her experience in life, assume this is what the therapist wants.

On the other hand, to be freed from illusions related to the internal mother, the patient needs reasonably accurate empathic responses. This feeling of being received and tolerated by the therapist can then lead to a sense of hope (the so-called "good enough mother" or "adequate container" experience).

If the process is reasonably successful, the therapist may become a vital bridge linking the terrified inner self to the outer world (the so-called "adequate father" experience).

Constantly pulling against the success of such an outcome is the fact that patients inevitably have a widely distorted picture of the trait they are afraid to reveal or exhibit (i.e., due to mother introjects).

In articulating this patient's specific "mirroring wish," the therapist is able to become the "missing "paternal self object" rather than remaining as the historically experienced transference figure. That is, the therapist comes to be seen as safe and accepting but "outside" at the same time.

When the therapist in this endeavor is reasonably accurate in interpretation, the patient will be able to feel understood and dare to reach out to connect with the therapist (i.e., without undue fear of usurpation or engulfment).

Kohut (1978) essentially characterized "the cure" as a process of "transmuting internalization."

This process is both defined and able to take place through the therapist's (yet) tolerable failures as a new object. Each additional tolerable failure allows the patient to take over functions previously located entirely in the mother—or, through projection, in the therapist.

Kohut also characterized this as learning how to "tolerate the object." Here, one is more and more able to go all the way to what is truly "out there" rather than continuing to distort the real in personal (or required) ways.

Largely freed from living forever in what Alice Miller called the "Prisons of Childhood (1981)" one is capable of discovering and being who one really is rather than living forever as one who was "assigned to be."

This, however, requires as well as enables an embracing of the entire real self, not just the portions acceptable to friends, colleagues, spouses, or parents.

And, it is largely impossible in the "highly managed" situation in which the therapist or insurance reviewer decides what should be given to the patient. Clearly, such a procedure simply duplicates the dictatorial situation which led to the original wound.

3. CONTEXT DILEMMAS

In addition to our personal problems as people, how did we, also as a culture, get into such a mess? How did this cultural context develop anyway? How have cultures gotten so out of touch with what is authentic around them —and why in the world do we as well as they seem to be striving to get more out of touch all the time?

Again, let us look at how such a situation developed in the first place—that is what sort of elements contributed to its development. Answers to such investigations seem likely to provide notions of how the situation might best be improved upon, resolved, or even redirected.

If this is true for individual persons, it appears to be similarly true for whole cultures, societies, and view-points. How did we ever get from there to here—from "dawn person" to modern "high-achiever?" How different are they, really?

Again, just how accurate or complete IS our conscious-ness—both high achiever and dawn person alike? How do we know?

It would seem obvious that present behavioral or conceptual maneuvers are (at least) heavily competed against by older patterns (whether or not such patterns are recognized as operative)—if not rendered outright useless by them.

And, it has been going on for a long time.

ANCIENT CIVILIZATION

Modern linguistic theorists, including "deconstructionist" types, have repeatedly sought to find the context surrounding the modern world. Such attempts extend from Worf's assertions concerning the numbers of words for "snow" among the Eskimos to Wittgenstein's famous observation:

> A picture held us captive. And we could
> not get outside it, for it lay in our language
> and language seemed to repeat it to us in-
> exorably...Philosophy is a battle against
> the bewitchment of our intelligence by
> means of language (1953, Secs. 115, 109.)

Foucault, throughout his work, has similarly pointed out that as one moves "back" hunting for "pure" beginnings, what one finds is increased chaos and fragmentation.

As an example of the nature of these suggestions, let us trace the development of Attic drama within the context of the shifting culture that produced it.

(I am worried it seems I look at Greece rather than other civilizations in the ancient world and give the impression such a development and transition was unique to them. It was not. The pattern I will discuss may be demonstrated to have existed through all archaic "human" societies. It is, nevertheless, true that developments arising directly from the Athenian culture, especially, formed the basis for our modern world.)

My comments will be largely based or related to research and comments made by A.M.G. Little (1967) and other writers.

Thus, in Greece, the primitive tribal culture that first extended from ancient Indo-European tribes initially inhabited and developed the new lands. Their most notable establishments were the cultures of the Minoan, centered on Crete, and the Mycenaean, centered in the Peloponnese.

In these cultures, which were rural, agrarian, matriarchal, and primarily concerned with the survival of life:

> Mythology became part of the pattern of
> tribal thought; it was received uncritically,

and, as a result, the tribal leaders, tracing their descent from gods and heroes, moved among their own generation with reflected glory...the belief which came from this experience became "cement for society." (Little, p. 6).

The history of the ancient world chronicles the fact organized democracy slowly outgrew mythology in terms of the culture (at least in terms of the major cities). This development represented the evolution of a great shift in basic conceptions about the world.

Thus rites, rituals, celebrations, and public displays in the ancient world originally contributed to the foundation for the development of the drama.

Attic drama...was the expression both of a society and of a psychology—of a society passing from tribal organization into political, from a tribal responsibility directed towards the group into individual equality before the law; of a psychology dependent upon this advance and fashioned by it, emerging from primitive methods into abstract speech. It became the key not only to a chapter in Attic society but to a chapter also in human thought (Ibid, vi).

Further:

[Attic drama]…was the projection of social conflict hidden and disguised from modern eyes beneath the mythological form of primitive thought. (Ibid, p4).

Thus, quite amazingly echoing principles clearly seen in modern depth psychology, the theater became a (major) method of re-adaption.

This may be seen in the case of tragedy, which (structurally) works on two levels--just as, it is suggested by implication, do we. These two levels are: (1) the plot (conscious mind), and (2) symbolic significance (subconscious).

Specifically, it was the use of The Chorus that played a pivotal role in Attic forms of drama. It is the Chorus that serves to bind the events on stage to the society.

Initially this Chorus grew out of the "Dyonysia," which was a festival that united the ten significant Attic tribes and slowly evolved into a contest of words and thoughts rather than action only.

It may be seen that Euripides, similarly to Plato, incorporated ancient myths into "present day" action. Further, Little stressed that this feature was the importance of Athenian drama: conflict was worked out on stage rather than on the battlefield (Ibid, p.11).

Gradual state recognition for the drama reflected a shift from "ritual forms" to a newer status. This was actually the beginning of secularization and led a movement away from the "religious mystery of belief."

In fact, it is with the work of Euripides in the fifth century BCE that tragedy ended as a reverence for the gods. The Athenians had outgrown this period. It is clearly the developing reverence for individual judgment that (at least on stage) "shut out the temple of the god (Ibid, p. 20)."

Thus, in sum, the ancient system of Greek (as well as many others) societies was composed of tribal leaders, the barter system, and an agrarian base. These ancient societies were directly shaped by mother rule, worship of totems, division into clans, and the law of exogamy (marriage within the clan was considered "incest"). This system was broken down by the development of the city-state, coinage, and a vigorous system both of trade and defense. These cultures were directly shaped by father rule, power, attainment of wealth, and—eventually—learning.

Thus in the new system order and power became central rather than revelation.

Such a difference may be seen in that early drama tended to be filled with "residues," whereas later drama was filled with "derivations."

What makes Athenian society remarkable is that it tried to fuse both.

Thus Athenian drama reflected the same "conceptual landscape" as modern psychology, especially the various forms of psychoanalysis. That is, it was/is felt there is a conscious, day to day, level of perception and simultaneously a subconscious influencing level that, largely unrecognized, focuses and informs much conscious activity.

PRIMITIVE AFTERMATH

As society slowly evolved from an agrarian-centered one to a city-state, the drama changed along with it—and thus reflects the character of this change.

This can be seen perhaps most clearly in the role and nature of the chorus. Whereas the chorus in early drama had brought the voices of mythology to bear on the present events, in later drama the chorus tended to evolve increasingly into functioning as the spokesperson for public opinion.

In drama itself, the progression might be briefly characterized as follows: In Aeschylus (born 525 BCE in Eleusis) the conflict swings on new social principles in opposition to the ancient codes. There was a shift from group to individual property ownership. Zeus was "expanded" into a "universal and moral god" that reflects the exchange of authority from fragmented tribal mores to the unified laws of the city-state. Aeschylus, thus, serves as adapter of old faith to new conditions.

At mid-fifth century, Sophocles (born 480 BCE) and Euripides (born 480 BCE) both wrote plays of a much more polished and concise form. This style reflected the shrunken area of social struggle in general. What these plays, perhaps most specifically, reflect is the slow evolution of the emphasis on the individual—who is beholden to higher laws than the state—rather than being an instrument of the social group.

This evolution also involved the development of comedy as a central form in addition to the earlier development of tragedy. The essential nature of comedy was looking forward whereas the essential nature of tragedy was reflective of the past. Thus, mythology was the essence of tragedy whereas it was increasingly a source of parody for comedy.

In the plays of Euripides, for example, the chorus is quite different from what was written and presented before him. Here, the chorus was no longer the dominant force in the drama but on the other hand took a background role in relation to the action of the individuals.

Euripides wrote during the long, indecisive period of the Peloponnesian war and also the period of resolution into democracy that followed.

It was during this period, Euripides became a strong voice for women when women were "voiceless sufferers" (see "Medea," and "Lysistrata." for example).

More than any other playwright, Euripides celebrated "the conflict of the human soul in the shattered ruins of a society (Little, p 58)."

After the fourth century BCE, it was a new world. There was great economic development, classes became distinct, education made great strides, and there was a marked increase in individualism.

The stage came to represent society, and there was a pronounced increase in realism (i.e., the "here and now"). Thus, drama, one might say moved away from the background themes of the culture and focused even more specifically on the city-state.

In this, it can be seen the development of Greek society during this time of transformation from its religeo-agrarian roots—i.e., tended to "dissever" itself—to an increasingly exclusive focus on the trade-militaristic societies of the central cities.

Thus, ancient Greece in its evolution tended to foreshadow our own progression—both in our culture as well as in our psychology.

Further, there were additional important differences between the primitive and sophisticated mind. In Greece as in our own time the growth of visual imagination tended to reverse that of verbal expression. Thus visual power became the complement to primitive speech (and "understanding").

The most obvious consequence of this shift was likely that the powerful symbolism of the primitive mind tended to become either sensationalism or realism in the modern focus. This resulted in an increasing secularization of themes—symbols were gradually "replaced" with "reality." ("Replaced" or just "occluded?")

In the theater, stage decor was more and more secular. The background increasingly came to represent the secular house. The chorus declined in importance; the musicians were gradually moved off stage, leaving the stage for actors alone; there was a move from an appeal to tribal aristocracy and ritual to democracy; the long sleeved Dionysian robe was worn by significant personages in the ancient drama, such robes came to be worn by the bourgeois in the modern period; and the use of masks to indicate the characters slowly gave way to mime.

It seems significant that in the ancient Greek culture as gradually in all cultures, there was a slow evolution of focus from an enactment and thus re-experiencing of basic human truths to an increasing focus on the external expedience of the immediately surrounding society.

This is important because along with this shift came a simultaneous evolution in terms of psychological focus. Gradually the focus shifted from directly "experienced" human truths of childhood and early development to a considerable usurpation of these direct "experiences" in favor of an increasingly exclusive concentration on the "here and now"—as if—then as now—the "here and now" were the whole picture, and there were no depth underpinnings at all.

My purpose here is to momentarily reverse this process and go back to discover what it is we have "advanced" beyond and then attempt to integrate this information into a wider view of reality and the self than external focus alone can provide.

We will do this by examining the characteristics that comprised the ancient notions of Dionysos.

4. DIONYSUS AND THE BACCHUS

The previous comments I have made can be illustrated remarkably well in Euripides' The Bacchae. But in order to understand this matrix more clearly, let us review some developmental and mythical elements evoked not only by the ongoing events of the Bacchae, but also the notion of the personality and fundamentally human elements "carried" in the figure of Dionysos.

In the comments below, I have relied heavily on in-depth accounts written by Arthur Evans (1988) and other writers.

Evans began:

In 406 B.C. the Athenian playwright Euripides died at the age of seventy-five in the Kingdom of Macedon, estranged from his homeland of Athens, which he had left two years before. Among the papers found in his Macedonian home at the time of his death was a heretofore unknown play: Bakkhai (or Bacchae with the Latin spelling). This play, whose title literaly means Women Possessed by Bakkhos, has long since struck [many] readers as one of the most bizarre ever written...(p.1)

Actually, much of the confusion stems from a common notion throughout the ancient world: that of "essential" or sacred wisdom disguised by metaphor from uninitiated eyes. (This procedure was followed also in Christian texts, for example, the extensive use of the literary device of parable.)

Such a phenomenon can be seen in modern psychology as well. For example, it is a common comment concerning psychological approaches that rely heavily on metaphor (targeting, for example: "inner" feelings, personal meaningfulness, the unconscious, &c.) to be criticized for not being testable in an entirely empirical or factually external fashion the same as properly external, factual elements.

Such approaches appear as so much nonsense to readers who do not grasp metaphor and thus spend their time in external, directly observable contexts.

Let us turn to the ancient myth of Dionysos in order to grasp the psychology as well as the dramatic sense of such a character.

According to Hamilton (1940/1942) Dionysos was brother to Demeter. His mother was a mortal, and his father was Zeus. He was thus part mortal and part divine. Dionysos was originally associated with the grape, whereas Demeter was associated with the grain. Food and liquid were considered essential for human life.

The grape was thought to have divine properties as it could carry people beyond the miseries of everyday life and give them a taste of the divine. By drinking wine, people were thought to ingest the God Dionysos himself. He showed them the portion of divine nature within them.

The God, as the wine, had two sides. One was the pleasure and transport of intoxication (i.e., taste of the world beyond), and the other was brutality and madness—as when one drinks too much. Nowhere in Greek mythology was anything all-blissful and all-good.

Dionysos died with the vines in the autumn and winter and was reduced to a stump of a shrub. He was reborn in the glory of the springtime when the Dionysian Festival was held. This festival was not held in a temple or in the woods. It was held in a theater where poetry and plays were presented.

Slowly the intoxication attributed to Dionysos shifted from the wine to poetry and the theater. That is where the experience was had and the insight was gained.

That Dionysos died each autumn and was resurrected each springtime along with his mortal mother made him an obvious model for the Christ.

In Eliad's (1957) language, Dionysos represented the sacred while his cousin Pentheus (King of Thebes, thus earthly power) represented the profane.

Euripides' Bacchae was a play dramatizing the interplay between these two regions. Also in this time the city-state and rational law was replacing ancient mythology and worship. Euripides' message is that just as the unconscious underlies reason and the illusion of control, the essential truths and rhythms underlie political structure. Either is ignored or mocked at one's peril.

The setting for the Bacchae begins in the distant past of Greece, during the last phases of the legendary era of Greek heroes and goddesses. The city in which the action takes place is Thebes.

Onto this scene comes an effeminate young stranger with long hair who confides to the audience that he is really a divinity in disguise--Dionysos (also known as Bakkhos and Iakkhos). The stranger insists that he is the Son of God, that his father is Zeus, the father of gods and men, who once slept with his mother Semele, a mortal from Thebes. As a result of this tryst with Zeus, Semele became pregnant, and when Zeus's jealous wife Hera found out, she was furious. So Hera plotted a vengeance worthy of a goddess. Appearing in human disguise, Hera urged Semele to ask Zeus a favor: to expose himself to Semele in all his glory as a god. After all, she insinuated to Semele, Zeus does so all the time for Hera, his wife. Is Semele to be less favored than Hera?

Semele swallowed the bait, and on her next rendezvous with Zeus begged him to please grant just one little favor. Beguiled, satisfied by his new playmate, and spent, Zeus nodded in assent. When Semele made her request, the god was aghast and tried to dissuade her, but without success.

Semele obtained her wish: ominous roaring of thunder filled the air, jagged bolts of lightning sizzled across the firmament, the earth heaved, and the great lord of Olympos was transfigured into the likeness of the sun. Semele herself was instantly burned to a crisp, expelling from her womb the fetus named Dionysos.

Zeus, in pity, took up the fetus and pressed it into the massive, fleshy folds of his thigh, clamping the skin shut with pins of gold. In time, Zeus went into labor, and from his body there was born a god with horns on his head and snakes writhing in his hair (Evans, p 3,4; see also: Hamilton, 1940,1942, and Stoneman, 1955).

This is the character who stands before the audience at the beginning of the Bacchae. Here, he is displaying his feminine character. Being a god, Dionysos is not subject to the either-or logic of the mortal "fact" world. Dionysos is neither this nor that; he is both. The route to the gods was, as Campbell put it, "through the pairs of opposites." That is, in Christian terms, to cross from the world of duality to the world of unity (the message of the Resurrection).

Here is a brief overview of the plot of the Bacchae.

Dionysus, the god of wine, prophecy, religious ecstasy, and fertility, returns to his birthplace in Thebes in order to clear his mother's name and to punish the insolent city state for refusing to allow people to worship him. The background to his return is presented in the prologue, in which Dionysus tells the story of his mother, Semele, once a princess in the royal Theban house of Cadmus. She had an affair with Zeus, the king of the gods, and became pregnant. As revenge, Zeus's jealous wife Hera tricked Semele into asking Zeus to appear in his divine form. Zeus, too powerful for a mortal to behold, emerged from the sky as a bolt of lightning and burnt Semele to a cinder. He managed, however, to rescue his unborn son Dionysus and stitched the baby into his thigh. Semele's family claimed that she had been struck by lightning for lying about Zeus and that her child, the product of an illicit human affair, had died with her, maligning her name and rejecting the young god Dionysus.

Dionysus's return to Thebes years later. He arrives in town disguised as the stranger, accompanied by a band of bacchants, to punish the family for their treatment of his mother and their refusal to offer him sacrifices. During Dionysus's absence, Semele's father, Cadmus, had handed the kingdom over to his proud grandson Pentheus. It was

Pentheus's decision to not allow the worship of Dionysus in Thebes. Dionysus tells the audience that when he arrived in Thebes he drove Semele's sisters mad, and they fled to Mt. Cithaeron to worship him and perform his rites on the mountainside. As the ruler of the state and preserver of social order, Pentheus finds himself threatened by the Dionysian rites bringing the women from the city into the forest. Unconvinced of their divinely-caused insanity, he sees their drunken cavorting as an illicit attempt to escape the mores and legal codes regulating Theban society. His response is therefore a political one, as he orders his soldiers to arrest the Lydian stranger and his maenads, whom he sees as the root of the troubles. Deviously, Dionysus allows himself to be easily arrested and taken to Pentheus with the others. In the first of three encounters, Dionysus begins the long process of trapping Pentheus and leading him to his death. The encounter begins with the powerful Pentheus thinking he has caught the delicate stranger. He orders his androgynous prisoner to be chained, bound, and tortured but soon finds it impossible to do so. When Pentheus tries to tie Dionysus he ties only a bull, when Pentheus plunges a knife into Dionysus the blade passes only through shadow. Suddenly an earthquake shakes the palace, a fire starts, and Pentheus is left weak and puzzled.

In their second exchange, Dionysus tries to persuade Pentheus to abandon his destructive path, but Pentheus does not relent. A cowherd arrives and describes his sighting of the maddened women of Cadmus. All the women were seen resting blissfully in the forest, feasting on milk, honey and wine that sprang from the ground. They played music, suckled wild animals and sang and danced with joy. But when they saw the cowherd, they flew into a murderous rage and chased after him. The cowherd barely escaped, but the herd of cattle was captured and torn apart by hand by the maenads, including Pentheus's mother Agaue.

Pentheus is left intrigued and excited by the messenger's marvelous and frightening tale. Dionysus takes note of Pentheus's interest and offers him a chance to see the maenads for himself, undetected. Pentheus, on the verge of launching a military expedition to arrest the band, suddenly cannot resist the opportunity to see the forbidden. He agrees to do all Dionysus suggests, dressing himself in a wig and long skirts. The effeminate Pentheus, stripped of his masculinity and authority, is revealed as a vain, boastful and lecherous creature. Once in the woods, Pentheus cannot see the bacchants from the ground, and wants to mount a tree for a better vantage. Dionysus miraculously bends a tall fir tree, puts Pentheus on top, and gently straightens the tree. At once the maenads see him, and Dionysus orders them to attack the vulnerable ruler. With rolling eyes and frenzied cries the women attack, bringing Pentheus down and dragging him to the ground. As he falls Pentheus reaches out for his mother's face and pleads with her to recognize her son. But Agaue, driven mad by Dionysus, proceeds to rip her son to death. At the palace the chorus is exultant and sings the praise of Dionysus. Agaue returns home with Pentheus's head in her hands. She is still deluded and boasts to all about the young lion she hunted and beheaded. Old Cadmus, who knows what has happened, sadly approaches his daughter and draws her mind back to the palace, her family and finally what she is holding in her hands. Agaue begins to weep. Cadmus remarks that the god has punished the family rightly but excessively. In the end, Dionysus finally appears in his true form to the city. He banishes Agaue from Thebes and ordains that Cadmus and his wife will turn into snakes, destined to invade Greek lands with a horde of barbarians (see Spark).

When Dionysos is brought before Pentheus in chains, it seems Pentheus is torn in his reaction. On the one hand, he is angered and repelled by the sight of such brash effeminacy standing before him and at the same time a close reading suggests he appears to be sexually aroused by the sight.

These polarities display the range of Pentheus' capacity. Thus, in Pentheus' time it was thought the epitome of shame for a man to display any so called "weak" traits of women—but to strive for strength and fearlessness instead (i.e., social rules imposed on natural process). Also, it appears the only response the king has toward women is sexual. Such creatures had no other utility to him.

Pentheus cannot go with the attraction pole and reacts with severe "masculine" gestures. He throws Dionysos in jail. Dionysos is also an affront to the civic rule of law.

In doing this, Pentheus committed the sin of Hubris. That is, he sought to match (or even surpass) the gods' power with his own human capacities. (It will be recalled Psyche did the same thing.) Hubris was always punished by the wrath of the gods (Nemesis). Thus Pentheus' act enrages Dionysos, and he begins to seek revenge.

It is significant that already Dionysos has managed to capture the sympathy of the audience. Thus when his rage is expressed the audience stays with him (a sort of support of the victim, if you will).

Actually, Dionysos had the same fate in store for women who had rejected him. He turned them into "mad women" and drove them to the hills where they have been since then.

It may be seen in the fate of both Pentheus and the mad women this is a dramatic statement of the consequences of ignoring the fundamental human truths that were glossed over in the development of the city state.

In psychological terms: emotional denial is an invitation to madness.

The women who followed the call of Dionysos (i.e., remained in touch with essential human truths and life rhythms), on the other hand, were called "Bakkai." These women went to the mountains and indulged in such things as wild dancing at night and the eating of sacrificial animals. The experiences of sleep deprivation, lack of food, strenuous exercise, exposure to cold, and suggestive music all led to a kind of altered consciousness.

What these women were essentially doing was throwing off the rule of men that had come upon them with the replacement of the old tribal orders by the city-state, where their status was low. In so doing these followers were able to renew deep, instinctual ties with each other and animals. They also experienced being possessed by a god.

Thus for the wives and daughters of the city-state who had essentially become non-persons in the eyes of the law, ancient rites were about the only places that allowed for a genuine outlet. This was especially true in terms of the "cults" of Demeter and Dionysos.

In light of these considerations, it may be seen Euripides uses the character of Pentheus as a representative of the "misogyny" of the Athenian civilization. His death, further, may be seen not so much as the madness of women but his own hatred for "the power of women when they act in groups independent of men (p 19)."

The madness illustrated here, the audience understood, was the madness of Pentheus.

It is interesting to note that such views have more or less been transferred into the "modern world" of the West. Thus when Christianity was made the state religion of Rome by the Emperor Theodosius, the Council of Constantinople condemned Dionysian rites as follows:

> Moreover, we forbid dances and initiation rites of the 'gods' as they are falsely called among the Greeks, since, whether by men or women, they are done according to an ancient custom contrary to the Christian way of life, and we decree that no man shall put on a woman's dress nor a woman clothes

that belong to men, not shall any disguise themselves with comic, satyr, or tragic masks, nor call out the name of the disgusting Dionysos while pressing grapes in the press or pouring wine in vats, thus ignorantly arid vainly committing insane errors (See Henrichs, 1977, p 158)."

So there.

Actually, transvestite practices were long associated with the rites of Dionysos in antiquity. Dionysos, who was capable of being very feminine, was routinely thought of wearing women's clothes.

The traditional costume of Dionysos on the stage [was]—a fixed style of garment of great antiquity—was a long, saffron colored dress (p 21)." This was often worn with a flowery sash and a wand.

By wearing these items, his followers directly imitated the god. These clothes formed, in other words, a kind of religious habit.

The "Christians were later scandalized that the Greeks [were so debased as to] worship a male god who wore a dress (p 21)."

Bourlet (1983, p 27) pointed out that in itself such a costume "invites" possession and ecstasy.

To the audience it is therefore significant that until the end of the Bacchae Dionysos disguises himself as a human being (i.e., the occluding of the old truths).

This point is the more remarkable as men, when they participated in Maenadism (Dionysian rites), were obliged to "lay aside all signs of male privilege and adopt a feminine persona (p 28)."

Of course, as the chief representative of the "new order," it is this that Pentheus abhors--that leads to his downfall.   Thus in a sense, the entire motion of The Bakkhai swings on Pentheus' refusal to join in the Maenadic rites (i.e., recognize the greater truths beyond the immediate).

Further, as a representative of this "new order," Pentheus displays an ambivalent attitude toward women. "His mind always turns to sex. But like [many] men with entrenched patriarchal values, Pentheus...[at the same time] has contempt for women...(p 29)."

Thus it may be seen that in terms of the "new order" any man who seems to look or act like a woman is degrading himself.

Evans argued:

> In effect, Dionysos is an expression of the sensual joys of life unrestrained by the state and unchanneled by the patriarchal family...For him, the primary purpose of sex is

not to beget but to enjoy…To Pentheus, with his straight jacket morality about masculinity, sex and the family, Dionysos naturally looks   like a raving lunatic hell-bent on overcoming civilization (p. 37).

The crux of the play—as well as much contemporary culture, many approaches to modern psychology, and the patients it treats (i.e., "us")—can thus be stated as follows:

…Dionysos rebukes [Pentheus] by pointing to his fatal flaw—he is so out of touch with his real feelings and needs, so repressed, that he is setting himself up for disaster. In short, he has violated the first rule of Euripides' friend and mentor, Sokrates: Know Yourself (Evans, p 37-8)."

This is where mythology meets psychology, the unconscious meets the conscious. To the patriarchal culture of the city-state with its upper class, conqueror deities (sky gods) the agrarian classes who honored earlier nature deities were an inferior group. And Dionysos was a Greek god who clearly came from and belongs to the earlier school.

Thus peasants (and also women) could identify with Dionysos and rallied around him as their deity, not Zeus. In this the aristocracy found itself confronted (much as many parents are with teenagers' music) by a powerful and alien god who would not go away and with whom they must come to terms.

In psychological terms, then, Dionysos represents the return of the repressed.

In mythological terms, he is "God made flesh, animal made human, the visible incarnation of nature's continuities (p 50)."

Moving, it seems in the opposite direction, the dominant classes slowly lost touch "with the earth, with animals, and with the great cycles of nature (Ibid)."

Segal argued (1982, p. 31), "The general tendency in the arts, literature, and philosophy of the fifth century [BCE] is to assert man's independence from nature, a tendency since then stamped on all of Western thought."

--Including psychology and our concept of the nature of people, I might add.

As an example, the "better" part of human beings was increasingly identified with reason, while sexual passion was more and more associated with animal behavior.

In the city-state qualities associated with women--softness, tenderness, physical reciprocity in the sex act, &c.--were looked down upon whereas qualities associated with men, especially men in war, were praised--aggressiveness, competitiveness, insensitivity to suffering, the active role in the sex act, &c.

It is easy to see that due to its associations with the lower classes and women, the rites of Dionysos were considered "inspired contempt" for the power structure in Athens. In fact when Dionysos attacks Pentheus' palace in The Bacchae it is a metaphor for the attack of his influence on the structure of the city state.

That is, it may be argued Dionysos reactivates those human dimensions increasingly shut apart by the development of urban civilizations and their codes of law.

Thus the old agrarian rites of worship expressed two essential forces, one male and one female. Here, grains and liquids are essential for human survival and thus the spontaneous emotional needs of their followers. Dionysos and Demeter were seen as suppliers of human foods necessary for survival, Dionysos in terms of the wine and Demeter in terms of the grain.

These were carried into Christianity in terms of the host and the sacrament.

In Greece, drinking wine was to be filled with Dionysos and a taste of his transcendent divinity.

Actually, a close reading of the text reveals Dionysos has a partner in his exploits: his mother.

Thus one might say the psychological condition motivating the demise of Pentheus (and by metaphor, the developments of patriarchal civilization in Athens and other large centers) concerns the certain consequences to his culturally "tangled" sexuality. That is he is drawn to women sexually, though his cultural ethos is to demean them at the same time. It would seem that, in this, he completely misses the real eroticism of women: with each other.

This above cited contrast came about as "Dionysos came from the town of Eleutherai" in the sixth century BCE, that is from the agrarian-based "outside." His rites spread to Athens where they were given a place to be practiced: the viewing space, "theatron."

Kerenyi (1976, p 331) argued that in this sacred spot in the latter part of the sixth century there occurred "the greatest miracle in all cultural history." This was that at some point in the rites "certain members of the Dionysian chorus stepped forth and began to recite individual lines in roles that were distinct from the chorus...With these developments, theater was born."

At the height of the classical Athenian society, the theater of Dionysos seated 17,000. Most of the 90 plays written by Euripides were performed there.

Interestingly, Evans argued:

[At his own theater in performances of the Bacchae]...Dionysos addresses the Athenian religious and political establishment in the person of Pentheus and says, in effect, "*You have repressed the sexual and emotional essentials of old agrarian religion and are ig-*

norant of your own inner self [italics mine].
The price for this repression is a madness
that will tear you and your civilization asun-
der (p 72)."

This is to suggest what he is saying is that the undoing
of Pentheus (and by extension the whole Athenian culture) is that their "sanity" is actually insane.

Thus the modern ability for conducting war replaced
older ("human rhythm") systems and became the essence
of "both political stability and economic development
(Evans, p 86)."]

In other words developing patriarchal societies tended
to define qualities, including both "masculine" and "feminine" in narrow and restricted terms that were against the
natural rhythms of everyone (as symbolized in the characters of Dionysos and Pentheus).

Thus Pentheus, who is barely out of his adolescence,
has a great need to prove his "masculinity" to himself and
others. Dionysos, on the other hand, represents what
Pentheus is most afraid of in himself.

This progression of restricted or narrowing range of
"approved" behaviors and attitudes resulted in a steady
decline in the status of women as well as any quality associated with them. It is easy to see that Judeo-Christian
values, including strong homophobia, stemmed from this
and similar devaluation of women in the patriarchy.

In fact the Christian church declared the "old gods" were demons in the service of Satan. What is truly ironic about this, as we will see next, is that many of the most essential Christian doctrines stemmed from that very "paganism."

Characteristics of Dionysos (presented in the Bacchae almost 500 years before the writing of the Christian texts) and Christian characterizations of Christ include:

The concept of Dionysos as suffering god. He was conceived in the body of a mortal woman impregnated by God. "He himself has taken on human flesh to walk the earth as a god incarnate (Evans, p 147)."

Dionysos was a god-man who shared the divine nature of his father and the humanity of his mother. He, thus, was bridge between the human and the divine. Dionysos is the god of wine and thus gives to it a "sacramental character." To drink wine in a rite of Dionysos is to commune with the god and take his power and physical presence into the body (i.e., become "one" with him). As descendent of the Minoan bull, Dionysos was associated with shepherds and stables. A favorite animal of Dionysos was the mule. Dionysos was famous for his hostility to war and thus was hailed as the "prince of peace." Dionysos liberates the instinctive life from bondage of social custom much like Christ liberated the instinctive life from the bondage of sin. Both, unjustly imprisoned, are set free by miracles to continue their work.

The development of Orphic religion (i.e., late Greek development) shifted several of these influences. Most notable are the following:

It changed the character of Dionysos to emphasize his role as the lord who conquered death. Orpheus was chosen due to his role in descending and rising from the underworld to rescue Euridice. Orphism became a male-dominated religion. Orphism moved in the direction of a salvation religion.

Orphism shifted the purpose of religion from a collective celebration of the joys of life to a purification of the soul and a reduction in the role of women.

It is certainly interesting the writers of the New Testament were at a considerable distance from the Greek developments and principles that they used. Not only that, but none of them knew Jesus personally.

Evans argued:

> To get a concrete idea of how far removed the New Testament is from Jesus, imagine for a moment that after Mohandes Gandhi died in India in 1948 all his immediate followers were wiped out and that nothing of his own writings survived. Then imagine that in 1968 an Englishman by the name of Paul, who never knew him, began circulating letters claiming that Gandhi had risen-

from the dead as was the world's savior from sin. Next imagine that after 1988 a number of conflicting short stories appeared out of London, written anonymously by people who likewise had never known Gandhi, claiming that he was the Son-of-God, born from a virgin. Finally, imagine that around the year 2118 four of these stories were declared to be the gospel truth for all future beliefs about Gandhi. Imagine this process, and you will be close to visualizing the emergence of early Christian beliefs about Jesus (p 166).

Further, it may be argued that the Christians took the last version of Dionysos and "split him in two." Thus they gave the "good" traits belonging to him to Christ and the "bad" traits to the Devil (see also Pagels, 1988-9 and 1995).

The consequence of this is the Christian world—and hence Western Culture—entered a vast power struggle between good and evil (controlled versus spontaneous). And with this development, the non-transformed traditions of Dionysos were relegated to the countryside and byways and have all but perished from awareness.

And thus, stated in the extreme…"From Europe through the Middle East to India and the Far East, the story has become a familiar one: early tribal cultures—relatively peaceful and agrarian [with generally] positive ideas toward sexuality and women—are transformed, often by conquest, into violent patriarchies (Evans, p 174)"

And the goal of patriarchies seems to be to glorify truncated views of the masculine and prove one's maleness.

Thus, a main consequence of patriarchal systems is that they tend to encourage objectification. And of course the problem with objectification of others is that one most typically ends up objectifying oneself.

Thus the pressures for conformity to the external culture underline the efforts of our society—and us. Especially in contemporary America, it is what is external, after all, that counts.

Richard Berman, a Washington, DC attorney, recently wrote :

> "Mind your own business" is out. "Mind everyone else's business" is in. Lighting a cigarette, sipping a beer, or simply relaxing over a high-caloric meal at the neighborhood restaurant are all becoming covert operations. If discovered, you await the inevitable condemnation of your "unenlightened" behavior (1997).

These so-called guardians of (proper) restricted patterns, "moral systems," or thoughts are those Berman called "behavior police." He suggested they are today's tyrants. Thus the pattern of "proper" patriarchal suppression continues unabated today as it did 2,500 years ago in Greece. Now, in fact, we are so used to it we even have trouble thinking it is not proper—or inventing some rational about why this approach actually makes sense.

Berman concluded his (newspaper) article as follows:

> When Thomas Jefferson wrote a good part of the Declaration at the Indian Queen Tavern in Philadelphia [hear! hear!], odds are he didn't sit in the no-smoking, no-poultry, no-milk, no-veal, no-meat, no-popcorn, no-perfume, no-beer, no-fat section (Ibid).

And if this isn't desperation about restricting and controlling everything in sight in order to please me or my group isn't enough, consider the runaway problems of drug incarcerations—or perhaps even better the different types of abuse.

Some "data" have apparently been collected concerning the latter, including:

> Learned at home: a child living at home with violent parents is 1,500 times more likely to become a victim of abuse. And 65% of the children who witness violence at

home are likely to become in abusive rela-tion-ships as adults.

Learned from society: patriarchal culture assigns a dominate [sic], controlling role to men. Abuse is reinforced by the community when police, families, friends or church leaders ignore or minimize it.

Why women [and others] stay:

Situational [sic]--No money, job or skills, no place to stay, fear of harm to children, losing children, social isolation. Emotional--Guilt, fear of loneliness, independence, be-lief that batterer [sic] will change, can't sur-vive alone (Baker, 1997).

It is easy to argue, of course, such comments apply to all of us, as this is—after all—the context in which we as well as our parents have been raised.

There is no need to go into our professions where re-strictions and threats seem to proliferate each year like mushrooms or viruses on the internet.

And, speaking of that, the content of the web seems, according to many, to be sadly overdue for shaping up.

So, what is the answer? Just let everyone run amok—as the over-control crowd fears?

Evans (who is not a mental health worker) wound down his discussions with this comment:

> To break through the old self and open up to the contingency and vulnerability of real growth, to take the decisive step into the risky formlessness of the re-creation of self —such is a process of revolutionary ecstasy: revolutionary, because transcending every external authority's definition, ecstatic, because transcending ourselves (p 192).

This comment is surprisingly similar to those we considered at the beginning of the week. Thus rather than running amok from our current levels, perhaps the resolution for finding meaning in our lives is to dig back through all the junk heaped on our heads by those who needed us to fit with them rather than learning how to manage and function in the real world with our real selves.

Just think, if they had done such a thing, perhaps we wouldn't be in this mess.

MEXICO EIGHT

1. PSYCHOTHERAPY, THE ENTIRE CONTEXT

There is an important difference between what happens on the surface and what happens in the depths of life and, indeed, throughout all reality. This clearly includes language, the device "through which" we see those above things in the first place.

In language, what is said is a surface consideration, and what such a saying is used to do (accomplish) are, clearly, different dimensions.

Once again…very briefly… descriptions, if considered linguistically, involve a factual use of language. Metaphors involve an evocative use.

Thus metaphors seek to create a direct emotional experience or connection rather than to describe something. For this reason, metaphors are ideally suited to the feeling life. And, in this way, metaphors always suggest an expansion beyond a simple descriptive view--to a more extensive context, if you will.

We may say metaphors are figures of speech in which separate elements are equated in a symbolic or evocative way.

Consider, for example, an early Zen poem by Muso Soseki:

> The bamboo--its heart is empty
> It has become my friend.
>
> The water--its heart is pure
> It has become my teacher.

This is a very different language usage from what a descriptive account might be, such as for example: "I like bamboo, and I learn (all kinds of quantifiable) stuff from water".

Specifically, metaphors may be seen to have a denotation and a connotation. The denotation is always some physical thing, but the connotation is always an emotion of some sort.

It is in this way metaphor functions as a bridge to the emotions and the heart (which is also a metaphor).

Description is the language of the "head" (i.e., "reason").

Without the development of metaphor, human history would only be a collection of facts. Yet with metaphor we additionally have mythology, religion, and--perhaps above all--poetry.

Metaphor and metaphorical thinking are the techniques that allow movement beyond the world of facts (or lower forms) in order to contact the world beyond (the higher forms).

Heinrich Zimmer (1971) said: "The best things cannot be said; the next best are misunderstood; and the rest is what we talk about."

The best things cannot be said because they are the denotations of the metaphor. The next best are the metaphors themselves. They are misunderstood because they are widely taken as descriptions rather than metaphors—and then the "doorway" closes. The rest are practical matters of transient importance, like "What is your retirement plan?"

The point is however we use it our language carries everything we do, everything we see, everything we understand. It is how we communicate and influence each other.

"Psyche," after all, is a Greek word that is taken as the symbol of the "indwelling self" and the "emotional nature."

Quite correctly, it would seem, Sweeny (among the nightingales) pointed out:

"I gotta use words when I talk to you."
(Eliot, *Fragment of an Agon*," 1936).

The issue is, of course, how we are using words when we talk. What are we really doing? What are we trying to do?

Hash and chaos is the inevitable result of interpreting a metaphor as a factual description. When we do this, the metaphor "closes" as it were, and there is no method of opening beyond the facts.

Of course, it may seem to us this proves what we have been taught all along, that there are simply two categories in awareness: facts and mush—as in, for example, the attempt to (factually or empirically) "prove" the existence of the unconscious.

Of such a project Wittgenstein said:

A [false] picture [Bild] held us captive. And we could not get outside it, for it lay in our language and language seemed to repeat it to us inexorably. (1953, sect. 115).

It is like [having] a pair of glasses on our nose through which we see whatever we

look at. It never occurs to us to take them
off (Ibid., sect. 103).

Yet it would seem much modern psychology, especially in this country is based on just such a project: the
avoidance of metaphor for an attempt to transform psychology away from the "dreaded darkness of the fuzz-
brained psychoanalysts (and similar others)" into the
"pure light of numerical printouts."

What such a effort urges, however, is primarily one
type of language use over another type, and, it turns out,
one sort of cultural tradition over another.

It is in this way, whether credited or discredited, it
might be said there is a surface and a depth or a
metaphorical and a descriptive, psychology.

If you will, there is a grammar that applies to the context of the surface effort (i.e., language game A) and a
grammar that applies to the context of the depths (language game B).

Let us look more closely at a fundamental shift in precisely these dimensions that has occurred through out recent history in our world, especially here in the United
States.

According to an excellent account by Langman (1997)
contemporary emphases on multiculturalism suggest that
in order to develop a more complete or sophisticated view

of the world, one must be able to describe with some accuracy both where one is and where one is not.

That "and where I am not" is the difficult part.

Thus it is felt that, for example, until I know where I am not; there is an important sense in which I won't really know where I am. That is, I won't know how or where what I do know fits into the larger context.

(The Mormons have a favorite saying: "I don't need to know anything else, because I already know the truth." Though this attitude seems to be catching on in our increasingly polarized society—especially among fanatical and right-wing groups—nothing more disastrous could be imagined! Clearly if all I know is what I know from where I am—or have personally been, I don't really know much of even that—because I don't know the context.)

In this sense, knowing the context is as important as knowing the focal topic.

I call this constrained view the "Tulsa phenomenon." (I call it this rather than the "Salt Lake City phenomenon" as it generates less local backlash.) So, imagine I have grown up and spent all my life in Tulsa. I attended Tulsa schools, follow the news as it is filtered through the Tulsa newspapers and TV stations, discuss the world as well as solutions to its most pressing problems with my Tulsa friends, &c., &c.

It is easy to see that in such a case I will not likely be able to understand (at least very well) the particular limitation or slant of my own viewpoint as, not having an external reference, I can't know the particular place of Tulsa's in relation to the whole or what life-long experience may be like in the context of the larger world.

Clearly this is intended as an analogy to a major problem all of us face, that of our own "approximate-ness"—and, because of this, our tendency to unwittingly assume the entire world is akin to our own idiosyncratic experience—or should be.

And it is in precisely this spirit that many writers have claimed psychotherapy and counseling are "extremely biased" products of the White (WASP) culture. They reflect the White culture's viewpoint, values, and biases at the expense of options.

Thus, Ivey (1995) suggested, "Traditional counseling and therapy are White, male, Eurocentric, and middle class in origin and practice" (p 55). Jackson (1995) claimed, "the counseling field is uniform in that it was developed from a single point of view, namely, an Anglo-European perspective" (p 12). Grieger and Ponterotto (1995) argued, "The roots of psychotherapy are White, European, and Western in origin" (p 366). And even the APA's recent publication on the history of psychotherapy—which underlined the importance for all of us of understanding the historical precedents for psychotherapy, as it has developed, echoed as well these same themes.

It would seem that all too often this view is simply assumed to be true—or seems to be true, and it is not examined further.

Well, let's examine it further.

Langman (1997) claimed that psychotherapy was not so much a product of the white, Anglo, middle-class, European culture as it is clearly the product of Jewish culture. It is clearly wrongheaded to assume, he argued, that similarity of skin color implies similarity of cultures.

Amazingly, even the APA's "authoritative" publication mentioned above does not cite any references to Jewish dimensions.

How important is this?

Actually, it would seem that the group that the above-mentioned writers among others have in mind concerning the origins of psychotherapy is in fact the WASP culture.

Let us explore how very different the WASP and Jewish cultural assumptions really are.

In so doing, the systematic bias that has tended to overwhelm contemporary American psychotherapy will (hopefully) become more clear.

So, what is necessary for someone to schedule an appointment with a psychotherapist?

First, one must feel there is a problem. One must also feel he or she is not capable of solving the problem him or herself. One must be willing to visit and disclose this dilemma to a stranger. Then, during the course of treatment, one might allow oneself to disclose significant areas of guilt and shame as well as discussing personal thoughts, feelings, dreams, and experiences.

One must also have the expectation or hope that the stranger might be helpful in some way.

In discussing this matter Langman (1997), interestingly, pointed to the book *People in Pain* (Zborowski, 1969) which is a large scale anthropological study of how people in different cultures respond to physical pain. His findings are helpful in thinking of the cultural aspects of psychotherapy as well.

Zborowski described the modal response to pain by WASPS ("old Americans"). In this group, he said, there was a "general reluctance to speak of, or to express, pain as this was seen as useless" (Langman p 209). The attitude here is largely, "Why cry; it accomplishes nothing." Self reliance was a strong value and people on the whole didn't want to look helpless or weak.

Zborowski noted that WASPS actually would speak to a physician about their pain, yet when they did so, they tended to be highly objective, minimizing, and "emotionally controlled" in their descriptions. Such an approach tended to hide pain, exhibit stoicism, and remain subdued.

Such tendencies also likely fueled the tendency of WASPS to avoid medical attention until they were suffering from a serious condition.

Similarly, McGill and Pearce (1982) stressed the prevailing individualism in the WASP culture:

> They tend to be good at self reliance, self-sufficiency, and self-control and rather less good at maintaining mutually giving relationships, tolerating dependency, and integrating and explaining emotional experience. Keeping a stiff upper lip, muddling through, and taking it like a man [for both men and women] all reflect English values (p. 458).

Zborowski (1969) reported the Irish characteristically added to even this position by claiming there was a "certain honor" in refusing to admit you had pain (even to one's family).

And, needless to say, in German culture there was a general "repression of emotion" often described.

So, we must ask, "Is this set of attitudes consistent with the process of psychotherapy?"

Clearly the answer is no. Thus, in spite of the widespread assumption that psychotherapy is a white, male, Anglo, traditional orientation, it would seem to be almost its opposite. Psychotherapy requires one (especially males) to give up one's hyper-stoicism and mute patterns to place oneself, horror of horrors, out of control (i.e., in the control of others).

In fact, such attitudes likely go a long way toward explaining the common stigma among certain cultural groups concerning the seeking of psychotherapy services, the equally common fear or ridicule of those (ding-bats) who practice it, and even the likely zeal in recent years for here-and-now counseling approaches, behaviorism, and (topological, "practical") cognitive techniques.

At any rate in its origin psychotherapy clearly does not represent typical White culture—or at least the significant elements of it that exist in the United States.

In contrast to the above, Langman (1997) claimed the Jewish culture was not as a rule rigidly stoic but, rather, people found value to expressing their emotions openly. In fact, he pointed out, compared with the stoic, stiff upper-lip approach, the Jewish culture seems almost routinely "theatrical."

For example, one patient said, "I rolled on the floor from this wall to that wall—chewing the carpet. For eight months" (p 210).

Thus Jewish families tended to share disclosures of pain and other significant emotions openly, and the family responded by becoming involved in helping the person involved. Here it can be seen that expression of emotion served not only an expressive but also a "connective" purpose. In fact such families tended to discuss and analyze problems at great length.

Another contrast between these general groups was that Jewish people tended to rely on experts, were highly verbal as a group, and tended to respond much more quickly to discomfort and pain.

Herz and Rosen (1982) claimed:

> For Jewish-American families, psychotherapy, particularly psychoanalytic psychotherapy, meshes with their ethic, beliefs, values, and practices. In fact Jews often see therapy as a part of life and will be disturbed if the children in the family do not accept its value (p 387)

Telushkin (1992) cited the common saying: "Every Jew is either in therapy, has just finished therapy, is about to enter therapy, or is a therapist" (pp. 30-31).

In fact, it is generally felt that modern psychotherapy began with Freud in Vienna at the turn of the century.

Freud who was raised in a culturally Jewish home was, it will be recalled, friends with a Jewish doctor Josef Breuer and his Jewish patient Bertha Pappenheim who under Freud's pen became "Anna O." When Freud traced the development of the (functional) symptom, it tended to disappear. This is often cited as the beginning of the "talking cure."

Freud did not dwell on his cultural roots, but it is known his father had an Hasidic background. Thus

Freud's father was steeped in Jewish life and especially mysticism.

Further all seventeen members of the first "inner circle" of psychoanalysis were also Jewish, including Sandor Ferenczi, Karl Abraham, Max Ettingon, Otto Rank, and Hans Sachs.

Later followers were Alfred Adler, Erik Erikson, Erich Fromm, Bruno Bettelheim, Theodore Reik, Willhelm Reich, A.A. Brill, Helene Deutsch, Melanie Klein, and of course Anna Freud.

Thus it would seem to be an odd error to assume, as initially stated above, that psychotherapy is the product of White, WASP, Anglo culture. In fact it would seem it specifically rose from European Jewish culture, and especially the influence on that culture from Eastern European countries.

Actually, it will be recalled that Freud's ideas were— and continue to be—routinely ridiculed and dismissed by the non-Jewish majority as being "anything from absurd to vulgar" (Langman, p 211). It will also be recalled how they were especially attacked with hostility and rejection for their ("shocking") views on sexuality.

Further, this attitude of minimization likely remains pervasive to this day in the "back seat" typically accorded psychotherapy in health care legislation as well as much public attitude.

Contrary to such a situation, however, it may be noted Freud was warmly welcomed and received by his own cultural community.

Let us examine why this state of affairs might be so.

In a very impressive intellectual tour de force, Bakan (1958) demonstrated that Freud had been familiar with Kabbalah (the mystical sect of Judaism) and argued that what Freud essentially did was to "secularize Jewish mysticism" (Langman p 212) .

What are the similarities between Kabbalah and psychoanalysis?

First is the notion of special knowledge. Thus in Kabbalah it is held there is a secret knowledge that is revealed to only a few. (This was actually a common notion in the ancient world across cultures (think, for example, of the Mysteries at Eleusis in Greece). The special knowledge notion was even extended into Christianity by the use of parables rather than descriptions in sacred texts. The point was that only those who could decode the parables would be privy to the secrets; others would be shut out.)

> The natural man receives not the things of
> the spirit…they are foolishness to him
>
> --I Corinthians 2:14

In Kabbalah it is (also) held that this secret knowledge was essential to arrive at an understanding of crucial aspects of one's identity. Further, such secret knowledge is only transmitted through oral transmission from teacher to pupil.

Clearly this transmission parallels the training of psychotherapists by those who are learned in the profession.

(As a student, my greatest amazement was that one could not learn these things from books.)

Further the traditional role of the Rabbi can be seen to actually involve extensive counseling and psychotherapy. Rabbis are trained in assessment, conceptualization, as well as intervention techniques.

Zborowski and Herzog (1995) stated:

> The worries, illness, misery, poverty—is his [i.e., the Rabbi's] realm. He will listen to the sobs of a childless mother who can "cry out" her heart to the holy man…His duty is to listen to the complaints, to hear pleas for help and comfort (p 171).

The task is to have "felt himself into his supplicant's position and reacted with compassionate concern" (Schacter and Hoffman, 1995, p. 65).

This, of course, is a quite good characterization of empathy.

The rabbi's efforts also relied on interpretation.

Here, it may be seen both rabbinical and psychoanalytic interpretive styles include two aspects of meaning: manifest and latent. Here the manifest level is that which would be comprehensible by anyone; it is often called "surface" or "overt" meaning. The latent level is the "hidden" level that only an expert might interpret.

Ostow (1982) commented that "Biblical exegesis and psychoanalytic interpretation...resemble each other in that both infer concealed meaning from manifest text" (p. 10).

Langman (1997) pointed out that in Kaballah interpretation was routinely extended from the text alone to the "rebbe" [Rabbi]. "As a holy man, his every utterance and movement was seen as imbued with significance" (p. 213). (Recall a similar development in Greek drama—as we discussed last year.)

> Every word the Zaddik [holy man] spoke, every gesture he engaged in, was taken as equal to the Torah in profundity and significance. We may say that Freud carried this tradition one step further. The Kabbalistic forms of interpretation 'were now to be used in the appreciation of any human being (Bakan, 1958, p. 246).'

Thus what began as a search for meaning in religious and mythological/poetic texts and was later extended to the words and actions of the "rebbe" now was applied to discover psychological meaning in what every person said and did. (Think of Freud's comments about slips of the tongue, mistakes, &c.)

As Langman pointed out, this was essentially a shift from focusing on a religious text to focusing on a human text.

The concept of the Unconscious is also to be considered. Bakan pointed out the concept of the unconscious can be found in Kabbalistic texts. "…a theory of repression and the role of the ego in repression are already germinally here" (p. 76).

Also the precursors of free association may be found in the Kabbalistic notion of the meditation techniques of "jumping and skipping."

> The "jumping" unites…elements of free and guided association and is said to assure quite extraordinary results as far as the "widening of consciousness" of the initiate is concerned. The "jumping" brings to light hidden processes of the mind (Scholem, 1954, pp. 135-136).

The notion of the unconscious appears in Hasidic "psychology" in the notions of spirituality and the soul.

> The Hasidic universe of discourse is like an iceberg. The world apparent to the eye is only a small fraction of the "real" world. The unseen is very real, since much real activity is transacted in it. In fact the rebbe, who has been called the geologist of the soul, does most of his work in these unseen regions (Schacter-Shalomi, 1991, p. 17).

Thus the Hasids tended to speak of spiritual health the way we speak of mental health.

In fact, Dream Interpretation is routinely spoken of in the Talmud. According to Bakan, Talmudic dream interpretation contained sexual symbolism, word play, and numerology, These elements all appeared in Freud's The Interpretation of Dreams (1900).

Langman (1997) pointed out "Jewish books on dream interpretation were common in Europe for several centuries before Freud" (p. 213).

And the amazing statement, "A dream uninterpreted is like a letter undeciphered," appears in the Zohar! (Vol 2, p. 200) The Zohar is a major Kabbalistic text.

Speaking of the Zohar, it is uncertain whether or not Moses de Leon, a brilliant thirteenth century Spanish

Kabbalist was in fact the author as he was reputed to be of what is repeatedly called the most important of the Kabbalist texts, the Zohar (book of splendor).

The Zohar describes the teachings of a second century sage who, in order to escape the Romans, lived in a cave with his son for thirteen years and wrote down his meditations.

The point of the discourses presented in the Zohar is the notion that "...observable things...[are] reflected in a higher world and that no thing or person survive[s] independently on any plane of existence, no matter how high...All souls form but one unity with the Divine Soul."

The whole point of life, thus, is to recognize this in the experience of union.

The Zohar goes on to state: "When a man has had a dream, he should unburden himself of it before his friends" (p. Vol 2, p. 259).

Further, there is a concept of Sexuality that is remarkably similar to Freud's in much of the Kabbalah.

> We find a conception of sexuality which is startlingly close to Freud's in the Kabbalistic tradition...Freud's use of the idiom of sexuality as the basic one for the expression of all the deeper and more profound problems of mankind is entirely in the spirit of Kabbala (Bakan, pp. 271-272).

Hoffman (1981) remarked "[Kabbalah] regards sexuality as a fundamental force in human life" (p. 79).

Further (and amazingly) Telushkin (1991) stated:

> Freud's notion of the id, the repository of aggressive instincts, energy, and amoral desires, is strikingly similar to the ancient rabbinical notion of the yetzer ha-ra, aggressive instinct that encompasses also the human predilection for evil. According to the rabbis, all people are born with the yetzer ha-ra, and only acquire a predilection for good—yetzer ha-tov—as they mature. (p. 544).

Thus, it would seem Freud's concepts of id, ego, and superego have precursors in the ancient rabbinical traditions.

Based on the above considerations it seems clear psychotherapy that ostensibly began in psychoanalysis—and in fundamental conceptions—has never left it, developed directly out of a Jewish context rather than a WASP, "White," or genetically "European" context.

To improve the contrast, let us now consider the development of main-stream American psychology in the first half of the century.

Under the influence of John B. Watson and later B.F. Skinner, psychology focused largely on objective measurement of observable behaviors. According to both, the goal of the study was the prediction and control of behavior.

Thus, does not behaviorism and the cognitively-oriented legacy it spawned and which flourishes to this day in fact closely correspond to Katz's (1985) characterization of White culture and its focus on the rational, objective, linear thinking, quantification, control, and mastery?

It may be seen in fact that each development in American academic psychology has originally been touted as the death blow to psychoanalysis—only to have such new developments incorporated within the fabric of psychoanalysis as each matures?

Hornstein (1992) claimed rather grandly:

> To the analysts, science had nothing to do with method, with controlling variables or counting things…Constructing a science of the mind could mean only one thing—finding some way to peer through the watery murk of consciousness to the subaquean reality that lay beyond. The efforts of the psychologists, with their bulky equipment and piles of charts and graphs, seemed superficial and largely irrelevant (pp. 254-255).

To practically all academic American psychologists, psychoanalysis appeared to be the direct opposite of anything remotely sensible. John Watson called it "voodooism" and compared it to phrenology and other fads (Hornstein, p. 256).

Imagine the attitude that would have greeted "secret initiation rites" and "secret knowledge!"

It would seem to be quite clear that what is present here, in addition to a clash of views, is a clash of cultures.

And in fact to this day psychoanalytic approaches to psychotherapy are preferred by Jewish families, whereas WASP patients (and managed care directors?) tend to prefer "objective" approaches that stress reason, discussion, education, task assignment and specific training exercises.

Another interesting point is that in the mainstream practice of psychotherapy in America a large portion of important contributions continue to appear from Jewish practitioners. Consider, for example: Aaron Beck, Donald Meichenbaum, Albert Ellis, Abraham Maslow, Arnold Lazarus, Victor Frankl, Irvin Yalom, Jacob Moreno, Nathan Ackerman, Salvador Minuchin, Kurt Lewin, Fritz Perls, Heinz Kohut, Otto Kernberg, Hans Strupp, Hans Eysenk, Joseph Wolpe, William Glasser, Alexander Lowen, Eric Berne, et. al.

As anyone can see, this is quite a list of talent. And… isn't it interesting   several of these people have been championed as the gurus of the WASP view of psychology!

At any rate, what I have tried to stress here is the difference between "ordinary," ongoing, WASP life and the ethos that gives rise and fashions the climate of psychotherapy.

Further, it would appear that much current thinking—as well as decisions governing "adequate care" made by managed care agencies—has little appreciation of the differences I have outlined.

As Langman noted, those who do not distinguish between the context of typical "White" (WASP) culture and the climate of psychotherapy simply do not account for:

> …how a culture that emphasizes self-reliance, hyperindividualism, controlled emotions, denial of pain, and avoidance of help-seeking produced the culture of psychotherapy which values self-disclosure, discussion of personal difficulties, emotional expression, and the use of outside experts for personal problems (p. 217).

Nor, might I add, do they account for the fact that psychotherapy persists and remains popular in spite of them and their frequent efforts to schematize and militarize its character.

Gill's comment is this: What Langman characterized as characteristically Jewish may be seen on closer look to be of much broader origin.

In fact, the (broadly stated) themes of the differences between rational, controlled, deterministic methods and emotional, unconscious, and receptive (i.e., Hermetic) methods are, I submit, constant throughout the ancient world, especially after the development of the city-state.

This in fact is what is known in the German culture as the Apollonion and Dionysian approaches. (See, for example, Hesse's wonderful novel Narcissus and Goldman.)

The difference swings on the same grammatical difference I have pointed to before: the difference between a (strictly) descriptive element and a metaphorical element.

Here the difference is the metaphor opens another dimension beyond the plane of the descriptive—precisely as psychotherapy opens another dimension beyond the surface—that which is simply noticeable by all. And...if the psychotherapy is of the "depth" variety, it opens dimensions beyond the surface indeed!

I further submit to you that a "human being" is more than a description or a surface, as the popularity of "religions" through time will easily attest.

To gain access to this complex creature, one simply must move beyond the surface, the given symptom or syndrome, &c., to get to the "true nature" of what such a life is really all about.

It is interesting in this regard to point out that the widespread use of metaphor was initially a device from keeping the "secret knowledge" from those who couldn't possibly understand it. Would those be precisely those who are primarily "self-reliant, hyper-individualistic, possessed of controlled emotions, denial of pain, and avoidance of open or surrendered disclosure."

This would seem to be so.

It is only by crossing the bridge, the tautology holds, that one can cross the bridge. The "modern" obsession with sealing off—as much as possible—the emotionally complex life would seem to have produced serious casualties for which the antidote would seem to be the other part of a complete human being.

As we shall see tomorrow, the mediaeval alchemists were often much closer to it than the stoic rationalists that followed them.

II: ATTACHMENT

One place where the fascination of "what on a depth level" goes with "what on a surface level," that is: what inheres in what else, what the components might be, how we got to be such and such a way, as well as what most profitably might be done about it—is in the general area of attachment theory—as well as the kind of thinking that initially developed it.

Thus, more than fifty years ago, the British psychoanalyst, John Bowlby was struck by Freud's notion that "individuals unconsciously orchestrate adult relationships on the basis of feelings and reactions originally evoked by childhood caretakers" (Bower, p. 94).

For example, why was it exactly that delinquent boys reported strikingly less involvement with their mothers, or that infants reared in institutions and cared for by a "rotating squad of nurses" exhibited a syndrome called "failure-to-thrive?"

Bowlby was also intrigued by what he called "caregiver-child attachments" in the behavior of several different animals, especially those whose young required a large amount of care. Experiments related to the "imprinting" of ducks and geese as well as those examining the result of deprivation—or cold (i.e., "wire") mothers on monkeys, among others, impressed him greatly (see Tinbergen, Lorenz, Harlow, et. al.).

Clearly there was a heavy investment in such bonds. This was of great evolutionary utility, reasoned Bowlby, and thus likely innate. Behaviors that tied individuals together in bonded units would be good both for the well-being of infants as well as the sexual drives of the adults.

From his growing pool of observations Bowlby deduced:

> On the basis of [the quality of] childhood ties to core adult protectors, he proposed, kids develop implicit expectations about how people operate in relationships. These working models of intimacy, which are presumably open to revision as one's social world expands, [ultimately, even] provide a blueprint for adult romantic pairings (Ibid.).

Thus Bowlby had framed the explanatory route in a slightly different way that did the majority of the work of Freud. Bowlby specifically focused on the initial interactions of caregivers and infants as the formative element in the development of what he called "working schemas" [that essentially function like "expectation sets"], whereas (strictly speaking) Freud's far more complex theoretical thinking essentially carried him to develop an interfacing system between neurological phenomena and learning.

Needless to say, Bowlby's hypothesis that there was an evolutionary attachment that effectively organized behavior from the cradle to the grave was not greatly popular among developmental researchers.

The majority of developmental types focused their efforts primarily on mother-infant interactions. There have been several attempts, however, to extend this interest to the effects of various different childhood interaction patterns on the subsequent interaction patterns of adults (see, e.g., Atkinson, et. al.) Many of these studies have followed the children observed as infants into adulthood and recorded their behavior patterns—precisely as Bowlby suggested.

Just what is the influence of early attachment on the subsequent life of individuals?

For the major source I used in preparing these comments, I am indebted to Dr. Charleen Weir who mercifully attempted to educate me—and just in the nick of time I might add!

The comments that follow are primarily based on material written by Kim Bartholomew of Stanford University.

Bartholomew (1990) distinguished between two different patterns of the "avoidance of intimacy" as he called it. (A third pattern has subsequently been added—more about this in a minute). Bartholomew's research would seem to speak directly to the WASP attitudes outlined above.

"…a fearful style that is characterized by a conscious desire for social contact which is inhibited by fears of its consequences, and a dismissing style that is characterized by a defensive denial of he need or desire for greater social contact. This distinction corresponds to two differing models of the self: people who fearfully avoid intimacy view themselves as undeserving of the love and support of others, and people who dismiss intimacy possess a positive model of the self that minimizes the subjective awareness of distress or social needs (p. 147).

Avoidance may be considered a "distortion between independence and dependence, or individuation and connectedness" (p. 148).

This roughly equates to the difference between the diagnostic categories of avoidant and schizoid personality patterns.

These concerns relate directly to what Bowlby (1977) called: "the many forms of emotional distress and personality disturbance, including anxiety, anger, depression and emotional detachment, to which unwilling separation and loss give rise" (p. 201).

In fact, the patterns that indicate the "quality of the attachment bond within a relationship" have been shown to be particularly vulnerable to "anxiety, fear, illness, and fatigue." Thus, when an infant experiences these states, he or she will initiate attempts to establish contact with attachment figures and thus regain a sense of stability. In this sense, the goal of the attachment system is to maintain a "felt security."

It is felt the degree of felt security one might feel in life, in attachments—as well as the particular "character" or "quality" of these connections—is rooted in the exchange between an infant and a care giver. That is, how much was the infant able to openly rely on the attachment figure as a source of security?

As you know, Ainsworth characterized infants who were, in her view, securely attached, i.e., confident of security, those who appeared to be anxiously attached and showed ambivalent behavior toward attachment figures, and the third category she described were infants who appeared to be avoidantly attached who were less disrupted by absence of the attachment figure but who as well did not as a rule seek proximity with such figures even when they were available.

Avoidance is typically accompanied by a preoccupation with inanimate objects which may be interpreted as a p p a r e n t l y bnormal exploratory behavior but which on closer inspection has a peculiar disorganized or mindless quality (Main, 1981; see Bartholomew, p. 131).

Bowlby argued persons who avail themselves of an attachment figure during periods of high stress are precisely those who experienced rewarding early attachment experiences.

He further argued that the one maternal variable that was most related to attachment patterns in children was "sensitivity to the infants' signals (see Ainsworth, 1978).

Thus mothers of securely attached infants tend to be consistently responsive to their infants' signals and show warmth in interactions. And in contrast, mothers of ambivalent infants tended to be inconsistent and inept in dealing with the infants. These mothers tended to show a "general lack of sensitivity to their infants' needs" (Bartholomew, p. 151). The mothers of avoidant infants were typically seen as insensitive and "rejecting." These mothers tended to avoid physical contact, were routinely critical and hostile toward their infants. They displayed blunted affects and tended to interact with the infants with "rigidity and compulsiveness in caregiving" (see Egeland and Farber, 1984)

And, though it is quite true that life events can affect attachment, children throughout childhood and beyond indicated that the stability of attachment patterns throughout this period was dependent on the stability and quality of "primary attachment relationships" (see Lamb, et. al., 1985).

Bowlby suggested that based on early attachment experiences children develop working models or "inner representations" (object relations) of themselves and others that are the key building blocks of later personality organization.

> Confidence that an attachment figure is, apart from being acceptable, likely to be responsive can be seen to turn on at least two variables: (a) whether or not the attachment figure is judged to be the sort of person who in general responds to calls for support and protection: (b) whether or not the self is judged to be the sort of person towards whom anyone, and the attachment figure in particular, is likely to respond in a helpful way. Logically these variables are independent. In practice they are apt to be confounded. As a result, the model of the attachment figure and the model of the self are likely to develop so as to be complementary and mutually confirming (1973, p. 204).

Working models shape both interpretations of social interactions and function to maintain an (accurate or not) sense of who one is and what the world is as well.

Thus securely attached children are more likely to play with a friendly unknown adult.

AVOIDANT PATTERNS

By contrast, it has been shown that abused toddlers were avoidant toward daycare workers who were warm and friendly toward them (see George and Main, 1979).

Sroufe (1983) found that avoidant pre-school students were most likely to be described by their teachers as either emotionally distant and withdrawn or overly hostile and aggressive. It has been suggested in this context that avoidant children fear others with act with reciprocity.

Bartholomew (p. 154-55) discussed a group of studies that had suggested avoidant children do not lack the desire for social contact. Avoidant children lack expressiveness, and both positive and negative affect are blunted. In fact, even when in distress, avoidant children tend not to seek their mothers either to express their distress or seek comfort.

It has been suggested that the intense focus on toys and objects is actually a form of displacement behavior. Stroufe and Waters (1977) found cardiac acceleration in avoidant infants who nevertheless did not behaviorally appear distressed. They concluded that avoidant behavior is actually a form of "active avoidance."

Further Ainsworth et. al. (1978) suggested "the behavior that best describes the avoidant group at home is anger directed toward the mother." Thus anger is often expressed in indirect and inappropriate ways at home.

According to Bowlby (1973) such behavior is also characteristic of infants who have been separated from attachment figures for a long time. He felt that in these situations anger was a "protest behavior" that was directed toward "increasing proximity with the caregiver."

And pre-school children previously classified as avoidant were rated by both teachers and observers as highly dependent (Sroufe et. al., 1983). In this instance it was felt avoidant children attempted to contact caregivers and teachers indirectly, but gave this up when it was not responded to or was deflected by another. From twenty to twenty five percent of the children Sroufe studied were considered by his team to be "clearly maladaptive!"

Summarizing the above kinds of observations, Main (1981) suggested:

> In response to separation avoidant infants feel angry toward the caretaker, but the expression of anger decreases proximity, so angry impulses are masked or cut off and replaced with a detached avoidance. Avoidance thereby prevents the infant from fleeing from or acting aggressively toward a rejecting caretaker. Chronically rejected infants experience particularly strong angry impulses with corresponding high levels of avoidance when the display of anger entails risk. However in less stressful situations, this anger is expressed indirectly...[thus]...avoidant in-

fants communicate less with their mothers
when upset (see Bartholomew, p. 156)

Thus it might be seen that avoidant children tend to internalize the same aversion to strong feelings as their mothers.

And under periods of high stress when there is no hope of gaining comfort, avoidant children are seen to shift their focus entirely to objects or engage is displacement behaviors that distract them from interpersonal frustrations. Bowlby called this an attempt to "deactivate the attachment system."

Such an explanation might be applied to the common phenomenon of "gaze aversion" among avoidant children. Thus by averting their gaze, it is possible to avoid the arousal that might accompany sustaining it.

ADULT ATTACHMENT

Bowlby (1977) suggested childhood attachment patterns underlie adult abilities to form affectionate bonds as well competent parenting. He even felt these early patterns accounted for (almost all) adult pathology.

Similarly, Weiss (1982) argued:

The defining features of infant-mother attachment characterize most love relationships: a desire for closeness to the attachment figure, especially under stress; a sense of security from contact and distress or protest when threatened with loss or separation (see Bartholomew, p. 158).

And Bowlby (1980) pointed to an adult pattern of "compulsive self-reliance" that is characterized by an "assertion of independence from emotional ties."

Main et. al. (1985) have developed an Adult Attachment Interview that elicits adult's representations of their childhood attachment patterns.

Here SECURE attachment was typically characterized by generally positive memories of treatment by parents and a valuing of attached relationships in general.

The Preoccupied or Enmeshed group (AMBIVALENT attachment) recalled a mix of closeness and frustration with parents, especially in the seeking of empathetic support.

The Detached or Dismissing of attachment group (AVOIDANT attachment) generally downplayed the importance of attachment relationships as well as the influence of their childhood backgrounds on present functioning. For this group, parents were typically described as cold, disinterested, or rejecting—especially concerning the seeking of empathetic support. (An interesting subgroup of these responders was a tendency to idealize parents "in spite of conflicting specific memories" (p. 159).

Further studies have indicated college students tend to rate the avoidant group as "hostile" and "anxious" relative to the two other groups. Such hostility is likely displaced anger toward frustrating and unavailable past attachment figures.

WHY DOES THIS MATTER?

Romantic love has been characterized as an attachment process. In a questionnaire developed by Hazan and Shaver (1987), the secure pattern was characterized as: "ease of trusting and getting close to others" (Bartholomew, p. 161). The ambivalent pattern suggested a desire to get close to another coupled at the same time with a comfort in distance and "a fear of not being loved sufficiently" (ibid.). Avoidant patterns were characterized more by a fear of closeness rather than a "detached approach to relationships" (ibid.).

For example, it has been argued (see Zeifman and Hazan) that consistently in cross cultural studies involving both men and woman, the most crucial qualities of a potential mate are reported to be "kindliness, empathy, and intelligence (see Bower, p. 94).

Clearly, such qualities similarly nurture secure attachment interactions in infants.

Insecure adults, on the other hand, "reported more negative experiences and beliefs about love, a history of shorter romantic relationships and less favorable descriptions of their childhood relationships with parents than did the securely attached adults" (ibid.).

Bartholomew (1990) suggested dividing the avoidant group into two categories: (1) those with behavioral tendencies to avoid close relationships, and (2) those with a subjective conflict between needs for attachment coupled with fears of intimacy.

The first group, those with behavioral avoidance patterns are thought to have developed a:

> "way of maintaining a positive self-image in the face of rejection by attachment figures [by]…distanc[ing] oneself and develop[ing] a model of the self as fully adequate and hence invulnerable to negative feelings which might activate the attachment system…over time, the strategies used to defend against the awareness of attachment needs become so engrained as to operate automatically and largely outside of awareness. Individuals with this style passively avoid close relationships; they place much value on independence

and assert that relationships are relatively unimportant (p. 164).

This pattern might be called *dismissing*. This is a way of avoiding without dependency. Here the child likely deactivated the attachment impulse as a protection from frustration and pain.

In extreme form, this pattern resembles Schizoid Personality Disorder.

The second group, the subjective conflict group, by contrast might be called fearful:

> Like avoidant children, these individuals experience frustrated attachment needs. They desire social contact and intimacy, but experience pervasive interpersonal distrust and fear of rejection. The result is subjective distress and disturbed social relations characterized by a hypersensitivity to social approval (ibid.).

Clearly, when pronounced or characteristic of an individual's adjustment, this pattern is Avoidant Personality Disorder.

And…to make matters even worse, childhood attachment patterns may be seen to figure strongly in individuation. Thus securely attached persons may be seen to have a relatively easy time with individuation, experiencing not only a secure base but support (both externally and introjected) for explorations.

Dismissing groups have "attained a sense of self-worth at the expense of intimacy, while the fearful have difficulties with both autonomy and intimacy" (p. 165).

Such patterns are not the result of specific untoward events in childhood but rather are slowly formed over time as a reaction to the general quality or climate of in-teraction patterns in the families in which they grew up. These interaction patterns are internalized as "working models" of self, others, and relationships between them. Further, as Bowlby (1980) argued, the strongest emo-tions, both positive and negative, as a rule appear within the context of attached relationships.

ADULT PATTERNS

Clinical literature affirms that, over time, individuals routinely tend to selectively develop interaction patterns that elicit confirmatory feedback from others. And of course, pathology may be seen as an excessive rigidity in the face of the ongoing fluidity of life and interaction demands.

Bowlby (1977) again suggested: "the deeper the rela-tionship and the stronger the emotions aroused the more likely are the earlier and less conscious models to become dominant" (p.209).

Bartholomew argued:

> In particular, adults that avoid close attachments may choose partners similar to themselves in order to maintain a safe interpersonal distance. Or they may choose partners who are inherently unavailable for intimacy by dint of such factors as physical distance, competing romantic attachments, substance abuse, or preoccupation with work (cf. Morris, 1981). Alternatively, avoidant individuals may choose dependent or preoccupied partners in order to validate their perceived need to maintain psychological distance—a pre-occupied partner may in fact desire[just the opposite:] a pathological level of closeness with romantic partners (p. 172).

Of course, the great danger is that a history of childhood rejection is highly likely to be passed on in angry and punitive parenting (Crockenberg, 1987).

At least in primary relationships, distancing may invoke intensified dependency needs in partners—that likely have the effect of fueling the distancing, &c. Thus a closed loop is unwittingly developed leading to misery on the part of all concerned.

Clearly, at any rate, the avoidance of intimacy and meaningful, trusting—or openly disclosing—exchanges, prevents the development of an experience that might be profoundly different, and thus capable of contributing to an alteration of the original attachment wound.

IMPLICATIONS FOR PSYCHOTHERAPY

The above comments would appear to apply wholesale to the practice of psychotherapy, where close, intimate interactions as well as the development of attached relationships are routine.

The obvious danger is, of course, that a therapist will unwittingly pass on an avoidant or ambivalent attachment pattern to a patient—by (unconsciously) allowing only a certain kind of interaction to take place.

This would duplicate the original experience of the patient, thereby reducing the possibility for progress or precluding it all together. And since what is known it typically thought to be ordinary, the patient may feel such treatment is simply the way things are!

It is easy to see where a WASP orientation coupled with an ambivalent or avoidant attachment style (i.e., "objective distance) would tend to encourage a very different experience than a depth oriented, more welcoming secure pattern might.

Objectivity and emotional neutrality do not especially tend to foster feelings of "welcome and safety," which would appear to be the precise elements that allow for a relaxing of current defensively maintained interactions.

Actually, since so many patient complaints have to do with the tragic effects of denial of genuine depth in interactions as well as interpersonal distancing either through fear of disclosure or displacement tendencies, it is easy to see why psychotherapy often continues to enjoy an uphill struggle.

Said differently, before I can operate from a genuine depth, I need to experience what that is, and before I can operate from a more secure attachment pattern, I need to have the experience of exposing my whole, true, rotten, untold self—and experience the life-changing miracle of being accepted rather than distanced by superficiality and surface comments, distance, negation, humiliation, open hostility (for some, even dying on a fence in Wyoming), or exploitation.

This would seem to be the essential challenge of a maximally helpful experience. How often—especially in our "modern" world of managed care—do such things happen?

Before, however, I can disclose my true nature or converse somewhat comfortably with depth, I need to have the experience of what these dimensions are like. And, since both seem uncommon in modern American popular culture, are they in fact receding even farther from our grasp?

NEXT

To consider elements of depth directly, I would next like to present some basic notions regarding the mediaeval development and practice of alchemy. Here, in a lovely and oddly profound way, it might be seen that the alchemists were, in an important sense, our "depth" predecessors: the gold they finally discovered by their great efforts was, remarkably, no less than the human soul.

Alchemy—along with the Tarot, the Troubadours, mystical tracts such as the Zohar and the like—was how notions of the Hermetic wisdom of ancient cultures, especially Egypt and Greece, were preserved and extended forward into the middle ages—right into the "heart" of hostile and repressive Christianity.

Tomorrow we will turn to this fascinating region. The next day I will present a fairly detailed analysis of alchemical examples—that directly pertain, I feel, to psychotherapy. And finally I would like to discuss with you some specific ways the ideas presented and considered here might be more directly incorporated into psychotherapy, life, and (gulp) relationships.

2. ALCHEMY AND THE UNCONSCIOUS

In order to understand the relationship of alchemy to psychology, it is necessary to first establish a meaningful context.

This context initially takes rise in ancient myths, rites, and symbols that concern the crafts of the miner, the smith, and the iron worker. Routinely, great spiritual significance was linked to succeeding discoveries in "their power to change the mode of being of substances" (Eliad, 1956, 1978, p. 7).

Actually, the first person of antiquity able to modify the state of matter was the potter.

Mineral substances were thought fundamentally related to the sacredness of the Earth Mother. Eliad (1978) stressed "Very early on we are confronted with the notion that ores 'grow' in the belly of the earth after the manner of embryos. Metallurgy thus takes on the character of obstetrics" (p. 8).

The miner and the metal worker intervene in the natural growth of ores, in short they accelerate the process.

> "In a word [therefore], man, with his various techniques, gradually takes he place of Time: his labours replace the work of Time" (Ibid.).

The miner, iron worker, and alchemist each directly involve themselves in a magico-religious enterprise where matter is held to be sacred and alive. Thus in their labors, they each pursue perfection and transmutation of the sacred and the alive.

It must be stressed, however, that alchemy was not an empirical science nor a rudimentary chemistry. Such developments only occurred after the collapse of metaphorical and religious thinking as it gave way to factual dimensions.

The difference between these dimensions is what Eliad (1957) thought of as the difference between the sacred and the profane.

> Unlike the practical chemist who is concerned with matter, the alchemist "on the other hand, is concerned with the 'passion', the 'death' and the 'marriage' of substances in so far as they will tend to transmute matter and human life" (Eliad, 1978, p 10).

Fabricius (1994) argued:

The art of alchemy is almost as old as human civilization itself. In their quest for metallic transmutation, the European alchemists or 'goldmakers' continued a venerable tradition originating as far back as the Greek and Egyptian civilizations...alchemy extends its roots into the tombs and labyrinths of Egyptian religion, and the Hellenistic figure of Hermes Trismegistus, who is the model for the medieval Mercurius, derives ultimately from the ancient Egyptian Toth, god of mathematics and science [and early muse of the Tarot] (p. 6).

How did it likely begin?

The ancient sensibility was obviously awestruck by meteorites. These were "stones of light" that came from high up in the heavens. They fell to earth carrying a sort of divine sanctity. That is, they were associated with a deity.

Meteorites, further, were the only source of iron for primitive people. "When [for example] Cortez inquired of the Aztec chiefs whence they obtained their knives they simply pointed to the sky" (Richard, p. 148).

Several cultures held meteoric iron to be more valuable than gold—and it was first fashioned into icons, ornaments, statues, and amulets.

It was not until the discovery of furnaces and the process of hardening metals by heating them to a white heat that iron developed and commanded a dominant position.

Further this development was only truly possible when, through smelting, iron became an industrial success—and based upon the sanctity of meteorites, there came to be a "terrestrial holiness shared by [all] mines and ores" (Eliad, 1978, p. 25).

Thus iron, whether it fell from the skies or was mined from the earth, was considered sacred.

A sword made of meteoric iron was sacred in this way. It was considered to be a weapon of light, a divinely originating article, "inspired" and certain of conquering all opponents.

(Is this the idea behind the "light saber" in Star Wars?)

Due to such properties, iron was therefore suitable for warding off demons.

Further, the tools of the smith: the hammer, bellows, and anvil were themselves considered to be miraculous objects.

Metals were thus considered to be sacred and sexualized (they were 'embryos' from the 'womb' of the Earth Mother. "[Thus it was held] everything that lies in the belly of the earth is alive, albeit in the state of gestation" (Ibid., p. 42). Metal-embryos, it was held, thus continue to grow ripe until they have attained a state of perfection.

Such considerations led to notions of the "marriage of metals." This is "a very ancient idea that was continued and brought to a conclusion in the mysterium conjunctionis of alchemy...the alchemist, that is, takes up and perfects the work of Nature, while at the same time working to 'make' himself." (Ibid.)

The first German book ever published on the subject of alchemy was the Bergbuchlein (1505). Here it was suggested ores are generated by the union of sulfur and mercury.

Further, Eliad (Ibid., p. 50) wrote the general notion of the time was: "If nothing impedes the process of gestation, all ores will, in time, become gold." "Lesser" metals were considered "younger," not ripe, not yet "mature," nor yet in a state of "perfection."

It was the work of the alchemist to speed this process of the aging and perfecting of metals.

The important point is that, in dramatic contrast to science that operates on factual compounds, alchemy was a venture into the mystic, spiritual realm of a living, higher "organic" unity.

Thus, the process of finding a mine site or a vein depended on the revelation of divine guidance. For this reason, the establishment of a new mine was always accompanied by a religious ceremony.

> ...the area to be entered is sacred and inviolable; subterranean life and the spirits reigning there are about to be disturbed; contact is to be made with something sacred which has no part in the usual religious sphere—a sacredness more profound and more dangerous. There is a feeling of venturing into a domain which by rights does not belong to men...(Ibid., p. 56).

Charged with this very same sacred quality, ores were transferred to the furnace and the "holy fire." The furnace was thought of as a special sort of uterus where the ore may complete its gestational destiny.

It is precisely through metallurgy that humans altered their mode of existence and "place" in the world—initially through elevation and gradually through desacrilization to consider themselves factual creatures living amid other facts.

And, it is no doubt for this reason, libations of beer were common at the furnace. (Hear, hear, there it is!)

It was from these sorts of concepts and these sort of operations that human beings got the notion they actually could intervene in natural outcomes. They could even bring about a birth (i.e., of the metal).

Thus humans could feel they were taking on the very work of eternity or time. This led to the notion human beings could be transmuted in the universe through the effects of the Philosopher's Stone (i.e., the culmination of the alchemical work). The Stone, that is, superseded time.

The alchemist, like the potter who predated alchemy, was considered to be the "master of fire". To be considered this was to be able to control the passage of matter from one state to another.

According to Eliad (Ibid., p. 79) the question was "how, without peril, to interfere in the process of the cosmic forces."

And ultimately, the goal was the capacity to be able to produce fire in one's own body and to find a way to transcend the human (or "lower") condition at last.

CHINESE ALCHEMY AND THE TAO

The above considerations are perhaps more easily seen in the alchemy that sprang up in China. This event occurred primarily in Taoist circles.

The traditional Taoist notions that all things are alive and in a kind of eternal unity easily held the idea that metals mature (along with all living things), and that the metallurgist or alchemist merely sped this process by reverent actions.

The Chinese knew that cinnabar (mercuric sulfide, which is bright vermilion in color) produces mercury when put in the fire. Thus cinnabar became the ideal symbol of regeneration or resurrection. That is, it went into the holy fire as an "ordinary" mineral and through "death" in the fire was transformed to an esteemed, precious element.

Due to such an association, it was thought mercury, being sacred, could ensure immortality in humans.

Fire thus had many "sacred" properties. Materials placed in it were reduced to their original condition of un-differentiaton. This corresponded to the pre-natal, embryonic state.

In India, alchemy was carried on by the yogis and its aim was, again, the attempt to purify the base materials.

THE WEST

Alchemy like agriculture and pottery before it were largely mysteries that implied if not directly focused on the sacredness of the universe and all things.

The alchemist, like the tiller and the worker of clay, felt he was entering into a "universe steeped in sacredness" (Ibid., p 143).

This is difficult to grasp and experience properly. Our age—and especially here in the United States—does not essentially live in a sacred world. When we experience nature or even look out of our windows, we do not primarily feel we are entering into a realm of the profoundly sacred, deserving of humbled awe.

As a rule, we are at most capable of an aesthetic experience.

Alchemy, in other words, arose in a context and from an experience vastly different from ours.

> "To symbolic thinking the world is not only 'alive' but also 'open': an object is never simply itself…" (Ibid., p. 144).

The point is crucial.

Think, for example, of a tilled field. In addition to a "patch of earth" as we might think of it, ancients directly experienced it as the living, receptive body of the Earth Mother.

It was precisely this kind of metaphorical immediacy that characterized alchemy.

> "We shall not find in alchemy any beginnings of science [as is often alleged]…At no

time does the alchemist employ a scientific procedure. The texts of the ancient alchemists show 'that these men were not really interested in making gold and were not in fact talking about real gold at all [real external gold]" (Ibid., p. 148).

The meaning of such mysteries and the direct experience of them was to transform human awareness, not to attain a "factual" result.

By entering directly into the experience, the ancients found transcendence beyond the factual, day to day world in front of them. They, in short, became immortal.

Gold, thus, was the symbol for immortality. This, not matter, was the goal of the opus.

[(I can't resist this.) A similar difference exists between the increase or decrease in the rate of some "problem" behavior and a profound inner transformation as the "result" of a meaningful therapeutic procedure.]

Fabricius claimed:

The first scientists of the West were philosophical and mystical types to whom practical alchemy was a branch of a comprehensive philosophical system. Their ideas rested on the Hermetic doctrines formulated by

Alexandrian science and Greek alchemy and [thence] disseminated throughout the Roman Empire on the wings of syncretism [i.e., a combination or reconciliation between differing religious beliefs in an effort to affect a compromise]…[in so doing] the European alchemists resuscitated the Hellenistic syncretism of the ancient world which the Christian Church thought it had exterminated for ever (Ibid.)

The Christian word for "perfection" is "redemption."

That death reduced entities to their original amorphous state suggested a return to the beginning in order to repeat the cosmogony. (Correct all the errors and faults and get it right this time?)

The point is that the alchemists, by pursuing the "perfection" of metals were really pursuing their own perfection.

There is a direct sort of correspondence between the work and the inner experience of the adept.

The adept must transform himself into the Philosopher's Stone. It was actually himself upon whom he worked in his laboratory.

The Philosopher's Stone was considered the "Elixir of Immortality."

For depth psychology, the importance of this is that the processes of the unconscious may themselves be expressed in alchemical symbolism.

In such a view as in alchemy, every initiatory experience may be considered to be a victory over death or temporality—that is, one no longer had to live a life confined to a particular "realm of experience."

To attain such transformation, one must experience the hieros gamos (higher union) of the opposites, typically symbolized as the unity of the King and Queen, in order to become the androgynous self—or the birth of the unified (sacred) self from the polarized (profane) self. That is, to move beyond the confines of the dual.

Yet ironically, in their efforts and desire to supersede time, alchemists actually foreshadowed the essence of the ideology of the modern age.

It was only by "taming" nature by one's own hand, through the efforts of one's physico-chemical processes, that one could become "Nature's rival without being the slave of Time" (Ibid., p. 174).

Actually, in all ages, people have dreamed of taming or improving on nature.

The shift in focus to a specifically scientific focus was possible only after the large-scale abandonment of the metaphorical view. Such a development occurred on a rather large scale in the West largely around the time of the Renascence and involved a wholesale destruction of the sacred mode of life (the hierophanies) as a base.

ALCHEMIC PROCESSES AND PSYCHOTHERAPY

The likely reason alchemical symbolism reflects the nature of the psychological processes of the unconscious so well is that the alchemist didn't really know the nature of matter. He had only hints. In order to grasp the significance of what he was doing, all that was available was his own comprehension, imagination, and experience.

Clearly, these were filled with projections—as that is really all he had. (And us?)

And of course, the way projections function is to transfer the contents of the unconscious to the external matrix.

> [Thus] While working on his chemical experiments the operator had certain psychic experiences which appeared to him as the particular behavior of the chemical process. Since it was a question of projection, he was naturally unconscious of the fact that the experience had nothing to do with matter itself. He experienced his projection as a property of matter; but what he was in reality experiencing was his own unconscious (Edinger , 1985, p.1).

Fabricius continued:

>...the production of silver and gold out of the metallic species remained a blind alley which led the alchemists still deeper into a mountain from which there was no escape into the sunlight of scientific understanding. Instead, the frustrated goldmakers got entangled in a subterranean labyrinth of fantasies, hallucinations, visions, and dreams. Thus, what appeared to be the greatest mistake of the alchemists actually was turned out to condition their greatest achievement: in the darkness of their blind alley the sons of Hermes at last came to discover the unconscious...The effect was the symbolized chemistry of alchemy which, in the last analysis, represents an alchemy of the mind (Ibid., p. 8, 11).

And:

>As gradually the alchemical laboratories changed into psychological laboratories and the alchemical work into explorations of the inner universe, the purgation and transformation of metals were 'translated' into symbolic procedures concerned with the purgation and transformation of souls. Thus the

meeting between the alchemists and the unconscious had a revolutionary impact on the
alchemical work, which at the end of the
Middle Ages began to develop into a mystical system …Finally, in the Thirteenth,
Fourteenth, Fifteenth, and Sixteenth Centuries the psychological experiences of gen-
erations of alchemists were brought upon a
common denominator and 'distilled' into a
mystical system remarkable for its theologi-
cal boldness and unity of doctrine: the opus
alchymicum (Ibid. p. 12).

If this is accurate, the images of alchemy serve to
"concretize" the processes and experiences that go on in
psychotherapy as well.

In 1914—fourteen years after Freud's publication of
'The Interpretation of Dreams'—the Austrian depth psychologist Herbert Silberer published a penetrating study
of alchemy called 'Problems of Mysticism and Its Symbolism.' Silberer…quickly recognized the unconscious
foundations of the opus alchymicum, whose images and
motifs closely resembled those uncovered by Freud
through his study of dreams. Silberer further
demonstrated alchemical symbols as eruptions of repressed unconscious forces…[he subsequently] succeed-
ed in unlocking their [i.e., the symbols'] unconscious
meaning and, thus, translating them into psycho-dynamic
terms (Ibid.)

Fabricius (1994) suggested:

The solution offered by the present study explains the individuation process and its alchemical reflection in terms of a sustained regression into the unconscious during which the imprints of the individual's entire psychological and biological development are uncovered in symbolic form (p. 5).

And…needless to say…the strong similarity of that which was experienced by the alchemist to that which may readily be experienced by all of us renders the whole process quite immediate indeed.

Thus progression through the alchemical opus points to the way for us as well to progress beyond the projections we have to a "higher" sense of the world and who we are.

"For the alchemist, upper and lower and inner and outer were linked by hidden connections and identities" (Ibid., p. 3).

Thus the thinking of alchemy is an extension of Hermetic thought from antiquity. Think of the Emerald Tablet of Hermes Trisgemistus.

That which is above corresponds to that which is below, and that which is below corresponds to that which is above in the accomplishment of the one thing.

Again, applied to psychology, the contents of the ego are actually "earthly representatives of transpersonal principles" (Ibid.).

The central image of alchemy is the opus. This, like the search for the grail, is a sacred work, a search if you will for that which is of supreme and ultimate value. (Think also of the ancient poem "The Pearl.")

Also, this is a metaphorical, solitary adventure. One alchemist said, "Now, the regimen is greater than is perceived by reason, except through divine inspiration" (quoted in Ibid., p. 6).

It is important that one must have the "equipment" for the journey. In addition to a personality sturdy enough to endure the frustrations, humiliations, and futility involved, one must have some sense of metaphorical thinking and experience—that is, for the region beyond the immediate context of the present-interpersonal (collective) dimensions and the logical and rational restriction.

In short, as one alchemist stated: "One must start with a bit of the Philosopher's Stone if one is to find it" (Ibid.).

This makes the Task similar to psychotherapy which is typically impossible for anyone to understand from the outside—or, I might add, to supervise very adequately at any significant level.

(Similarly, lovers are always being asked, "So, what have you been doing lately?"—as if there were really some way to answer that.)

Think of the Gospel According to St. John:

> If you belonged to the world, the world would love its own; but because you do not belong to the world, because I have chosen you out of the world, for that rea-son the world hates you. (15:19)

In other words, one must not be swallowed up by the social (collective) statistical standards. (Paradoxically, St. John urges a very different sort of experience from that which is so often suggested by modern Christian practices.)

It may be said, collective thinking is frequently re-vealed by a preoccupation with whether or not one is normal. Yet to the extent that one is a separate, unique world of being, there can be no norms, since a norm is an average of many...For the scales to be [genuinely] bal-anced, the individual must be of equal weight to the world (Edinger, p. 9).

Throughout the ancient world, there was a notion of a kind of "primary matter." Thales of Miletus' famous dictum: "All is water," as well as Heracleitus' notion "All is fire" are examples of this tendency.

He [Thales] said that the world is held up by water and rides like a ship, and when it is said to 'quake' it is actually rocking because of the water's movement (Seneca, Qu Nat. III, 14; K 90).

These notions from antiquity influenced the alchemists who concentrated on the prima materia or the original substance. It was thought that for a given substance to be transformed, it must first be returned to its original, undifferentiated state.

Thus, in therapy one's blocks, defenses, distortions, and limitations must be worked through ("durcharbeitung") before the essence of the "real" self can be uncovered.

"[In psychological dimensions] Innocence corresponds to the undifferentiated state of the prima materia," claimed Edinger (p. 11).

The problems inherent in this include the phenomenon of prima materia being found everywhere—that is, no matter where we look, our perceptions include or are significantly colored by (i.e., by projection) our own individual state, though we typically don't notice this. It is also why it is so difficult to find and treat.

190

In a passage I have always thought was unusually articulate, Beier (1966) said:

> [We are our own prophets.] Through the responses [one] elicits, he constantly obtains proof that the world is exactly the place he thinks it is (p. 13)!

Also, though it is of incomparable inner value, the prima materia is typically avoided by us, abhorred, "cast into the trash heap," &c. Thus the prima materia is treated, in short, like the suffering servant of Isaiah. This essential commodity is therefore typically to be found in the shadow, the rejected, denied, and disowned part of ourselves. Further, it is that element in our personalities that is routinely considered most despicable.

This is partly why psychotherapy is such a struggle. As patients, we struggle like fury against owning those elements of ourselves that we despise (and have usually either denied or projected—such is our primitive status).

Even once the prima materia has been found, it must be subject to the operations and procedures necessary to transform it into the Philosopher's Stone, the true, integrated Self.

This is what the alchemists were doing. In their laboratories, what they finally discovered was actually no less than the human soul.

SEVEN STAGES OF THE WORK

In the symbolism of alchemy there are many operations and images—many of which overlap. It would seem, however, that there are seven basic categories of the work.

In most accounts, the work begins with Calcinato—or sometimes Solutio—but in reality any operation can be the initiating point. The other steps may follow in any order.

Let us consider these in turn and discover how they relate to the process of psychotherapy and the development of the truly human Self.

After all, in psychotherapy, if one goes at all deep, one sets in motion profound and mysterious events and experiences.

I: CALCINATO

Calcinato is based on the chemical procedure of calcination. This entails the heating of the material to an intense heat in order to drive off water and other components that will volatilize.

Thus, any image that contains an open fire that affects substances will be related to the calcinato.

In psychological terms, calcinato would apply to the defeating of the supremacy of the ego-consciousness, or the present conceptions of the self and the world.

It is the death of certainty that ushers in a necessary regression to a more "pure" state—that is to a more fluid, primitive, and less determined state.

The King or the "present concept of the self and others" is preoccupied with desire. For what? For the things of the physical world, what is immediately known. It is precisely this quality that must be "burned away" (purged).

In alchemical images, desire is represented as a dangerous wild creature, for example a wolf as in the image from Maier, of 1618. This is the lowest level of development.

The next level is represented by the lion or the fire (it is the lion that eats the wolf and the fire that destroys it).

This second level is actually a descent from the first level of aware desire. Thus, the loss of the present orientation plunges one into uncertainty and chaos. And though one likely functions more poorly following this descent, it is an advance as the iron grip on the present orientation has been loosened.

The following illustration is a picture from the Rosarium philosophorum, of 1550 of a lion devouring the sun (lower desire-guided awareness consuming the great light of higher understanding and life).

Ich bin der war grün vnnd guldisch Löwe ohn for-
(gen/
Inn mir steckt alle heimlichkeyt der philosophen
verborgen·

The highest level is often represented as the level of the king. The king is the overseer who symbolizes the highest state. (It will be remembered that a typical conception in earlier societies virtually equated the king with a/the deity. The king and the deity were thus held to be in accord.)

Edinger consequently explained:

> ...the calcinato is performed on the primitive shadow side, that harbors hungry, instinctual desirousness and is contaminated with the unconscious [i.e., unaware of the true source of its impulse]. The fire for the process comes from the frustration of these instinctual desires themselves. Such an ordeal of frustrated desire is a characteristic feature of the developmental process (Ibid., p. 21-2)

The calcinating fire only destroys the impure and base elements, leaving that alone which is "pure" and capable of ascent.

Think of the furnace of Nebuchadnezzar. In the biblical image, Nebuchadnezzar demanded everyone kneel before his golden image. Shadrach, Meshach, and Abednego refused and were thrown into the furnace. When Nebuchadnezzar checked the furnace, he found the three, now joined by a newer fourth, sitting calmly in the fire, as it were having a grand old time.

Being "higher," they could not be destroyed by the "lower" fire.

The lack of vulnerability to fire is made up from an immunity to rule by base or blind desire.

Isaiah claimed the "eternal fire" was the means by which one is punished for "belonging to oneself." The Christian concept of the fires of hell similarly punish rampant self-focused desire.

It is, therefore, personal pleasure, power, wanton destruction and harm, &c., that must be "cleansed" by the calcinato.

Images of fire are always associated with the end of the world.

Frost (1923) wrote:

> Some say the world will end in fire,
> Some say in ice.
> From what I've tasted of desire
> I hold with those who favor fire.
> But if I had to perish twice,
> I think I know enough of hate
> To say that for destruction ice
> Is also great
> And would suffice.

Throughout the Bible, there are numerous images of fire and metallurgical metaphors.

I will turn my hand against you. I will
smelt away your dross in the furnace. I will
remove all your base metal from you (Isaiah, 1:24-25).

I will lead...[them] into the fire, and re-
fine them as silver is refined, test them as
gold is tested. They will call my name and
I shall listen; and I shall say: These are my
people; and each will say, "Yahweh is my
God!" (Zechariah, 13:9)

You tested us, God, you refined us like
silver, you let us fall into the net, you laid
heavy burdens on our backs, you let people
drive over our heads; but now the ordeal by
fire and water is over, and you allow us
once more to draw breath (Psalms,
66:10-12).

In the Gospel of Thomas, there are several references
to fire as purifier, for example,

Jesus said, "I have cast fire upon the
world, and see, I am guarding it until it
blazes" (10).

As early as the Iliad of Homer there is mention of fire
as the purifier of the soul.

The Homeric Hymn to Demeter recounts her being taken in by the king and queen of Eleusis and given the task of tending the young prince. She is thrown out, however, when it is discovered that she puts the baby in the fire every night in order to render him immortal.

In Christian terms the purifying fire is projected onto the afterlife as purgatory.

Sometimes fire is symbolically equated with blood, as in blood baptism," (i.e., the ordeal of intense affect).

The end product of calcinato is the white ash. This signifies the albedo. The ash is the incorruptible "glorified body" that has survived the purifying ordeal.

The Biblical image is the "crown of glory."

In psychotherapy, one must have the necessary ego strength to endure the endless frustrations and assaults to the ego and one's current adjustment pattern to rid oneself of distortions and contaminations in order to enable one to move to a "purer" state, less driven by unknown unconscious processes and risen above a consuming demand for ego-pleasure and ego-power.

The outcome is that when one is rid of bondage to the lower fire, "fire" may then be considered the higher passion or higher purifier. In Christian terms, the Holy Spirit.

II: SOLUTIO

Solutio has to do with turning a solid into a liquid.

> Just as calcinatio pertains to the element fire, coagulatio to the element earth, and sublimatio to the element air, so solutio pertains to water (Edinger, Ibid., p. 47).

Solutio, in psychological terms, would have to do with the dissolving of the ego-consciousness or present view and understanding in the unconscious so that it might be born again without the errors it has now.

It is typically terrifying to lose one's capacity into a boundless sea of chaos (drowning is an often-used image of solutio), and this is usually experienced as massively anxiety producing. Immature or substantially primitive people, on the other hand, may view with blissful pleasure the opportunity to surrender to a sweet regression and containment. One envisions handing one's coping capacity to another and letting them handle everything.

This immature position is, however, very dangerous. It corresponds to what Neumann (1954, see esp. pp. 16-18) called uroboric incest that consists in surrendering to the Great Mother's wish the child not separate, but remain part of her forever.

For the personality that is able to withstand the solutio and the terror that accompanies it, such dissolution enables the process in which one form is able to disappear and a new form is able to be born or regenerated in its place.

In alchemical symbolism, solutio is often performed on the king. The king drowns.

The dissolution of the old form is often called nigredo. And often, the solutio that leads to this is symbolized by love. Love sets the heretofore stagnant life free to live more fully.

With regard to metals, solutio is thought of as liquefacatio, which is smelting or sometimes called "ceration."

Psychologically, the dissolving agent is seen as a superior or broader viewpoint. This greater context can then function as a containing dimension for the growth of the lesser element.

> Whenever a one-sided attitude encounters a larger attitude that includes the opposites, the former, if it is open to influence, is dissolved by the latter and goes into a state of solutio (Ibid., p. 57).

In religious contexts, the image is often baptism. In Christian terms, baptism unites the individual with Christ, that is—in Jungian terms--unites the ego with the Self.

Another image of the solutio, one more cosmological, is the catastrophe by flood. In dreams, for example, floods often suggest major life transitions.

Actually, to be "in" anything: in love, in transition, in pain, in torment, in hysterics, &c., is to be surrounded and contained by the dimension. This also is the action of solutio.

In Greek terms, solutio is associated with the moon. The moon was considered to be the source of dew, "an agent of healing grace and identical with the aqua permanens" (Ibid., p. 74).

Also, dismemberment (one method of solutio) is associated with Dionysos. This is what happens to Penthus in Euripides' play The Bacchae.

The Dionysian energy is fluid, demonic, and ecstatic. It is directly opposed to clear, structured meaning. "It is in the service, not of safety, but of rejuvenation" (Ibid., p. 64).

It will further be recalled, the wine of Dionysos and the blood of the Christ are the same image symbolically.

Neitzsche pointed out in Also Sprach Zarathustra: "… man does not possess creative powers, he is possessed by them. (1954).

An additional refinement to the symbol is suggested by the notion of the "Red Sea." This is seen as the universal solvent and is therefore the liquid version of the Philosopher's Stone.

Perhaps the most beautiful image of solutio is found in the Tao te Ching.

> The best (person) is like water. Water is good; it benefits all things and does not compete with them. It dwells in (lowly) places that all disdain. This is why it is so near to Tao. (Chan translation, 1963, p. 113).

And again in psychological terms, cleanliness suggests not literal purity but the awareness of one's own dirt. Thus, if one is psychologically clean (aware), one will not unwittingly contaminate the environment with shadow projections.

In sum, there are seven major aspects of solutio symbolism: (1) return to the womb or primal state; (2) dissolution, dispersal, dismemberment; (3) containment of a lesser thing by a greater; (4) rebirth, rejuvenation, immersion in the creative energy flow; (5) purification ordeal; (6) solution of problems; and (7) melting or softening process (Ibid., p. 78).

Further, these dimensions overlap, but it is basically the confrontation of the ego-consciousness or current viewpoint with the wider-reaching unconscious that brings about the solutio.

It must be stressed however that in psychotherapy not only the patient but also the therapist must submit to solutio. "Thus, both patient and agent must be soft and fluid" (Ibid.).

And again, the lower solutio concerns the reduction of the ego-consciousness or present state to the unconscious, and the higher solutio concerns the flowing together of the body and spirit at the same time.

This procedure leads to the Self, the transpersonal center that "unites and reconciles the opposites." This is the Philosopher's Stone, the aqua permanens, the elixir, the "tincture," the "universal solvent," &c.

The Gospel According to St. John states:

> Whoever drinks the water that I shall give him will never suffer thirst anymore. The water that I shall give him will be an inner spring always welling up for eternal life (4:14).

III: COAGULATIO

Coagulatio is the process that pertains to the earth.

The chemical model here is that of turning a liquid into a solid by cooling. Thus a solid that has been dissolved in a solvent reappears when the solvent is evaporated.

Thus coagulatio is essentially the process of turning something into earth. For this reason, coagulatio is equated with creation.

In psychological terms, to become earth is to have achieved a concretized or "localized" form. It has, in other words, been attached to an ego.

According to many myths, coagulatio is promoted by action, such as storm. "The churn of reality, solidifies the personality" (Edinger, Ibid., p. 85).

Dictum Eleven of the Turba Philosophorum, an important alchemical text presents this recipe for coagulatio:

Take quicksilver [mercury], coagulate in the body of Magnesia, In Kuhul (lead), or in Sulphur which does not burn; etc (See Ibid.).

To alchemists Magnesia was a general term for "various crude metallic ores or impure mixtures." Lead was "heavy, dull, and burdensome. It equated with "heavy reality." Sulphur whose yellow color and inflammability equated with the sun.

Psychologically this points to the amalgamation of mercury which signifies the very spirit of Mercurais which, in Jungian terms, is the "autonomous spirit of the archetypal psyche" with (1) impure mixtures, that signify the incomplete developmental state of us; with (2) lead that signifies the heaviest and most burdensome part of us; and (3) with sulphur that does not burn (which does not exist in this world and is thus suggesting a psychological dimension) which may well signify those elements that rightfully would earn us a place in Christian hell—however combined with mercury that does not burn suggests purely temporal dimensions.

In psychotherapy coagulatio begins with the establishment of transference desires. The lure of desire, after all, is the "sweetness of fulfillment."

Hamlet protested:

> Oh, that this too too solid flesh would melt,
> Thaw, and resolve itself into dew! (Act I,
> Scene II, Line 129)

In the extreme, coagulatio is associated with evil. It is common in accounts since antiquity to equate matter (the things of the earth) with evil.

In the Gospel According to St. Matthew it is stated:

> Do not save riches here on earth, where
> moths and rust destroy and robbers break in
> and steal. Instead, save riches in heaven,
> where moths and rust cannot destroy, and

robbers cannot break in and steal. For your heart will always be where your riches are (Good News translation, 6: 19-21).

The developmental point is that growth of the ego is necessarily accompanied by shame, carnality, and guilt. And for this reason, awareness of one's own evil—that is, the "shadow" element—coagulates.

This is why, again, Jesus is reported to have said, "Resist not evil" (Matthew, 5:39). It is always dangerous to be too one-sided—even if that one side is good.

Symbolically in alchemical figures, guilt is represented by chains and jail (think also of Prometheus).

Coagulatio is typically followed by mortificatio and putrefactio. That is, what is now fully concretized must be transformed.

Mythologically, femininity is the dimension associated with relationship. Relationship coagulates.

Furthermore, it soon becomes apparent that it is not only an external relationship that coagulates, but an internal one does too.

Emotions cast about until they concretize in some fashion—as do clothes.

Perhaps the best image of coagulatio, however, is the notion of the parent complex. Here, significant relations with the transcendent or archetypal dimensions are negatively impacted by prior coagulated experiences with one's concrete parents.

Coagulatio is always experienced as bondage, because it confines to immediate reality. We say "She was bound to do that!"

In the Phaedrus, section 250, Plato spoke of the soul being "enshrined in a living tomb which we carry about, now that we are imprisoned in the body, like an oyster in his shell."

But perhaps the most striking image of coagulatio is in the first of the Gospel according to St. John: "And the Word became flesh and dwelt among us" (John, 1:14).

This, or the crucifixion at which The Christ was nailed to a cross.

Also Adam and Eve eat of the fruit. Eating incorporates a substance and coagulates it into body. What nourishes the body belongs to this same imagery.

The Christ was born of a virgin. The image for this in alchemy is "white foliated earth." A famous plate from Maier, 1618, suggests "Sow your gold in white foliated earth." (Since typical coagulated earth is black, white earth suggests purification—similar to the calcified white ash that remains at the end of the process.)

The Gnostic poem "The Pearl" ("The Soul") recounts a similar story of descent, the purification ordeal, and assent.

In both the Christian and Gnostic traditions, incarnation or descent is specifically for the purposes of "rescue" (Edinger, p. 106).

> [Thus] the alchemical operation of coagulatio, together with the imagery that clusters around this idea, constitutes an elaborate symbol system that expresses the archetypal process of ego   f o r m a t i o n (Ibid., p. 115).

V: SUBLIMATIO

Sublimatio is the portion of the work that pertains to air. It turns the material under consideration into air by volatilizing and elevating it.

Thus, as Edinger (Ibid., p. 117) points out, the essential quality of sublimatio is that it translates a lower form into a higher form by ascending movement.

And, for this reason, images that are associated with elevated movement: ladders, stairs, mountains, flying, &c., belong to sublimatio symbolism. It is the process of moving higher rather than lower.

The tower is a sublimatio symbol par excellence (think of the Tower of Babel or Key Sixteen of the Tarot Higher Arcana).

The alchemical vessel was routinely equated with entirety or the macrocosm. The lower part suggested the earth; the upper part, heaven.

> [For example,] The "expulsion of quicksilver" is done by sublimatio, which releases the spirit hidden in matter. In the largest sense, this refers psychologically to the redemption of the Self from its original unconscious (unaware) state (Ibid., p. 123).

The point is that the body is "made perfect" by spiritualizing it.

And in this regard, the "white soul" is often represented as a white bird (dove) rising above the material being heated.

Dream images of birds suggest sublimatio, whereas bird-phobias may suggest defenses against a necessary sublimatio.

Since antiquity, birds have been considered to be messengers from God (or Gods).

In psychological terms, it is the process of "rising above" the problem for a more synoptic or clearer view which indicates the sublimatio. That is, it is meta-logic rather than logic; meta-grammar rather than grammar, &c.

> Sublimatio is an ascent that raises us above the confining entanglements of immediate, earthly existence and its concrete, personal particulars (Ibid., p. 118).

In Jungian terms it is a shift of perspective from the individual psychic context to a consideration of the "archetypal context."

Thus the alchemical notions of sublimatio have nothing to do with the Freudian notion of "sublimation." Clearly, for example, sublimation can be a "lateral operation."

The history of the development of human awareness and culture is the history of a process of sublimatio in which succeeding developments allow progressively expanding awareness of ourselves and the world around us. Reason, for example, enables a separation from personal likes and dislikes.

In Christian terms, sublimatio has to do with the translation to eternity. This is the greater sublimatio as opposed to a lesser sublimatio.

In all these cases, rising motion eternalizes whereas descending motion personalizes.

An alchemical instruction is "Sublimate the body and coagulate the spirit."

Repeated ascendings and descendings are called circulatio.

In chemistry, circulatio suggests a process where substance is heated in a reflux flask. Thus the vapors ascend and condense and are then returned to the globe of the flask, over and over.

The fourth paragraph of the Emerald Tablet says:

> It rises from Earth to Heaven, and then it descends again to the earth, and receives Power from Above and from Below. Thus you will have the Glory of the whole World. All Obscurity will be clear to you. This is the strong Power of all Power because it overcomes everything fine and penetrates everything solid.

Perhaps the best example of this is the Tarot sequence of the higher arcana of cards. Here, The Fool, having attained reunion with eternity, is seen joyfully stepping off of a cliff in order to descend to the lowest point of the world and awareness. There The Fool is incarnated as The Magician, who might be described as the earthly potential of all eternal dimensions.

Through the stages this potential rises until at its apex where it disappears through what Joseph Campbell called "the vulva of eternity" and is reunited with the undifferentiated totality (the eternal) (in terms of Kabbalah: from "ain" to "ain soph.")

Over and over in continual process this movement takes place (circulatio).

These examples illustrate the difference between the Hermetic and Christian reference point. The Christians only speak of a one-way ascent to heaven. The Hermetic view is always circular.

The shift in viewpoint is critical. The alchemists were not working for personal redemption as such. They were endlessly devoted to "the liberation of God [the eternal] from the darkness of matter" (Ibid., p. 144).

3. ALCHEMY AND THE UNCONSCIOUS TWO

VI: MORTIFICATIO

As we have seen so far, the purpose of alchemy was to "free the light from the stone." That is, free the higher radiance from the merely concrete facts. Unlike the aims of Christianity, which were essentially based on the same symbolism, alchemy and Hermetic thought sought to unite lower and higher "regions" together, not rise from one and disappear into the other.

One common conception of the alchemical opus was that it essentially consisted of three stages: nigredo, albedo, and rubedo: the blackening, the whitening, and the reddening.

Mortificatio concerns the first of these: the blackening.

(An overlap does exist in alchemy between mortificatio and putrefactio.)

There is no chemical analog for mortificatio. What it concerns is "the experience of death." Putrefactio, on the other hand, concerns "rotting."

Mortificatio is the most negative operation in alchemy. It has to do with darkness, defeat, torture, mutilation, death, and rotting. However these dark images often lead over to highly positive ones—growth, resurrection, rebirth—but the hallmark of mortificatio is the color black…

[The point is] That which does not make black cannot make white, because blackness is the beginning of whiteness, and a sign of putrefaction and alteration, and that the body is now penetrated and mortified…Putrefaction is of so great efficacy that it blots out the old nature and transmutes everything into another new nature, and bears another new fruit…[it] takes away the acridity from all corrosive spirits of salt, renders them soft and sweet (Edigner, 1985, pp. 148-9).

It is the law of opposites that awareness of one side of necessity consulates the contrary.

Often, throughout ancient mythology, it is the dragon that must be killed in order to rescue the maiden, as in the accounts of the hero who must slay the dragon (i.e., individuate) (See Neumann, 1954). But perhaps the most common symbol used in this context is another: this concerns the King or Sol (the sun) who is to be killed. Sometimes it is even the Lion or an Eagle that must have its wings clipped.

The dragon suggests the regressive pull of the Great Mother not to break away from the mother-symbiosis. The King, sun, lion, and eagle suggest the conscious ego and the "power instinct."

Most commonly, therefore, mortificatio of the King or the sun points to the "death and transformation of a collective dominant or ruling principle" (Ibid. p. 151).

When something white has been killed, it putrefies and turns to black. That is, what was once valued is debased.

Such images are common in the Christian scriptures where fear is routinely linked to wisdom. "The fear of the Lord is the beginning of wisdom" (Proverbs, 1:7).

Perhaps the most famous reference in this regard is from the Gospel According to St. John:

Truly, truly, I say to you, unless a grain of wheat falls into the earth and dies, it remains alone; but if it dies, it bears much fruit. He who loves his life loses it, and he who hates his life in this world will keep it for eternal life (12:24-25).

As in this case, images of death and burial have routinely suggested the planting of seeds and their subsequent germination (think, for example, of the Hierophant's lifting of an ear of corn in the rites at Eleusis).

An almost universal dictum from antiquity is simply: the old must die in order for the new to be born. In accord with this dictum, the notion in alchemy is that death is the conception of the Philosopher's Stone.

Actually, the repeating cycles of germination and decay, light and darkness, all forms of death and rebirth belong to lunar symbolism (Edinger, p. 163). The moon dies and is born each month in an endless cycle.

Further, it is also likely the earliest forms of religious practice concerned burial rites. Symbols from ancient mortuary symbolism (see Bachoven, 1859, 1967) have appeared as symbols in alchemy as well.

Adjusting one's sensibility to the necessity of the whole cycle is seen as crucial. Not only is this an adjusting to the world that is there (actually present), but a development of the capacity to endure the contradiction posed by opposites serves to enlarge perceptual capacity and thus "nourishes the Self." (In addition to helping greatly on the Miller Analogies Test.)

[Another term for nigredo is "corvus" which means crow or raven. Not only is this bird black but it is known to be a carrion eater.]

It will be recalled that Plato, in fact, specifically connects death with the birth of wisdom. Philosophy, he held, can only come about in any significant form upon the death of the body and a "life of lower forms." In the Phaedo, for example, the following notion appears:

"Putrefaction, as we saw some time ago in our discussion, consists in separating the soul as much as possible from the body, and accustoming it to withdraw from all contact with the body and concentrate itself by itself, and to have its dwelling as far as it can, both now and in the future, alone by itself, freed from the shackles of the body (Collected Dialogues, 67c).

A similar point was made by Jung when he said: "The experience of the self is always a defeat for the ego" (Mysterium Coniunctionis, par. 788).

We might say any encounter or confrontation with the unconscious is an overwhelming and typically wounding experience. That is, one learns what one doesn't want to learn.

Amazing nigredo and mortificatio images occur in modern poetry. For example, Roethke wrote:

> In a dark time, the eye begins to see,
> I meet my shadow in the deepening shade;
> I hear my echo in the echoing wood—
> My shadow pinned against a sweating wall.
> That place among the rocks—is it a cave,
> Or winding path? The edge is what I have.
> (In a Dark Time, 1964)

And in East Coker, Eliot wrote:

   I said to my soul, be still, and wait without hope
   For hope would be hope for the wrong thing; wait
without love
   For love would be love for the wrong thing: there is
yet faith
  But the faith and the love and the hope are all in the
waiting.
   Wait without thought, for you are not ready for
thought:
  So the darkness shall be the light, and the stillness
the dancing.

(1942)

Also:

   In order to arrive at what you do not know
   You must go by a way which is the way of
   ignorance.
   In order to possess what you do not possess
   You must go by the way of dispossession.
   In order to arrive art what you are not
   You must go through the way in which you are not.
   And what you do not know is the only thing
   you know
   And what you own is what you do not own
   And where you are is where you are not. (Ibid.)

And, of course, mortificatio leads directly to the symbolism of the Passion of Christ and the psychology of sacrifice.

Meister Eckhart said:

> Suffering alone is sufficient preparation for God's dwelling in man's heart...God is always with a man in suffering; as he himself declared by the mouth of the prophet, 'Whosoever is sorrowful, I will myself be with him (Jeremiah, 31:25) (I:263).'

PART VIII: SEPARATIO

Alchemists thought of Prima Materia as a jumble of elements that must be subjected to a process of separation.

There are many physical analogies of this.

The method for producing metals from crude ore consisted of pulverizing, heating, or chemical means.

Many substances when heated will separate into a volatile part which vaporizes and an earthy residue which remains behind. Amalgams, for instance, when heated release their mercury as vapor and leave the non-volatile metal at the bottom of the vessel (Edinger, p. 183).

The parallel is that in separatio, order is brought about from a state of confusion much as—according to creation myths—the universe was brought about out of the original chaos. And for human beings, the sense is that of separating the gold of the self from the mere vapor of its contamination.

In mythology, many creation myths begin with a "cosmic egg." There are also mentions of the "Philosophical Egg" in alchemy.

The Emerald Tablet states:

Separate the Earth by Fire: the fine from
the gross, gently and with great skill.

The psychological point concerns the development of the capacity to become aware of the elements of the Self, including, of course, the opposites (i.e., the development of the capacity for and the expansion of conscious awareness) rather than living in a primal, undifferentiated or unaware mass—where nothing can be accounted for, understood, nor predicted.

(Some (see Buber, Edinger, Kernberg, et. al.) have argued the position that the first phase of separatio with regard to human consciousness is the differentiation of the "thou" from the "I ." In other words, the separation of the elements "me" and "not-me.")

As Neumann (1954) has detailed, the extent to which the opposites remain unconscious is the extent to which one remains in a state known as participation mystique. One consequence of this is that, as I have not differentiated an individual identity as yet, I may remain "fused" with one side of a pair of opposites and project the other side onto other persons or the world. This was the state in which "Primitive Person" lived before attaining a knowing consciousness.

Further, such a process clearly does not end with increasing consciousness. Thus it would seem obvious that each succeeding aware discovery or aware encounter with an area of the heretofore unknown unconscious would seem to require a crucial procedure of separatio.

Symbolically, swords, knives, and sharp cutting edges of various sorts are suggestive of separatio. (Think of the suit of Swords in the Tarot.) Thus, separatio is often thought of in terms of a death or a killing.

But perhaps the greatest agent ever of separatio has been the development of grammar.

This is reflected in the famous first sentence of the Gospel According to St. John:

In the beginning was the Logos [Word], and the Logos [Word] was with God, and the Logos [Word] was God (1:1)

"Logos" in Greek is the capacity for knowledge and knowing, i.e., the awareness that brings understanding.

The author of the gospel then adds: "The same was in the beginning with God" (1:2).

Edinger (Ibid.) added:

> By separating the opposites, the Logos brings clarity; but, by making the opposites visible, it also brings conflict (p. 191).

This comment looks to a theme that occurs throughout the Synoptic Gospels as well as in the Gnostic Gospel of Thomas. For example:

> I have not come to bring peace, but a sword. For I have come to set a man against his father, and a daughter against her mother, and a daughter-in-law against her mother-in-law; and a man's foes will be those of his own household Matthew, 10: 34-36).

> Jesus said, "Men think, perhaps, that it is peace which I have come to cast upon the world. They do not know that it is war. For there will be five in a house: three with be against two, and two against three, the

father against the son, and the son against the father. And they will stand solitary (Thomas, 16).

In Greek mythology, Eris, the Goddess of Discord, governs separatio. Eris is the sister of Ares.

Heraclitus argued:

War [between the opposites] is the father of all and the king of all, and some he shows as gods, others as men; some he makes slaves, others free (Fragments, 53).

The point is: how we deal with the opposites is the truly important issue.

Counting, numbering, measuring, weighing, &c., are all methods of separatio.

Notions of law and justice as well are based upon the mean or balance between the pairs of opposites. In Jungian terms, the "Golden Mean" may, in a similar light, be thought of as a maximized relationship between the Ego and the Self.

This notion of law, justice, and the golden mean of life is suggested by Key Eleven of the Tarot: Justice.

Of course—on the other hand, separatio can be used destructively as well as constructively.

Thus, artificial or forced divisions (such as, for example, imposed equality or arbitrary quotas) may function to tear away rather than be an aid to aware consciousness.

It is, in fact, too much focus and concern on separatio that gives rise to the constellation of its opposite: coniunctio. Here, Mercurius changes from being the "logos-cutter" to the "Eros-glue" (Edinger, p. 200).

Such shifting may be seen to be in the service of the notions of "justice" mentioned above.

The reason separatio is a necessary condition for coniunctio is the goal of separatio is to reach the state of the indivisible. The indivisible commodity is the individual.

This is why, for example, the sudden death of a parent, child, lover, or spouse shatters profound states of identification and the participation mystique. "The ego's unconscious connection with the Self is embedded in these primary identifications, and therefore the occasion of such a death is crucial. Either it will lead to an increased realization of the Self, or, if the potential consciousness is aborted, then negative, regressive, and even fatal effects may follow (Ibid., p. 203).

It is a critical factor in the consciousness of the modern Western viewpoint that Christianity focused directly on the opposites. Increasingly, however, "Justice," i.e., balance, is not suggested as the outcome (that "ought") to be achieved.

For example, rather than a reconciliatory union or an optimal balance, Christianity has increasingly suggested further polarization, especially in terms of the dimension of "good and bad." One is exhorted to embrace good and avoid evil (i.e., shift from being the A-half to being the B-half rather than "realizing" the AB whole).

For all these reasons, separatio might most profitably be suggested to be a necessary cleansing dimension in preparation for the greater conuinctio.

PART IIX: THE CONIUNCTIO

The coniunctio is the culmination of the opus, the goal toward which all prior efforts have ultimately been directed. Again, it involves an external laboratory analog and also a profound inner transformation.

> The alchemists had the opportunity to witness in their laboratories many examples of both chemical and physical combination in which two substances come together to create a third substance with different properties (Edinger, p. 211).

An important example of this was the formation of amalgams by the union of mercury and other metals. "The common alchemical image of the sun and moon entering the mercurial fountain had its origin in the dissolving of gold and silver in mercury" (Ibid.).

There were two forms of coniunctio considered. The first was the lesser coniunctio that consisted of the fusion of two not-yet completely pure substances. The result of this fusion was mortificatio and a continuation of the refinement process.

The second was the higher coniunctio that was the goal of the opus.

In psychological terms, the need for further procedures in the case of the lower coniunctio has to do with instances in which the conscious component of the ego remains unwittingly identified (unknowingly influenced) with some element of the unconscious. That is, one's consciousness is contaminated by primary process material and thus not yet fully separate.

The higher coniunctio essentially consists of a final union of purified opposites, an experience that forever eliminates any one-sidedness.

Experienced psychologically, each of these procedures is initially experienced as being emotionally as well as conceptually thrown back and forth again and again, from pole to pole, until, gradually, it becomes possible to experience each side of the polarity at the same time. It is this new standpoint that is called the coniunctio.

Jung said:

> The one-after-another is a bearable prelude
> to the deeper knowledge of the side-by-side,
> for this is an incomparably more difficult
> problem (Mysterium Coniunctionis, par.
> 206).

The "philosopher's stone" constellates the same idea. The stone, which is a portion of matter par excellence is at the same time taken to be a symbol of aware and transcendent unity. Thus the higher and the lower are linked together as suggested, for example, in the Emerald Tablet.

In this sense, the alchemical notion of the philosopher's stone foreshadows the modern notion of the psychic process.

The stone most often described in terms of the philosopher's stone is the lapis. Lapis is a royal blue stone with flecks of gold inherent in it. Thus the gold is embedded in the supporting color of the regal and the feminine.

The most common alchemical image of the fusion of the coniunctio is the marriage and sexual intercourse of Sol and Luna (don't tell the Republicans or the U.S. House—we will get busted for pornography and have to fib our way out of it).

It is a critical element of these notions that one be aware of the fusion discussed. Thus it is the conscious ego that creates the known Self.

That this is not simply a cognitive exercise, as for example a digression into Hegelian-type (i.e., conceptual) logic, may be seen from the stress that is placed on love.

Love was in fact seen as the very glue of the coniunctio.

This was essentially object-love in the case of the lower coniunctio. That is, love was projected outward and focused on external elements.

In the case of the higher coniunctio, however, love concerned the inner union of the (entire) Self through the process of individuation.

Thus object love is often conceived as the extroverted aspect of individuation whereas inner union and awareness of the Self is often conceived as transpersonal love.

The extroverted aspect of the coniunctio promotes social interest and the unity of the human race; the introverted aspect promotes connection with the Self and the unity of the individual psyche (Edinger, p. 223).

This difference can be seen clearly by reading (again) the Symposium of Plato. I hope you do this. It is a profound discussion of the importance and character of love.

Yet perhaps the best expression of (at least transpersonal) love (at least in Western writing) is a description from the Apostle Paul:

> If I speak with the tongue of men and of angels, but have not love [charity], I am a noisy gong or a clanging cymbal. And if I have prophetic powers, and understand all mysteries and all knowledge, and if I have all faith, so as to remove mountains, but have not love, I gain nothing. Love is patient and kind; love is not jealous or boastful; it is not arrogant or rude.
>
> Love does not insist on its own way; it is not irritable or resentful; it does not rejoice at wrong, but rejoices in the right. Love bears all things, believes all things, hopes all things, endures all things (I Corinthians 13: 1-7).

The Philosopher's Stone, once created by such deep emotional devotion, may be employed to transform any base matter into the noble.

Such a transformation is carried on completely by the Lapis or the Elixir; the alchemist does not participate in this event.

(Imagine, for example, the different "world-perspective" typically experienced by persons who have spent a considerable time at a university. It is a common occurrence for one's view to undergo considerable shift from the portions of the world experienced before college. Thus, following such an experience, the new world-view operates "automatically:" it requires no effort.)

When such an idea is applied to psychotherapy, it speaks to the notion of the influence of one's experience. That is the context available for introjection.

And, in like fashion to the alchemists' notions, in order for the patient to be able to benefit from the experience, his or her mind must be open. He or she must be able to be receptive.

But, it is crucial to add the transference element: the therapist must be open as well. In this way, by mutual development, the two can unite in the kind of interaction that points toward newly-discovered growth rather than backward to regression.

Jung argued: "You can exert no influence if you are not susceptible to influence" (The Practice of Psychotherapy, par. 163).

An alchemical text, The Golden Treatise of Hermes, contains a very similar comment which is:

Understand, ye Sons of Wisdom, the Stone
declares: Protect me, and I will protect thee;
give me my own, that I may help thee (see
Atwood, 1850-1960, p. 128.)

And the following statement from Proverbs suggests,
from another background position, this same caution:

Forsake her not, and she shall preserve
thee; love her and she shall keep thee...Ex-
alt her, and she shall promote thee: she shall
bring thee to honor, when though dost embrace her (Proverbs 4: 6-8).

Again, in psychological terms, the fundamentally reciprocal nature of reality suggests that the unconscious will
adopt the same attitude toward the conscious awareness
as the conscious awareness adopts toward it. The act of
befriending the unconscious, therefore, aids the Ego.

An alchemical verse quoted by Jung (The Practice of
Psychotherapy) is as follows:

Heaven above
Heaven below
Stars above
Stars below
All that is above
Also is below

Grasp this
And rejoice
(par. 384)

In sum, it is now possible to decipher the (metaphorical) meaning of the text held to be most sacred to the alchemists: the ancient Emerald Tablet of Hermes. This text is actually a recipe for the second creation of the world and self realization. The Emerald Tablet, which is likely in Greek, and specifically Alexandrine in origin, was first translated into Latin in the seventh century.

THE EMERALD TABLET
by Hermes Trismegistus

Truly, without Deceit, certainly and absolutely:

That which is Below corresponds to that which is Above,
and that which is Above corresponds to that which is Below,
in the accomplishment of the Miracle of One Thing. And just
as all things have come from One, through the Mediation of
One, so all things follow from this One Thing in the same way.

Its Father is the Sun; its Mother is the Moon. The Wind
has carried it in his Belly. Its Nourishment is the Earth.
It is the Father of every completed Thing in the whole
World. Its strength is intact if it is turned towards the
Earth. Separate the Earth by Fire: the fine from the gross,
gently and with great skill.

It rises from Earth to Heaven, and then it descends
again to the Earth, and receives Power from Above and from
Below. Thus you will have the Glory of the whole World. All
Obscurity will be clear to you. This is the strong Power of
all Power because it overcomes everything fine and pene-
trates everything solid.

In this way was the World created. From this there
will be amazing Applications, because this is the Pattern.
Therefore am I called Thrice Greatest Hermes, having the
three parts of the Wisdom of the whole World.

Herein have I completely explained the Operation of
the Sun.

This is, in a nutshell, the basic outline of the system of
alchemy. Not only did it preserve and extend into the
middle ages the Hermetic view of life so common in the
ancient world, but it focused on and articulated issues
which would play a central role again in modern princi-

ples of psychotherapy—especially psychotherapy of any significant depth.

For those who may be interested, tomorrow we will journey to Bucerias where we can enjoy my favorite joint, drink a lot, eat a lot, discuss a lot, and generally enjoy an unspoiled vista of sea, sand, and sky.

When we meet again here the following day, I will discuss some specific alchemical examples, so you can brush up on your developing symbol language skills as well as go through the opus in what seems to me quite a clear way. And, if we have time, I will also introduce you to a new Tarot spread which I recently learned, entitled: The Hermetic Cross of the Golden Dawn.

(The Tarot also follows and "realizes" the Emerald Tablet.)

Then, finally we will put this all together in fairly specific—and hopefully useful—psychological terms.

Questions?

4. AN ANALYSIS OF THE CONIUNCTIO OF ALCHEMY

Now we have reviewed some foundations of "depth" clinical issues and gone over the system of alchemy as it developed in the middle ages as well as the early post-renascence period, let us look today at some specific examples of alchemical symbolization. Tomorrow we will then tie issues discussed so far to specific clinical examples and issues that may be used directly in psychotherapy (and life).

THE CONIUNCTIO

Why alchemy—of all things? As was stated yesterday, alchemy presents a unique sort of glimpse into the depths of the human unconscious psyche, a glimpse according to Edinger (1994), "no other body of symbolism provides in quite the same way."

Thus, for example, if we pay serious attention to alchemical images, we will find ourselves confronted by the same material that occurs in our dreams.

As we have seen, it has been argued that, in essence, our psyches are necessarily comprised of opposites. The very beginning sentence of Jung's Mysterium Coniunctionis is as follows:

The factors which come together in the coniunctio are conceived as opposites, either confronting one another in enmity or attracting one another in love.

The trick, of course, is that true or developed consciousness requires a "simultaneous experience of these opposites—as well as an acceptance of that experience. Furthermore, the greater the degree of this acceptance, the greater the resulting consciousness,

The ten Pythagorean opposites which, if you think about it, appeared at the beginning of distinctly Western consciousness, were these: limited/unlimited, odd/even, one/many, right/left, male/female, resting/moving, straight/curved, light/dark, square/oblong, and good/bad.

(It is interesting that, of these, the one most stressed by Christianity is the last: good/bad—that and possibly male/female.)

The reason for stress on these opposite polarities is related to the logic of grammar. (Grammar, as explained below, is the device that allows for an awareness of opposites in the first place.)

Thus, it may be seen that along about sixteen to eighteen months of age or there-about, infants have finally internalized enough grammatical structure to be able to begin to use words correctly. This is what parents call "learning the names of things."

Things don't really have names. Of course, we could name them. We could name the floor "Charles." We could even name it "Floor." But then we wouldn't say, "There is the floor." We would say, "There is Floor (capitalized)."

So, when the child utters something like "milk" in the proper grammatical context, we tend to celebrate this for the big deal it really is.

What the child has really demonstrated is something quite remarkable: before I can correctly use the word floor (i.e., in the proper context and not in improper contexts), I need to have some sense both of what floor is as well as what floor is not.

That is, grammar implies, and requires, an opposite. Words are meaningful in the same way rules are. Thus there needs to be a way to do it right and a way to do it wrong. Words as well as rules would be meaningless if it simply didn't matter where or when I used them (i.e., they could be used correctly in any context).

This is why the opposites are important to consciousness. My grammatical boundaries become sharper as my language skills improve. This is precisely the same way my ego boundaries become sharper. Think, for example, of the dimension of "form level" on the Rorschach.

Edinger (1994) said:

> The young ego is obliged to establish itself as something definite and therefore it must say, "I am this and I am not that." No-saying is a crucial feature of initial ego development. But the result of this early operation is that a shadow is created. All that I announce I am not then goes into the shadow.

> …The very survival of the ego depends on how it relates to [good and bad]…for the young ego can tolerate very little of the experience of its own badness without succumbing to total demoralization (pp. 13,14).

Thus it might be said that early in our development, our relationship to the notions of good and bad resembles a pendulum. We are this or that (exclusive or). If maturity is able to progress, one slowly develops the capacity to own up, to take the bad on oneself. Thus one is able to stop projecting the bad or blaming others. One sees, as Gloria Steinem was able to see (The Enemy Within, 1997) that the problems are not "out there" but are rather "in here." If this developmental progression is played out to its higher manifestations, one would end up with some truly profound developments. Edinger (Ibid.) added, for example:

> When one is able to acknowledge one's evil, one becomes a carrier of the opposites and in so doing contributes to the creation of the coniunctio [the supreme goal of alchemy] (p 14).

Jung called it a shift from the "one-after-another" to a deeper knowledge of the "side by side" (Ibid.).

The reason this is critical is that when we fall into one pole of a dichotomy, we lose the ability to function as a carrier of the opposites—and we, therefore, constrict consciousness—which in fact almost seems, at times, to be the American character.

Thus we might say individual subjective consciousness is powerfully drawn to the opinions and positions of the collective (social) consciousness—and these collective opinions and positions tend to be introjected early on where they continue to function forcefully, often just beyond awareness.

Yet the only way the self can retain its integrity is to maintain a balance, as Joseph Campbell (The Power of Myth) said, "between the pairs of opposites." Further, this can only be done if one maintains a significant consciousness of both possibilities.

Edinger (1994) pointed out in this context that games were considered sacred to the gods. Sporting contests actually "work out the drama of the coniunctio (p. 16). Here, within the game, the opposites unite. The point is that while it surely is a good thing to win, it is also critical that one lose. The reason for this is to avoid losing in the game threatens to result in a similar loss of an immediate sense of the opposites. And it was for this very issue that resulted in defeat being considered the "gateway to the unconscious (Ibid.).

One way you find out what the particular opposites are that directly pertain to you is to scrutinize, for example, what you love and hate—that is: where do I place my identity?

The point is, as Edinger (Ibid.) pointed out: "Whenever we take too concretely an urge to love or hate, then the coniunctio is exteriorized and thereby destroyed."

Rather it is possible to see that we are bound to that which we hate as surely as we are bound to that which we love.

This capacity to contain the opposites is perhaps the fundamental discovery of the alchemist's laboratory.

[The coniunctio] is the entity, the stuff, the substance that [was] created by the alchemical procedure when finally it succeed in uniting the opposites. It is a mysterious, transcendent thing that can be [must be] expressed by many   symbolic images (Ibid., p. 18).

Some of those images are: the Philosopher's Stone, an incorruptible body that unites all things, the aqua permanens (also sometimes called the tincture), that is either permanent or penetrating water, tinting everything with its color, the filius philosophorum, the son of the philosophers or the savior of the world, the pharmakon athanasias, the medicine of immortality, the cibus immortalis, the food of immortality, &c. (Ibid.).

I hope you see the point. The coniunctio is consciousness, albeit a "higher" consciousness.

And since the alchemists were known as philosophers, the filius philosophorum, the son of the philosophers, was clearly the developing consciousness of the philosopher. Thus the son was created [uncovered] in the laboratory— and created from the unconscious. The work "releases" this and makes it articulate.

Consider the following alchemical recipe quoted by Jung in his Mysterium Coniunctionis:

> If thou knowest how to moisten this dry earth with its own water, thou wilt loosen the pores of the earth, and this thief from outside will be cast out with the workers of wickedness, and the water, by an admixture of the true Sulpher, will be cleansed from the leprous filth and from the superfluous dropsical fluid, and thou wilt have in thy power the font of the Knight of Treviso,

whose waters are rightfully dedicated to the maiden Diana. Worthless is this thief, armed with the malignity of arsenic, from whom the winged youth fleeth, shuddering. And though the central water is his bride, yet dare he not display his most ardent love towards her, because of the snares of the thief, whose machinations are in truth unavoidable. Here may Diana be propitious to thee, who knoweth how to tame wild beasts, and whose twin doves will temper the malignity of the air with their wings, so that the youth easily entereth in through the pores and instantly shaketh the foundations of the earth, ands raises up a dark cloud. But thou wilt lead the waters up even to the brightness of the moon, and the darkness that was upon the face of the deep shall be scattered by the spirit moving over the waters. Thus by God's command shall the Light appear (par 186).

Edinger translated this passage as follows:

There is a fountain whose water is polluted. A winged youth burns with love for this fountain and, actually, the fountain is meant to be his bride. But, there is an evil thief who is the polluter of the fountain, and he prevents the approach of the winged youth. Then, with the help of Diana, the youth enters the pores of the earth adjacent to the fountain and this union causes an earth-quake and raises up a dark cloud. When things have settled, the waters of the fountain have been purified and the world has been created (as in the first chapter of Genesis, where the spirit of God moved on the face of the waters and the darkness vanished and light appeared) (p. 21).

Here the language is clearly symbolic.

Kermode (1979) in a superb volume entitled The Genesis of Secrecy pointed to and detailed the ancient practice of using symbolic language and metaphor to keep the truth in the hands of the informed and initiated—and to exclude the rest (who, for example, might think God were a fact or the self is irrelevant since it can't be counted or rated for short term improvement). Kermode (p. 1) reminded us of I Corinthians 2:14:

> The natural man receives not the
> things of the spirit...for they are
> foolishness to him.

To decode the above described alchemical recipe, consider the goal to be precisely the coniunctio, and the opposites that unite within it are the fountain and the winged youth. Other pairs of opposites are also represented, for example, water and fire, mercury and sulfur, and the moon and sun. Yet before the great union can take place the thief must be dealt with. In the Mysterium Jung called the thief a kind of "self robbery" due to collective [social] thinking. In the example the thief is characterized as crude sulfur as opposed to true sulfur.

Here sulfur represents the "active substance of the sun" or the impulse of consciousness. The crude sulfur is directed toward the conscious ego (often from the collective consciousness) whereas the true sulfur is directed toward the unbounded self—and thus includes, for example, the "emotional awareness."

And in plain psychological terms the results of the operation of the true sulfur is the ability to stop projecting one's shadow contents on others but to carry them and endure them in one's own "burden of darkness."

Such an ability purifies the world for everyone.

THE ROSARIUM PICTURES

Let us turn now to the Rosarium Pictures and follow them as our guide to our own personal transformation and realization of Self.

And if, as Kohut argued somewhere, the goal of psychoanalysis is to learn to "tolerate the object" (i.e., embrace that which is actually there), such a realization will serve as the goal of psychotherapy as well as alchemy.

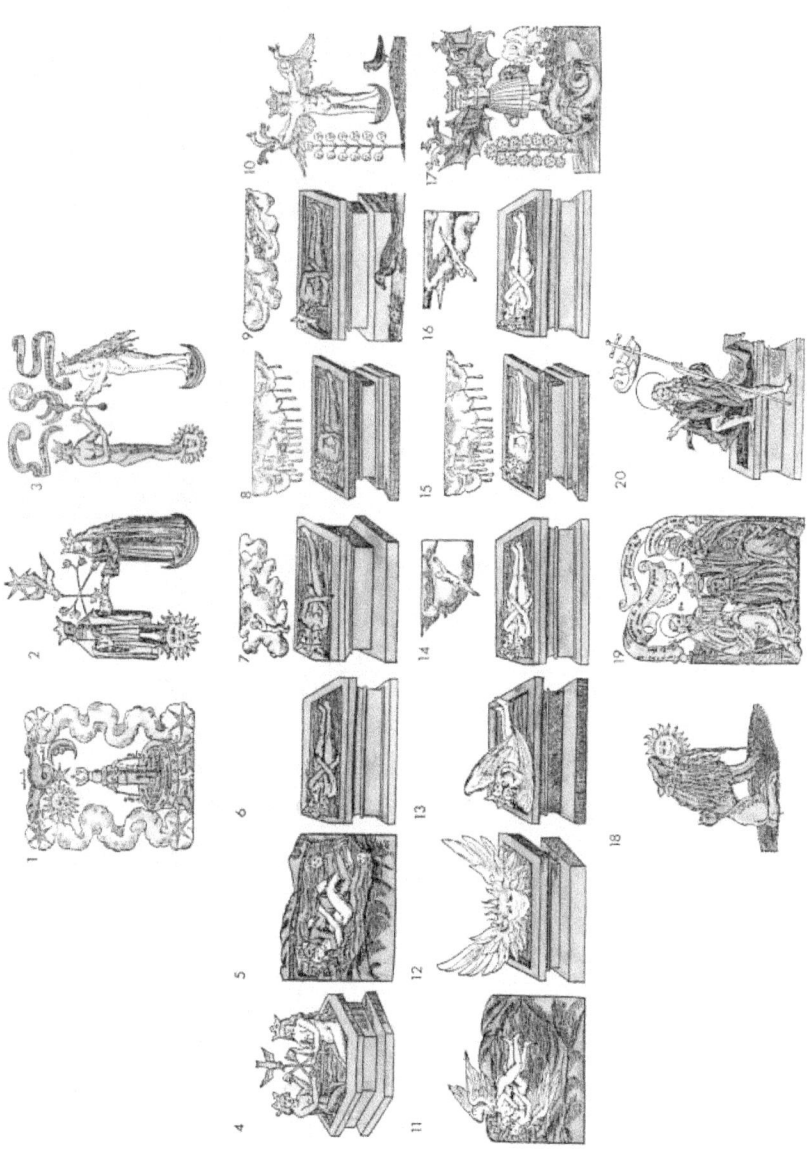

The Rosarium Pictures

The Rosarium pictures will be considered one at a time in an attempt to decode the symbols uses for our "modern sensibilities. Hopefully, it will become possible to see how these images actually apply to everything--but especially to the structure of what might be called the distinctly personal journey of understanding. As in the comments above, my descriptions will be largely based on additional work by Edinger (1994).

With the Rosarium Pictures, the focus shifts directly to the human dimension. It is the distinctly human transformation that will be the main theme here.

PLATE ONE: THE MANDALA FOUNTAIN

Here we see a fountain with a flower design on top of it. Three pipes spurt liquid into a containing basin. This is surrounded by a kind of square design with the opposing heads of a two-headed serpent on top, each one spewing a vapor. In each corner of the vapors there are four six pointed stars.

At an initial level, the vapors and polarities of stars may be seen to represent the ancient notion that the four elements originally derived from two vapors, a smoky vapor and a watery vapor. The smoky vapor divided into earth and air, and the watery vapor divided into fire and water.

Encased by the vapors and above the fountain there is a fifth star separating the sun and moon. This star repre-

246

sents an amalgam or unification of the four elements. Thus the vapors represent prima materia and the fifth star represents ultima materia. In other words, this is the alpha and the omega, the beginning and the end of the mystery.

Clearly this is the Mercurial Fountain. (Think of Key One in the higher arcana of the Tarot cards: The Magician, who may be thought of as Hermes Mercuries in descended or incarnate form). In strictly psychological terms, the Mercurial Fountain, as well as the Magician, illustrate what might be called the "pure state" of the beginning, thus the unconscious before the development of the conscious elements, or in Jungian terms the psyche before the development of the ego.

In one's youth, the sense of self may be said to be still poorly differentiated and so one lives largely in identification with that which is around and available to one.

This is seen in Picture One in that the three spouts pour the life giving fluid into the pool that as yet has no reflection (three spouts from one fountain beneath two images of sun/moon and serpent's heads surrounded by the four elements and capped by the opening of the higher star (thus, 1,2,3,4, and pointing to 5). The three fountains pour "virgin's milk," "vinegar," and the "water of life." These are symbols of the aqua permanens, the liquid version of the philosopher's stone.

PLATE TWO: EMERGENCE OF THE OPPOSITES

Edinger (1994) describes this picture as follows:

> Here we have a robed king and queen, each crowned. The king stands on the sun and the queen stands on the moon. They hold each other's left hand and in the right hand of each there are long stemmed white flowers which cross. Above them is a six-pointed star. Since this star is central we can assume it derives from that fifth quintessential star in the first picture. Below the star, a dove descends with another flower in its beak which crosses the other crossed flower stems (p. 44).

Thus the original unity has now been split in two.

The King and Queen face each other, and this facing takes place under the "motivation" of the third thing: the white dove. Thus, compared to Plate One, this represents the separatio. It reflects the primal separatio: the separation and delineation of the sun and moon, that is light and darkness, masculine and feminine, and the basic model for most ancient creation myths.

"The creative act of separatio means consciousness has been born, and consciousness means human beings" (Ibid.). Yet the King and Queen are not quite human beings yet; they are rather primary archetypes. In this capacity, they can function as the gateway to the unconscious (the fact they are holding left hands symbolically signifies that this is an unconscious function).

Initial meetings such as this are typical in alchemical symbolism.

They are standing on the sun and the moon. Sol and Luna represent, in general alchemical symbolism, all the pairs of opposites.

The dove has been interpreted both as the Holy Ghost and also as the Dove of Aphrodite. Regardless of the preferred interpretation, the dove descends from the star as a messenger of the transpersonal or cosmic Self.

PLATE THREE: STRIPPED FOR ACTION

Here we see the same figures standing on the sun and moon, but now their clothing has been removed. Also, the nature of their connection is different. In place of the left-hand connection of Plate Two, the King and Queen are connected by the two flowers they are mutually holding. The dove remains above with its additional flower crossing the flowers of the King and Queen. The star has been eliminated allowing concentration to be focused (for us as well as the King, Queen, and dove) on the six pointed flower that connects all elements together.

The figure six represents union. That it has moved from the heavens in the figure of the star and reincarnated in the earthly form of a growing flower indicates the plane of focus has shifted from the higher to the lower. That the lovers are finally "fully" grasping the flowers indicates they are finally committed to them. "...you could say the Imago Dei has fallen into the human realm" (Ibid., p 52).

Flowers might be considered to be the "erotic or [physical-sensual] aspect of the motivating energy" (Ibid., p. 50).

Also there is another addition. A huge one. Here words have been added. Each of the three figures is making some sort of statement, and so language has appeared.

The scrolls may be decoded as follows: Sol is saying, "O Luna, let me be thy husband"; Luna is saying, "O Sol, I must submit to thee"; and the dove is saying, "The spirit is what unifies" Ibid.).

Plate Three suggests arrival at the honest embracing of what exists in this world. Jung (1953-79 "The Psychology of Transference") referred to this plate as "the naked truth." Thus the image of nakedness suggests psychological "openness" or honesty. The pretenses have been shed, and "the process is going to proceed in earnest" (Edinger, p. 53).

PLATE FOUR: DESCENT INTO THE BATH

Plate Four depicts a basin filled with water. The basin in a hexagonal shape that preserves the motif of the six pointed star. This theme continues to be depicted as well by the flowers held by the couple and the white dove. The naked king and queen are both in the basin.

Here the process has taken another step. Now the couple is not only united by the flowers they are holding but by the water as well.

This is to enter a state of mutual solutio. "Solutio is an image of a descent into the unconscious that has the effect of dissolving the solid, ordered structure of the ego" (Edinger, 1985).

In alchemical terms solutio is a return to undifferentiated matter, the prima materia.

Water was typically thought of as the womb, and to enter the water was to return to the womb for rebirth.

The dissolution of the Sol and Luna symbols upon which the king and queen have been standing suggests a chemical reaction well known by the alchemists. The sun and the moon symbolize gold and silver. How to unite these two disparate elements? One way that was discovered was to amalgamate them with mercury to produce an amalgam that consisted of both gold and silver.

Another way to interpret Plate Four is to consider it to symbolize a fusion and merging with the Great Mother.

Yet as Neumann (1970) has pointed out: how one responds to the fusion with the Great Mother [the transcendent or archetypal sense of the feminine—thus the "higher" rather than the "lower" mother]—how one responds to the Great Mother depends upon one's degree of ego development.

Thus for an immature ego, fusion with the Great Mother is a return to a state of bliss and protection. For a more developed ego, however, this is a bittersweet bliss as it carries with it the forfeiture of a developing autonomous existence.

And of course these considerations also apply to the relationships in our lives. Profound "releasing" to another is blissfully consuming for the immature ego. It is a somewhat risky and tormenting state for the more mature ego that fears for the loss of its autonomous identity.

The king and queen have entered a state of participation mystique.

In short, this plate suggests the process of getting wet with the unconscious. What will happen? Either this will lead to a rebirth and an enrichment or to a dissolution, destruction, and death.

The images of the flood, tidal waves, whirlpools, &c., suggest this state.

Actually, the two states are components of the same thing. Typically—as Zen notions tell us—it depends on whether one has adopted a short or long term view.

Thus what might seem like destruction in the short range might actually turn out to be the first stage of a new transformation or assimilation.

PLATE FIVE: UNION, MANIFESTATION OF THE MYSTERY

Here the two figures have completely submerged in the basin of the fountain. They are under water and not visible at all. The scene depicted in Plate Five is revealed to us by the actions of the mystery.

There is no dove, no star, no longer a flower pattern. The sun and moon are seen here as they have descended with the figures—who are seen in the act of intercourse.

Notice that the moon is now full. The depths of the water are of course the feminine element, so it stands to reason the moon would here be full.

This plate, as it were, consummates what has gone on in the first half of the process. It is the celebration of the heiros gamos [the higher or sacred marriage] as opposed to the lower or physical marriage. (I was told by a Greek psychologist that gamos actually, literally means "fucking.")

There is an interesting developmental point to be made at this point. Typically, this stage is lived through but it is not made conscious.

So it is with much sexuality. One simply finds pleasure, satisfaction, or whatever, and then starts over (i.e.,
back to Plate One). The veil does not lift. One just does
it over and over.

Such a state is certainly the case during the first half of
life.

At some point, the veil opens and one experiences the
great mystery of the opposites working. This allows for
the realization of the attainment of the state of mutual
identification—that is to say, profound psychological unity.

The development takes place under water to, again,
suggest its unconscious nature. It is actually a major
threat for the so-called solar consciousness [where
thought and rationality is the most dominant element].

A parallel picture in the Rosarium depicts the sun being eaten by a green lion. Thus the instinctual nature here
consumes higher or synoptic generative awareness. Instinct has taken over.

The point must be stressed that intercourse between the
ego and the anima or animas components is very different
from intercourse between two figures other than (i.e., outside) the ego. Here the image suggests the joining of the
opposites. [This is a similar notion as that suggested to
Parsifal by Gournamond.]

PLATE SIX: IN THE TOMB

Plate Six presents the united hermaphroditic body of the King and Queen lying dead on a mortuary slab. Edinger (Ibid.) said, "…this shows the effect of witnessing what happened in [Plate Five]. It literally strikes one dead."

Seen from this view, Plates Five and Six present the inevitable consequences of "seeing into the dynamism of the opposites. Once you really see how that works, you are knocked out by it, so to speak" (Ibid.).

The outcome of being able, at long last, to grasp the dynamic conjoining of the opposites involves a blurring of the polarities upon which rational (i.e., conceptual, descriptive) thought depends.

The Jungians point to this as the "death of the ego… upon the encounter with the self" (Ibid.).

At any rate it is to be able to move beyond polarized, exclusive awareness to a metaphorical, inclusive awareness. This is to be able to transcend the awareness level at which one has been living. It is a life transforming thing.

Stressing the importance of this transformation, the poet Rilke wrote in the first Duino Elegy (1922/1939):

Yes, but all of the living
make the mistake of drawing too sharp distinc-

tions.
Angels (they say) are often unable to tell
whether they move among living or dead. The eternal
torrent whirls all the ages through either realm
for ever, and sounds above their voices in both
[my italics].

In alchemical symbolism this is represented by the co-niuctio that results in the mortificatio.

It is, if you will, a joining of marriage and death.

Thus, as in Tristan and Isault or Romeo and Juliet for example, it is the inevitable fate of the lover to die. That is, the individual identity dies so the joint identity or "higher entirety" can be born. Typically, it is only after the individual identity has been abandoned and the process of merging with another that forms an "us" or "both-as-one" identity has occurred that awareness of what has somehow (mysteriously) happened is able to finally develop.

Another way to think of this image is that one finally achieves what one has so desperately desired for so long —and finds it isn't what one wanted after all.

In a profound sense, though everything has changed, nothing has changed. This is, thus, the breakdown of the projection. The psychic energy that was invested in the external is rediscovered in the internal. The projection is integrated.

Ego-centricity is destroyed.

Typically in alchemical treatments, it is the King who undergoes mortificatio. Here, in the Rosarium sequence, in is Sol and Luna simultaneously.

In sum, the image of death—as in dream imagery—suggests not obliteration but transformation. It is the first step in transformation, the necessary prelude to rebirth in the new form.

PLATE SEVEN: SEPARATION OF SOUL AND BODY

Here we see the same hermaphrodite body lying on the same slab, only now there is a small figure ascending from the body into a cloud that has appeared overhead.

It is a standard, long-standing image of the soul leaving the body at the moment of death. This image can be found all the way back in ancient texts, as is seen for example in Homer.

One way to think of the process involved in Plate Seven is to think what it is like when someone (external person) you love dies. There is left a hole in the exterior, but there is also a hole left in the interior. The part of our own energy, our own self, that has been attached to that person is also lost. It feels as if it has died.

Through the process of grief, over time, we will reclaim that part of ourselves, yet we will reclaim it in transformed state. Only then we can feel more or less complete again.

In Plate Seven the energy that has been lodged in the external leaves.

Plates Six, Seven, Eight, and Nine together present a sequence that illustrates the processes of death, separation and ascension of the soul, and finally the return of the soul.

In addition, and somewhat similarly, Jung claimed the alchemical coniunctio actually took place in three stages (see Mysterium Coniunctionis, last chapter).

Stage One: union of soul and spirit. When the soul leaves the body it rises to join with the spirit, the unio mentalis.

Stage Two: the unio mentalis reunites with the body.

Stage Three: the soul-spirit-body combines with the world and brings about the unus mundus ("one world").

The issue is this: in order to bring about the possibility of reunion, the mind must be separated from the body. This is often called the "voluntary death." The issue here is to free the mind from the body-influences, the "bodily appetites and the heart's affections." Such an event allows for a perception of a spiritual dimension that is "supreordinate to the turbulent sphere of the body" (Ibid.).

Charitable readings hold this is what Christian theology has primarily been up to: a separation of the mind from the appetites of the body. It is what led Nietzsche to say, "Christianity is Platonism for the masses" (Beyond Good and Evil, 1966, p. 3).

In the next step, that which has been separated to attain a sort of individuated purity is rejoined. The opposites are reborn, one might say. Only now, they are rejoined with an aware consciousness of their dimensions as well as their true individual natures.

Stage three points to an experience quite beyond grasping. Joining with all things is likely only possible in any full sense in a profound sort of mystical experience or in death.

Psychologically, the first stage of coniunctio is associated with the withdrawal of the projections.

And the emergence of the symbol of the homunculus figure might most properly been seen as the birth of the divine child, or the "inner person." This is born out of the "death of the body" which is, of course, associated with the death of the concrete level of human existence." The divine child points toward an experience of the participation mystique.

You know, rising above and beyond the mall-crowd.

A final comment on Plate Seven: the cloud that appears overhead is an ancient symbol of the "transpersonal reality." It is how the eternal or the transcendent forms manifest themselves.

PLATE EIGHT: GIDEON'S DEW DRIPS FROM THE CLOUD

The homunculus has disappeared into the cloud, and the dual-body remains on the slab. The feature added here is that dew begins dripping from the cloud.

Thus, in the last plate, the movement was from lower to higher. Here it is reversed, and the movement is now from higher to lower.

Further Plate Eight is not called "Dew Drips From the Cloud," the image explicitly is entitled "Gideon's Dew..." This is a specific reference to a specific dew.

The account of Gideon's Dew is found in Judges, Chapter Six.

That the poem that accompanies Plate 8 specifically mentions "Gideon's Dew" instead of simply "dew;" it suggests the alchemist is living out the myth of Gideon.

The story of Gideon is fairly long and complex, but the essential point might be summed up by stating Gideon was a young Israelite who received a sign in the form of dew upon a fleece from God that showed that if he raised an army he would be victorious against the invading armies from the East, the Midianites.

Thus the point about dew is that it is a "sign of divine intervention, it is the moisture that heralds the return of the soul" (Jung, "Psychology of the Transference").

In other words, dew functions symbolically in a similar fashion to rain, but dew is more mysterious than rain. Dew was associated with the moon, and "moon-dew" indicates the effects of grace. And, throughout antiquity, the relation of the moon to the soul was stressed.

Jung said: "As the water of ablution, the dew falls from heaven, purifies the body, and makes it ready to receive the soul; in other words, it brings about the albedo, the white state of innocence, that like the moon and a bride awaits the bridegroom" (Mysterium).

In Plate 8 the dew "descends and purifies and revivifies the dead body" (Edinger, p. 85).

The body here, remember, is an image—it is not actually the real body. Perhaps the best way to think of it is to think of the ego (the thinking, secondary-process part). The ego might be called the body of the psyche.

The purified ego (body) is one that has resolved its contaminations from the unconscious. That is, it is a healthy, worked-through ego.

The German word for "working through" is "durcharbeitung."

In Jungian terms, the process of purification must dissolve the identity of the ego and the self, so it is its own unified identity.

Edinger pointed out: "[Similarly] everything occurs on the exterior at first" (Ibid., p. 87). Even the unconscious is (thought to be) external. This occurs, again, because so much of what is unconscious is projected. Thus, in significant part, it is the "taking back of the projections" that finally reveals the dimensions of the unconscious.

Hint for the reasonably strong: when something "out there" evokes a response from me, it actually shows me a piece of my own psyche is out there.

PLATE 9: REUNION OF SOUL AND BODY

Here is illustrated the same slab, the same dead unified body, the same cloud—but now the homunculus is seen returning.

It would seem that it is finally safe for this to happen as the body has now been purified.

At the bottom of the plate two birds have been added, one buried up to its neck in the ground and the other looking down at the first.

Symbolically it might be stated that the birds duplicate the scene occurring above them. That is, the buried bird may be thought to be equivalent to the dead unified body on its way to being born out of its buried, "earth-bound" state. The bird looking down at it may be thought to be akin to the returning homunculus (the creature of the air appears to free the creature surrounded by soil so it can fly as well).

In alchemical symbolism, ash was considered equivalent to the dead body. The text accompanying Plate 9 quotes the alchemist Morienus as saying, "Despise not the ash, for it is the diadem of thy heart."

Another alchemical interpretation of the ash was that of "white foliated earth." This is purified earth—the purified body.

Ash is, after all, the whole ultimate goal of earthly existence. It is the incorruptible, glorified body that has endured the entire process. It is, thus, of superior value.

Similar symbolic references may be found in the Bible. Isaiah, for example, promises to give the mourners "a crown for ashes, the oil of joy for mourning, and a garment of praise for the spirit of grief" (61:3).

PLATE 10: RESURRECTION OF THE UNITED ETERNAL BODY

The united body is now alive and erect. It is standing on the moon that is suspended above the earth. There is a chalice in the right hand that contains a three headed serpent. All these heads are crowned. Twined around the left hand is a fourth crowned serpent. Looking at the plate straight on, out of the ground on the left is a tree that sprouts faces. This is actually the "sun and moon" tree, though it doesn't exactly look like it. (The image is much more clear in Mylius' 1622 plate ten.) On the right side of the picture is a bird standing on the ground.

The plate as a whole represents a union of the united body-soul-spirit entity. It is a cosmic union. Further, the unified entity is standing on the moon—and the moon is also the fruit on the tree.

The point may be summed up by stressing the idea that the entire "cosmos   is [really] a single organic process" (Edinger, p. 96)".

The bird likely represents the successful fusion of the two birds in Plate 9.

The three headed serpent suggests the Greek image of Cerebrus, the three headed monster who guards the entrance to Hades or the underworld (i.e., the realm of the dead). The single, entwined serpent, on the other hand, is the symbol of Zeus, the symbol of life. (Thus the three headed serpent is associated with death, and the entwined serpent is associated with life—as is the uroboris.)

In sum, Plate 10 may be described as suggesting that awareness of the true, unique, incorruptible self has been attained. This self is a unification of all polarities of opposites. It has a lower and higher (earthly and eternal) dimension, a masculine and feminine dimension, &c. It is holding "polar symbols"—and thus exists (suspended) between life and death, and also exists (suspended) between the earth and the heavens.

Also, throughout ancient symbolism, the moon was typically taken as suggesting the earth (it is a "lower" body); whereas the sun typically suggested the eternal realm. So, the figure standing on the moon (lower form) and rising toward the sky (higher form), again, spans these dimensions.

Additionally it is suggested that such a supreme achievement of self realization and individuation as that illustrated in Plate 10 cannot help but reverberate and influence others, that is, to multiply.

Finally, the rising figure may also be thought of as the philosopher's stone. One quality of the philosopher's stone was that when ground into a fine powder and thrown onto base matter, anything the powder touched also turned into philosopher's stone.

Symbols for the philosopher's stone include the risen Christ as well as the lapis, which was the element frequently considered of highest value in antiquity—and often reserved for royalty alone.

The suggestion to grasp is of course that through this process, the philosopher's stone could belong to each of us.

5. THE ANDROGYNE

In transcendence, both male and female roles are by-passed. In mysticism, seekers go through the experience of divine love and marriage, in which they become the ravished spouses of the godhead.

The androgyne is the symbol of supreme identity in many early religious systems. It corresponds to the number 0 (+1 -1 =0).

In Hindu it is Siva.

It is Dionysus in Greece, where it was also called the the Hybrid or the Man-Woman.

"The complete androgyne wades blissfully through the world of change." It is "samsara," balancing action and inactivity (i.e., the polarities).

The power that can heal us from our partial sex roles is not reason, but plastic imagination.

In mystic Hebrew, God's name is IHVH. The Kabbalist reads I=father, H=mother, and VH=the androgyne cosmos or Son-and-daughter, who were joined back to back, but in the process of cosmic development are separated and then unite face to face. IH is the primal manifestation of divinity, VH is the consequent uniting.

Adam was androgyne; Eve split off to create duality. What heals them is imagination.

Hermaphroditus was son of Hermes and Aphrodite. He lived in Crete where he was brought up by his foster mother, Mt. Ida. He was bathing at the pool of Salmakis, the water nymph, when she twisted herself into his body and begged to remain there. Her wish was granted. After this all who bathed in these waters were turned into hermaphrodites.

The myth of Eros and Psyche should be read as that of hermaphroditus. Psyche corresponds to Salmakis, and Eros to Hermaphroditus.

Eros is equated frequently with Hermaphroditus, and Eros and Psyche were originally (or ideally) one.

The flowers that symbolize androgyny in Western Art are the Columbine and the Lily.

Human life can be defined as the constant and endless process of healing an inner split.

In Hindu, the process is thought to be a constant process of spliting and healing (as Siva).

In alchemy there is a life giving androgynization going on constantly. The offspring of the sun and the moon is

Mercurius, essence of transmutations. He/she joins with salt, the fixing agent.

In Egyptian mythology, the Merceuius figure is Thoth.

Jung stressed that in an intimate encounter between a man and a woman, there is always a decussation (crossing) between the man and his feminine soul, or anima, on the one side, and the woman and her masculine soul, or animus, on the other.

To relate to the core of cosmic life is the aim of the initiate. He identifies with Mercurius, the fluid androgyne principle of reality.

In alchemy, the angelic mercurial androgyne, that is the "homunculus" rises from the androginization.

6. BRINGING IT ALL TOGETHER: TREATMENT OPTIONS

A: APPROACH TO PSYCHOTHERAPY

Let us try now to put all of this together. I have attempted to present linguistic, cultural, and mythological support for the importance to both psychology and our individual lives of that which lies beneath the surface.

The task is now to focus on specific ways in which such notions might be used to make a helpful difference.

For example, consider: What does it actually mean to say a patient comes to treatment voluntarily? What is really implied in a free ability to choose?

Imagine, for example, there is a huge social stigma regarding the issue for which the patient seeks treatment. Against the background of such stigma, how free might someone actually be?

In some extreme cases it may even seem—upon close look—that the patient's ability to choose has for all intents and purposes been successfully eradicated--or at least highly diminished--by negative social messages and contexts that may be surrounding and influencing the patient.

In other words, as Yarhouse (1998) has argued: "various environmental stressors constrain a person's ability to choose freely..." (p. 249). Clearly for all of us, constant pressure from without must be responded to in some way.

Extending from insights developed in terms of family dynamics and experience, it would seem, for example, a young person has three possible choices in responding to such contextual pressure:

(1) Comply with the pressure (i.e., go along with the suggestion).
(2) Rebel (behave in a fashion that opposes the suggestion).
(3) Withdraw (avoid the suggested dimensions as much as possible).

As an adult, some persons are able to develop additional options, for example:

Go underground (go along with the suggestion on the surface, while pursuing one's own "reality" nonetheless.

Go away or transcend the family matrix all together—for every practical purpose (i.e., "divorce" the family and leave them behind.

Significantly, however, each of these choices involve some reaction in a more or less direct fashion to the original input.

This points to the necessity of finding just what impetus the person may actually have for seeking treatment. Especially if the issue has resulted in contextual censure, it is highly likely there is guilt and shame on board in not-insignificant amounts.

Humane treatment requires that the guilt and shame be addressed and methods for managing these dimensions be found before progressing with the issue or issues proper.

After some resolution or at least empathic "holding" of the guilt and shame issues, it is likely there would be more voluntary involvement than otherwise might be possible.

Clearly, the therapeutic environment that would seem to be most helpful is one that does not unwittingly duplicate the wound that brought the patient in for help in the first place.

Further, it is highly likely that the wound in question is in fact a product of the skewed context in which the person was required to live during formative years. Thus, if no anger is tolerated in one's childhood home, anger must be expressed or dealt with in alternative ways. (It doesn't just go away—though that may be the external view.)

If the therapist is (also) eager to avoid anger, the context that contributed to the patient's wound is unwittingly duplicated.   In such a situation, the patient will likely think such an environment is normal as it duplicates the only environment that is known.

Guarding against this unwitting and iatrogenic mistake would seem to be critical to help the patient experience a context that is not distorted in similar ways to his or her childhood background—to which he or she was required to adjust in some way in order to survive. Now, however, the "survival strategy" that worked in the original situation doesn't work, and new patterns must be developed.

Why is this therapeutic issue such a big deal?

In 1996 Strupp reported the results of his recent research into psychotherapy efficacy and included the following two points related to what we have been discussing:

> 1. Therapists rapidly develop a generally positive or negative attitude toward a patient. This phenomenon occurs within the first few minutes of an interview and tends to persist.

> 2. This attitude has profound influence on the therapist's diagnostic and prognostic judgments about the patient, treatment plans, and—what struck me as particularly important—the empathic quality of the

therapist's hypothetical communications of the patient (p. 135).

Strupp went on to argue that the therapist's attitude, and especially the empathetic qualities displayed, is clearly communicated to the patient "who will [tend to] react reciprocally" (Ibid.).

Such exchanges will likely have a cumulative effect on therapy, the nature of the relationship, and the outcome as well.

A powerful few minutes indeed!

Based on such discoveries, Strupp reported he had begun to feel that therapeutic technique in itself had little to do with the outcome. He felt "...that the greater weight was borne by the quality of the emerging patient-therapist relationship" (p. 136).

Strupp did acknowledge, however, that therapeutic skill was also an important factor.

Part of this problem, he reasoned, was due to recent tendencies in diagnostic practice.

I, for one, remain convinced that "my kind" of psychotherapist treats persons who suffer problems in their interpersonal relationships rather than from disembodied "dis eases" susceptible to "managed care" (Ibid.).

Indications have been that "even a small number of pejorative communications by the therapist has highly deleterious effects on the patient-therapist relationship" (Ibid.).

The danger, of course, is when the patient unwittingly tries to get the therapist into a conflict based interaction—as this may be the modal pattern of interaction in the patient's corner of the woods.   When the therapist unwittingly joins in this conflict situation, he or she will tend to duplicate the environment that prevailed in the patient's background.

Strupp stressed empathetic listening in treatment. He argued: "…empathy is the single most important human and technical tool at the therapist's disposal" (p. 137).

Strupp then outlined his view of empathetic listening that he felt was optimal.

As far as possible, leave the initiative with the patient. This approach, he reasoned, displayed the greatest respect for the patient as a person of equal worth.
Stimulate the patient's curiosity about him or her self and his or her interest in collaborating with you.

Listen for the theme or themes of the hour. Be sparing in your communications without being monosyllabic or silent for long periods of time—which is typically experienced as rejection. Use non-technical language, and—clearly—avoid making dogmatic statements.

Be patient! This is the hallmark of a good therapist. Pay close attention to the countertransference issues. Be aware of your own limitations. Acknowledge your powers are limited. Scrutinize your intended communications to make sure they are in the patient's best interests rather than serving your own purposes.

Assiduously avoid criticisms and pejorative communications. There must be a genuine commitment to the patient on the therapist's part. Treatment should never be experienced by the patient as being routine or a business process. (p. 137-138).

In time, good clinical skills tend to become a part of the therapist's very being, rather than being an idiosyncratic activity—they tend to be repeated throughout the therapist's interactions.

Thus, Strupp concluded, we should be training persons, not technicians.

For all intents and purposes, what Strupp has here described is a context that would seem to foster secure attachment connections on the part of patients.

That is, the context Strupp thought optimal seeks to develop a sort of respectfully supportive and yet non-binding interaction.

In a similar vein, Bowlby (1988) argued it is the erroneous equation of intimacy with fusion and the concomitant loss of autonomy that has come to characterize the mental health field.

Actually, spending all one's time making sure one doesn't "hurt someone else's feelings," for example, is the exact opposite of how a secure attachment might be characterized, which is:

"A secure connection to an accessible and responsive attachment figure fosters a sense of felt security, open communication, and autonomy" (Johnson, Maddeaux, and Blouin, 1998, p. 239).

Here, it might be seen that autonomy and secure connectedness are two sides of the same coin—not conflicting opposites. The implication is, of course, that insecurity and fears of disengagement are actually a source of stress—and lead to separation and attachment difficulties.

In anxious attachment, which is also called ambivalent or preoccupied, the attachment figure, who is a potential source of emotional comfort and nurturance, is both longed for and obsessively pushed away and mistrusted (Ibid., p. 240).

It actually seems this pattern of interacting becomes a characteristic of the personality, so such people actually tend to treat everyone and everything in the same way.

It would seem to be security and autonomy that lead to optimal adjustment, not fused togetherness.

B: AN OBJECT RELATIONS AID TO DIAGNOSIS

As I am sure you know very well, there has been a constant (and increasing) mismatch between direct treatment work, especially of any involved sort, and the increasingly "topological" character of the diagnostic manual.

Beginning with DSM III, diagnostic categories were no longer presented in terms of what might be called "fundamental dynamics," but were presented as empirical descriptors.

Perhaps the great utility of such a system is that it is appealing and understandable by reviewers and insurance companies. Perhaps the great drawback of such a system is that it largely ignores the whole "genotypic/phenotypic" distinction.

Thus, it is a fact known since the time of Mendel, that organisms with the same depth or structural make up (genotype) may nevertheless appear quite different (phenotype). Conversely, two individuals that appear remarkably alike (phenotype) may in fact have widely different depth structure (genotype).

The consequence is, of course, that one cannot tell from looking at the surface of some phenomenon just what the basic structural make up is. Further one cannot know what the depth structure of some phenomenon is and be able to therefore predict somewhat accurately what the precise appearance of that phenomenon will be.

All of this, of course, applies directly to the diagnostic system. As anyone who works in the field knows all too well, someone may appear, say, quite borderline—or "dependent"—but at the structural level have an entirely different make-up altogether.

In such cases (as Kernberg, 1975, among others, has argued at length) the topological diagnosis may be little or no help in treatment itself.

In an interesting attempt to rectify this problem, Wells and Glickauf-Hughes (1998) presented a "two-part diagnostic model of ego-object relations development and character organization" (Ibid.).

Here, an attempt was made to distinguish between "three broad structural organizations (i.e., borderline, pre-neurotic, neurotic) and six character styles (i.e., schizoid, hysteroid, narcissistic, masochistic, obsessive-compulsive and hysterical)" (Ibid.). And, because one paper can't cover everything, the authors did not consider either normal or psychotic.

The assumption is that a person's level of ego development is centrally critical to treatment strategy.

For example, lack of certain support and feedback (typically called "therapeutic abstinence") will likely be productive for patients functioning at the neurotic level of organization—as the resulting tension will likely encourage the space to be filled by the patient with highly relevant and meaningful material ("grist for the mill").

Creation of the same void with a patient functioning at a borderline level of organization, however, will likely produce splitting and decompensation as the capacity to tolerate and make use of tension is typically beyond such a person.

The three levels of organization might be called a "vertical dimension" (i.e., an increasing ability and breadth).

Further, each level of ego-development organization discussed above may manifest different "horizontal" patterns or "styles."

At base, it is possible to distinguish between polarities that describe persons who tend as a rule to over-rely on others and others who tend as a rule to over-rely on themselves (i.e., rely for rewards and comforts Millon, 1981).

For this reason, at the borderline organizational level, both schizoid and hysteroid styles are encountered. The schizoid style is one in which a person tends as a rule to over-rely on him or herself. The hysteroid style is one in which a person tends as a rule to over-rely on others.

Here, the hysteroid style may be described as one in which there is "emotional lability and vacillations between intense demands around needs for support and hostile, denigrating attacks" (Wells and Glickauf-Hughes, p. 43).

By contrast, the schizoid style may be described as one in which there is "emotional detachment and isolation, a preoccupation with inner life, and an exaggerated reliance on thought processes...[where]...relationships manifest an underlying lifelessness and social communications are typically irrelevant or tangential (Ibid.).

Thus, for the schizoid style, the central fear is likely related to threats of engulfment and loss of self, and for the hysteroid style the great need for others is tempered by an equally great fear of abandonment and feeling bereft.

At the pre-neurotic organizational level, both narcissistic and masochistic styles are differentiated. Here, the schizoid person's central defense of emotional withdrawal is replaced by the narcissistic person's grandiose false self structure on the one hand, and on the other by the hysteroid person's defenses of acting out and "globalized splitting" are replaced by the masochistic person's central defenses of masochistic splitting and reaction formation.

Thus these pre-neurotic styles tend to focus on inner feelings or inferiority, unworthiness, and worthlessness.

Narcissistic individuals typically attempt to defend against such feelings by "attachments to admiring/admired objects who feed the narcissists' grandiosity, reinforce their self-confidence, and provide psychic direction...[if this mechanism fails, narcissistic persons tend] ...to either choose new admiring/admired objects or to rely on the invocation of their grandiose self structure" (Ibid., p. 44).

And, "while the grandiosity of the narcissist revolves around personal perfection ("I am the greatest"), the grandiosity of the masochist focuses on goodness ("I am the most generous, giving, and loyal of all") (Ibid. p. 45).

Thus, while the narcissistic person typically feels entitled to admiration and adoring because his or her regard for the self is one of regard for personal perfection, the masochistic person feels entitled to a loving relationship "because of the compensatory illusion of control related to the myth of fairness and reciprocity" (Glick and Meyers, 1988).

It might be noted the masochistic character is essentially directed to the task of obtaining "love from a predominately hurtful love object...as [a] reward or compensation for great effort suffering, or submission" (Wells and Glickauf-Hughes, p. 45).

Problems along the way are typically encountered by such people as a result of passive-aggressiveness, care taking, high degree of control (stiffness), endless power struggles, &c.

At the neurotic level, obsessive and hysteric styles have been outlined.

"The obsessive tends towards a more microscopic, detailed[,] precise cognitive style in contrast to the hysteric, who tends more towards a macroscopic, global, impressionistic cognitive style" (Shapiro, 1965).

Thus, such persons are constantly losing the forest because of the trees and maintaining a characteristic over-involvement with details and rigorous compliance. They also tend to indulge in excessive rumination due to an unusually harsh and severe super ego.

Here the narcissistic person's grandiose false self has been replaced by intellectualization and isolation of affect. Thus while the narcissistic person wishes to be perfect, the obsessive person's focus has more to do with "doing things perfectly" or "being right."

"The neurotic obsessive has an overdeveloped need for control because of deep seated insecurities about the self and the world. This is where the "super-moralistic rules" come in. These allow such a person to be technically correct, often without consideration of what is emotionally needed.

Obsessive people tend to wrestle with the dilemmas of compliance versus defiance, orderliness versus messiness, as well attempting to keep quiet about "intense feelings of insecurity, shame, and anger" (Wells and Glickauf-Hughes, p. 46).

The hysteric replaces the masochist's over-reliance on reaction-formation and masochistic splitting with pseudo-emotionality, repression, and cognitive fog…[such people are seen to be]…" (a) hypersensitive to the feelings, motivations, and expectations of others, (b) trend or fashion-consciousness, (c) extremely emotional, (d) flighty, (e) engaging, and (f) dramatic" (Ibid.)

Hysteric persons, in other words, typically overlook details and may appear unusually vague or imprecise.

Such persons constantly try to please others in order to gain their love and approval. To accomplish this, dependent childlike and seductive roles are typically used.

The hysteric personality is also organized around a number of polarities that can be seen in what Krohn (1978) termed the hysteric's myth of passivity.

As a result of feeling unprepared to cope with life, desiring to be taken care of, and centering on the love object, the hysteric minimizes his or her own substantial capabilities and presents an interpersonal style described and dependent, superficial, and affectively shallow (see Mueller and Aniskiewicz, 1986).

Such a person will as a rule therefore tend to appear externalized and also, at the same time, as a helpless victim.

In significant relationships, hysterics are thus often caught between their wishes and their fears, between their dependency needs and their anxieties about being controlled (Ibid.)

In sum, consideration of these preceding issues should make it possible to see how a diagnostic pattern may emerge from an object relations account that is based on both ego-structural developmental level as well as motivational theory.

Here the focus is on elements that may be seen to be directly helpful in treatment considerations rather than simply being further topological efforts primarily designed for chart-reviewers and insurance companies.

It also helps each of us to remember that what we are is "clinicians who treat people," not "providers who treat syndromes."

C: THINKING OF PSYCHOTHERAPY IN TERMS OF VOICES

Finally I would like to discuss with you an heuristic or device that frames interactions in a different sort of way that can encourage new ways of seeing and appraisal: exercises that may be unusually helpful in your own lives and/or work.

In principle, it is certainly not a new trick to think of the various influences or inputs from our own psychological makeup as VOICES.

Think back to suggestions of Eric Burne, for example.

"Voice talk" can be helpful in all likelihood due to the common tendency in our culture to think of everything as a fact. ("Just give me the facts, ma'am," said the serious Joe Friday.) Thus we tend to think, for example, if we have an "id," it must be a thing and it must be somewhere. That is, we cannot allow "id" to be what John Austin calls a "trouser word" (1965), that is a "constellating" or substantival term that "wears the trousers" for (i.e., makes concrete) a collection of (amorphous) forces.

Thus, it is somehow easier for us to think of a "voice" than a "valence."

(With unparalleled fondness,) I call my own particular "head-word" device "The Committee."

That is: imagine there is a committee room in your head. There is a committee table in this room, and seated around the table are four people.

The first is the person who likes you, who thinks you are special, a being worthy of love and life. (This is actually a characterization of the "praising superego precursor" or the interject of how I was praised and valued as a child.)

The second is the person who thinks you are very bad. ("All-bad" as Dr. Copeland would say.) This person repeatedly claims you are worthless, stupid, laughable, &c. The "bottom line" seems to be the notion that ultimately you will be hurt. As shorthand, I call this person "the head voice" or "put-down voice." (It is actually a characterization of the punishing super ego precursor or the interject of how I was punished as a child.)

The third person simply wants to go to the beach now! That is, this is the pleasure voice who only seems to be able to think of pleasures, impulses, and seeking satisfaction. (This is a obvious characterization of the unmodulated id, and typically includes the spontaneous, basic instincts and impulses, as well as the genuine material excluded by the "put-down" voice—what Neumann and Jung called "the shadow.")

The fourth person is you (executive function). And you are the only person who is able to leave the committee room. (The rest of the committee has been in the room since you were about three years old—and have not been out since.)

This is how life goes in terms of such a cartoon: you go out into the world, and something happens. You bring a report of that happening back to the committee so the committee can, for example, vote on it and determine how you are going to feel as well as what you are going to do about it.

(This all happens in a split second, but let's slow it down.)

The early analysts employed the term balance as in, for example, "She had a very 'balanced personality.'" If this term were to be used in terms of the head-committee, it would imply an equal input from each of the committee members.

In reality this rarely happens, and the most common cases seen in psychotherapy are likely those in which all committee members get a vote, and the put-down voice gets 2,114 votes. And then, as a result of this vote, the put-down member is commonly believed to be correct.

Thus, in such situations, the self tends to be held hostage by the negative interject—that is a common element in cases of depression and/or anxiety.

What is the virtue of this weird head-formulation?

Realizing the put-down person is not oneself is usually a very helpful event. Thus the put-down voice is the put-down voice and I am me—a different creature.

Such a move enables me to think of the put-down voice in a more objective, even "distanced" fashion than I would be able to do if I continued to think—as many do —that the put-down voice IS me.

Thus it is always prudent when one has a thought (any thought—but especially a judgmental thought, and especially a judgmental thought that is applied to the self) to ask the question: who's speaking? This allows me (for the first time—as I now have a "tool") to realize it is the negative interject and not my own thought who is usually speaking (especially in the case of judgments). Such a realization allows for a sense of self at a distance from the thought it is hopeless to ever stop deferring to the negative interject.

Another formulation is one recently suggested by Honos-Webb and Stiles (1998). Here assimilation analysis is conceived somewhat similarly to the above, and also in terms of voices.

Thus "voices" here are used in much the same way as "objects" in object-relations theory, as "personal archetypes" in Jungian psychology, as "automatic thoughts" in cognitive therapies, &c.

Thus, Stiles, et. al. (1990) suggested schemas:

> A schema is a frame of reference that organizes perception and experience. Schemas include prior beliefs that determine what material is wanted and therefore attended to. Schema-inconsistent experiences might be warded off, distorted, or experienced as problematic. (Honos-Webb and Stiles, p. 24).

Here, therapeutic progress consists of the assimilation of problematic experiences into a person's schema.

This assimilation takes place in levels that I will describe for you in a minute. These go from the first level where the problematic experience is warded off as much as possible to the seventh level where mastery of the problem or conflict is realized.

To think of this system in terms of voices, imagine "the problematic experience is considered as a separate, active voice within the person, rather than an abstract memory or a passive packet of information "(Ibid., p. 25).

Examples of problematic voices might be the products of (1) an isolated event, (2) a set of series of related events, (3) an older voice that has now become problematic due to a change in life circumstances.

Here, the self might be seen as a "community of voices."

The trick is that voices may be vestigial, implicit, or not in (conscious) awareness. In such cases, unheard voices may seek expression in symptoms for which one cannot seem to account.

A symptom can therefore be understood not as a pointless affliction, but rather a manifestation of a warded off voice (Ibid.).

In this view awareness is maintained by beliefs that are challenged by the emerging material, experience, or voice. If not for this held view against which the emerging entity might be judged, we would in all likelihood simply experience it rather than listening to the belief that contradicts and interprets it as problematical.

Thus, "As an unwanted voice emerges into awareness, a specific voice that opposes the emerging material [i.e., the specific voice that opposes the new input] is called forth from the community of voices" (Ibid.).

The process of assimilation of the new voice into the community of voices typically takes place as a kind of "interior exchange" between the contradictory established voice and the emerging voice.

Here, the emerging voice is outcast as it conflicts with the established voice.

This actually constitutes, if you think about it, our natural resistance to change. Thus the resistance to confront trauma is as potent—if not more potent—in creating psychological damage as is the original trauma.

The fatuous sense of being in control is due to one's alignment with the established voice and the subsequent dismissing or disenfranchising of the emerging voice.

Clearly the more intrusive a symptom (voice) is, the less it has been able to be assimilated.

The Seven Levels:

Level 0.   Here the emerging voice is not observed. Symptoms might be apparent, but the voice itself is occluded. Further the precise opposing voice has not arisen, at least into consciousness, to defend the current system.

A person's discussion about loss of control serves as a marker for level 0.

Level 1. The unwanted voice begins to emerge into awareness but is not yet taken as a topic for discourse. This level is associated with fear—specifically the fear of losing control. One identifies with the strengthening established voice. He or feels it should be possible to cope with the situation (under-valuation) but does not consider the issue to be psychological in origin. One may vow to "soldier on" or "tough it out."

The emphasis is on controlling or suppressing painful emotional input or, for example, maintaining an objectified and distanced view by what Kohut called "externalization" of the issue.

Here one worries about what is "out there" (e.g., situational or environmental factors) in order to avoid self awareness. ("The devil made me do it.")

The transition from Level 1 to Level 2 requires the person to give up some measure of control.

Level 2. The emerging voice presses further into consciousness. This level is characterized by intense emotional pain and confusion. The person is distressed but can't identify the problem. Here the emerging input disrupts the previous unity within the individual. Still, greater weight is given to the established voice—but it is beginning to appear that the situation is complex, not simple.

Moving from Level 1 to Level 2 requires the person to tolerate disorder and disequilibrium. If not, defenses are further marshaled in the service of denial.

Level 3. Here the person explicitly recognizes the problem. This results in a "direct confrontation" between the emerging and the established voices. It is significant that at this level, the person can become aware of the operation of the two opposing forces or voices rather than simply identifying with the established voice. That is, objectivity is allowed to begin. One is able to talk about the dominant voice rather than only being able to talk out of it. In Level 3, both voices tend to have equal weight, though the more or less clear identification of the dominant voice, clarifies the problem.

A marker of Level 3 is that the person feels at an impasse or "stuck."

Level 4. Beyond the level of cognitive understanding in and of itself, what is required here is "an empathetic understanding between the separate voices" (Ibid. p. 29). Thus, each voice is able to see the other's contribution. This level is characterized by mixed affect and greater psychological complexity as a new element is allowed to become a part of the self. The pain associated with hearing the emerging voice in prior stages is absent here. Thus allegiance to one position as opposed to another is no longer required.

Levels 5-7. These levels involve the application of the new adjustment to the real world. Typically, one's behavior becomes more flexible and less defended.

Here optimal adjustment entails the capacity to tolerate the enlargement of the self in the service of more developed awareness.   As individuals, we differ most profoundly in what we can see. The opposite of defending, according to Freud, was "reality testing." That is learning more about what is.

What I have been suggesting here is that what is goes beyond being a WASP and the attempt to live a topological existence, or the attempt to function in such a way that one is "on top of it at all times," "in control," or— perhaps worst of all—"distortion-free."

It goes beyond physiology and conceptual learning, S.E.S., gender, self help, and organized religion.   It depends on the nature of my foundation and capacity for any of these things as developed and introjected in my attachment history.

It goes beyond descriptive reality to the dimensions of the unconscious, the "collective archetypes," and what Joseph Campbell called "the song of the blood," that is what it is to be a human being.   Tapping into this profound dimension requires an expansion beyond the cultural inflections of the present, about ninety percent of what one learned in school, an even higher percentage of what one sees on TV or—God help us—increasingly in films, and, yes Virginia, it even goes beyond managed care guidelines for proper treatment protocols and scientific experimentation.

It lies, as they say, in the heart—where we, our friends, our patients, our families, our deepest longings have life. It is what we live for. And, as we have seen through the Tarot, the countless examples from ancient Greece, and now through the extension of Hermetic thinking into the middle ages (and thus the "modern world"), it is eternal. Only the metaphorical "carriers" change to protect the innocent.

It has been shown to be THE most important element in psychotherapy, and I would suggest in parenting and teaching as well.

And, as Kohut saw so clearly, it is really who we are.

MEXICO TEN

1. INTRODUCTORY REMARKS

Welcome back. Or welcome. This is our tenth year meeting! The idea to create this trip began one winter Wednesday in my supervision group. I told Mary Talboys about it, and together we patched together that first trip. We came here: to Cancun. None of us knew what we were doing (which has not changed much), but the trip was a huge success and became the source of legends, tall stories, lies (bull shit), and distortions galore.

After trip number four, which we took to Mazatlan, Tom Wolfe took over the logistic details of pulling the trip together. This is a role he has continued to the present with, I must say, amazing energy, thoroughness, grace beyond belief, and high style.

The first year Joe Culbertson and I commandeered the bar in the hotel where we were staying and talked about borderline personality disorder and the relationship between shame and narcissism. I used some mythological examples to illustrate these points, and this seemed to be a highlight.

Bill Watts, my beloved teacher from UCLA, was there. He lit a candle. Bill died two years ago.

After that first year the focus of the presentations has been two fold. The first emphasis has been to clarify and describe a more expanded context of the disorders and conditions frequently seen in psychotherapy. I have tried to present, in hopefully clarified terms, the depth dynamics that apply to these disorders/conditions as well as how to work with them more effectively.

A second emphasis has been to find mythological examples to illustrate such dynamics. I have tried to show the amazing similarity of ancient myths and contemporary discoveries related to psychology and the human soul (especially in "depth psychologies" and psychoanalysis). (Last year, for example, we focused on the Tarot and the year before on Alchemy.)

It also has became clear that two or two and a half hours of drivel was overwhelming enough, and the rest of the day needed to be devoted to eating and drinking--in order to confront and endure the following day's presentations.

Each year we have taken a day off for sightseeing, excursions, and side trips. This year Tom and I are trying to arrange a trip to Tulum and Koba for those of you who would like to come along. Tulum is among the most picturesque of the ancient sites, and Koba is a city that is in the process of being excavated from the jungle as we speak. We will keep you posted.

Thank you all for joining us on this adventure. Both Tom and I hope you have a great time. And...we will keep you informed about the future. We have lots of ideas for a new series of adventures. I mean, after all, we don't want to stop now!

2. KOHUT

(This material is excerpted directly from: http://www.s-fu.ca/~psimpson/kohutppr1.htm#to)

It became clear to Kohut that disorders most commonly diagnosed by Freud were no longer prevalent, due to historical changes in society and family. [This, he held] required a turn away from established psychoanalytic theory and a return to observing data in clinical experience with contemporary clients to generate new theory and treatment (Kohut, 1959/1978).

Kohut went on to declare empathy the defining scientific method (Kohut, 1973/1978) for the investigation of complex mental states; Kohut who held degrees in both medicine and neurology, was opposed to an objective medical model for treating complex mental states (Kohut 1981, in Lichtenberg, 1984). Kohut further upset the psychoanalytic establishment by declaring that empathy as an overarching methodology made the "tool-and-method" distinctions between their profession and that of clinical psychology no longer relevant, and that it could form a framework within which many treatment techniques could be used (Kohut, 1973/1978).

"For reasons that I cannot explain, I have, so far as I can judge, ever since my childhood been familiar with the relativity of our perceptions of reality and with the relativity of the framework of ordering concepts that shape our observations and explanations. I had always assumed that everybody else shared this knowledge. [I found myself set apart with] my clearly established knowledge that reality per se, whether extrospective or introspective, is unknowable and that we can only describe what we see within the framework of what we have done to see it . ...I was completely unprepared personally for the misunderstanding from the side of my colleagues of the issues ... that I had presented to them (Kohut 1981, in Lichtenberg et al , 1984, p.90-91)."

[Compare this to the Introduction of Wittgenstein's Philosophical Investigations as well as Flax (1990).]

A great deal of Kohut's obliviousness to peer reaction can be explained by his upbringing, unusual even by Viennese standards in the 1930s. He was the only child of a concert pianist and the daughter of an exceedingly rich merchant family, the Lampls. Born in 1913, ...Kohut's early years were separate from his father, who soldiered on the Russian Front. He remained very close with his mother (whom he once fondly characterized as "crazy" [Strozier, in Goldberg, 1985]). Like Freud, Kohut was the first son of a young mother, and remained a prince for life.

Kohut's crucial tale about his young self was of going down to the train station in 1938 to, in generous tribute, demonstratively take his hat off to Freud as the old man steamed off into exile. This was when he vowed to follow Freud, whom he had never met (Strozier in Goldberg, 1985). (Whether this tale is true or false is debated.)

Arriving [in the U.S.] with 25 cents in hand, Kohut rapidly obtained an internship [at Chicago], followed by a residency in neurology, which he served together with Thomas Szasz, and then by an assistant professorship in neurology and psychiatry in 1944 at the age of 31 (Strozier in Goldberg, 1985). When he completed his psychoanalytic training in 1949, he was immediately invited to join the staff of the Chicago Institute.

His Eurocentric intellectual foundations were already established when he came to the U.S. Like the Gestaltists who fled Europe with him, he was steeped in the history of philosophy, and at home with the idea of a science of spirit legitimately separate from a science of material things. Thus, while not unaware of issues in American psychology (it is worth noting that he did use the word "operationalism", which is Behaviorist in origin for his definition of psychoanalysis [Kohut, 1959, 1982/1984]), Kohut remained free of the historical burdens of American psychology: extreme positivism, blinkered operationalism and the romance with quantification and statistics.

When he made his 1957 call for psychoanalysis to be limited to human experience accessible to empathy (Kohut, 1959/1978)2 , Kohut was literally screamed at from the floor of the Chicago Institute...

This devastating lack of receptivity shook Kohut badly... As a consequence, Kohut retreated to proving his loyalty through zealous organizational work and to his own private analytic and data-gathering work for about ten years. He also confined himself to expressing his ideas within the vocabulary constraints of Freud's drive theory. Not until 1971 did Kohut publish his first book. While Anna Freud tried to ignore its logical consequences, others did not: at meetings, many colleagues would no longer even look at him (Wolf in Hunter, 1992). It was not until 1977 that he freed himself to declare openly that he was abandoning drive theory (Kohut, 1977).

By the 1950s, like Balint and Winnicott in England (Bacal & Newman, 1990) and the Blancks in New York (Blanck & Blanck, 1974), he was among the earliest to notice the disappearance of classical neurotics from his caseload, to recognize the therapeutic inadequacy of classical Freudian interpretation based on a view of humans from a former Zeitgeist (Kohut, 1984a), and to see a significant pattern: a new historically-situated shift in forms of psychological misery (Kohut, 1973/1978, p.680). The Blancks (1974) called these new patients "Watson's babies," products of the cold upbringing so successfully promoted by Behaviorist John B. Watson.

It is also possible that he was hardened against his older mentors by his clinical experience: many of his analysands, suffering as he insisted from unempathic upbringings, were the adult offspring of psychoanalysts, or psychoanalysts who needed to repair the effects of their training analyses (Kohut in Goldberg, 1980).

It seems that Kohut's intellectual immunity to peer pressure, and his ability to see the historical breadth and significance of this trend, may have been rooted psychodynamically in his isolated, intellectually-immersed upbringing with its one-to-one relationships to the exclusion of embedded group relatedness.

Despite the rarified air of a psychoanalytic institute, it is hard to imagine that Kohut, who had initiated the joint training program in psychiatry, psychoanalysis, social work and student mental health clinic at the University of Chicago (Elson, 1987), was unaware of Carl Rogers, who also worked there in the Counselling Service in the late 1940s and early 1950s.

...the hostile reception to his first statement of fidelity to phenomenological ideals in 1957 effectively blocked... [his earlier]...personal ambitions...This personal blow seems to have forced Kohut to authentically immerse himself in the process he started. As a result, he achieved a more profound commitment to theory-making integrated in the living reality of his patients, and in the time and tide of history. It may have been the best thing that could have happened to Kohut, in the sense of seeming to have firmed up his core self, a person who could trust to process, personal or intellectual, without losing cohesion.

In the beginning, Kohut's "hard-ball" competitiveness (Wolf in Hunter, 1992), and personal arrogance (Strozier in Goldberg, 1985) invited normal envy, not to speak of narcissistic rage and spitefulness, in the psychoanalytic hierarchy. Following his first rebuff by the older generation, Kohut's "inner circle" of admiring younger men initially repeated the patterns of Freud's circle (Grosskurth, 1991), including the hostile departure in 1973 of one of his first adherents, John Gedo, labelled by the young circle as "the Jung of the group" (4) (Wolf in Hunter, 1992, p.493) .

Taking a wider angle perspective on Kohut's life affirms what he himself hinted at in "The Search for the Analyst's Self" (Kohut, 1978a, p.931), making it clear that his own personal journey was the moving force of his theoretical process, as John Gedo points out (Gedo, 1986).

Kohut, in Eriksonian terms (Erikson, 1982), was "redoing" in slow motion, the developmental tasks of adolescent identity formation, with its vitalizing element of fidelity to self-chosen ideals. In Kohut's middle age, this process was neither easy nor painless. The price, in terms of loss of established career, prestige and connectedness were inevitably higher than for an adolescent just starting out in life.

Referring back to Kohut's selfobject theory, a parent who is sensitive to their child's developmental needs will be growth-promoting if they transform their role from mirroring or soothing to modeling, as the child's emotional use of them shifts from taking in admiration and giving idealization to skill development for the future. This shift to working side-by-side with a parent Kohut called the twinship selfobject experience, which parallels Erik Erikson's concept of the shift from the Oedipal play age to the age of industry as school begins. Kohut insisted that this is the source of joy, not pain, in the Oedipal period (Kohut, 1977).

Lastly, evidence of Kohut's personal shift lies in his redefinition of psychological health. This definition had always been one of "good enough" living, that is, when the client had developed a reliable internal source of energy and initiative in one of three spheres of life (ambition, ideals and skills/talents), corresponding to the three self-object experiences for all of which the client had previously been completely dependent on others to provide (Kohut, 1977) (in contrast to classical analysts' insistence on "complete" working through of all spheres of conflict).

To Oedipus ("Guilty Man"), he contrasts the story of Odysseus (Tragic Man"), whom he waggishly called "the first Modern Man, a draft dodger". Odysseus faked insanity to avoid joining the insanity of the Trojan War. He was faced with the choice of either continuing his symptomatic, compulsive ploughing or killing his baby son, who had been flung into the furrow ahead of him by his fellow Greek rulers. And so he ploughed a semicircle around the baby, thus choosing to risk his own future death in war over the immediate certainty of death for the next generation. This circumscribed life choice, which is paradoxical in a life of individual striving, Kohut called the "semicircle of mental health" of "Tragic Man" and:

...a fitting symbol of that joyful awareness of the human self of being temporal, of having an unrolling destiny: a preparatory beginning, a flourishing middle, and a retrospective end; a fitting symbol for the fact that healthy man experiences, and with deepest joy, the next generation as an extension of his own self. It is the primacy of the support for the succeeding generation, therefore, which is normal and human, and not intergenerational strife and mutual wishes to kill and to destroy -- however frequently, and perhaps even ubiquitously, we may be able to find traces of those pathological disintegration products of which traditional analysis has made us think as a normal development phase, a normal experience of the child. It is only when the self of the parent is not a normal, healthy self, cohesive, vigorous, and harmonious, that it will react with competitiveness and seductiveness rather than with pride and affection when the child, at the age of five, is making an exhilarating move toward a heretofore not achieved degree of assertiveness, generosity, and affection. ... It is a remarkable fact that nobody, as far as I know, has pointed out, at least not in an effective way, a feature of the Oedipus myth which refers to the intergenerational relationship--an aspect of the story which is truly remarkable, especially by comparison with the parallel aspect of the intergenerational story about Odysseus and Telemachus as told to us by Homer. ... Is not the most significant dynamic-genetic feature of the Oedipus story that Oedipus was a rejected child? ... Does our attention to [the rest of the story] not allow us to see King Oedipus' "Oedipus complex" in a different light? And does it not, by stark contrast, illuminate even further how Odysseus' normal intergenerational response, the semicircle of his plough, lead to a relationship between father and son ... which, I submit, is the true and nuclear essence of humanness. This nuclear essence of man is not a surface phenomenon, not part of a precariously maintained civilized crust of the personality or of a reaction formation. It constitutes the essential nucleus of the self and the access to it in our patients is often attained only with the greatest difficulty (Kohut 1981, in Lichtenberg, p. 96-98).

What makes Kohut's myth so vibrant for us all is that it is immediately recognizable as the central metaphor of his life with all the significance that such a metaphor signals:

It is precisely at the level of these reified images that the subjectivity of the theorist becomes most apparent, for they can be shown to vividly reflect his personal solutions to the nuclear crises of his own life history (Stolorow & Atwood, 1979, p. 23).

It is my speculation that Kohut attained this definition of psychological health through his own very slow personal journey with his students and followers, in addition to his experience as a father.

Today, many other theorists long divided from Freudian currents, are now taking an interest in self psychology.

One area of psychoanalytic/psychological thinking that has not warmed to self psychology is that of ego psychology and object relations (Kernberg, 1984; Masterson, 1985; Rinsley, 1982). Both of these currents find their roots in the feuding tradition of psychoanalysis, a barrier hard to overcome. But other barriers exist. Margaret Mahler's 1950-1970s research in infant development proved that academicially sound, direct observational research could be done within a psychoanalytic framework. This gave an enormous boost to the prestige of ego psychology, and re-legitimzied, in modern terms, Freudian/Kleinian drive theory, within which Mahler worked. This sharpened the differences between Kohut and others in psychoanalysis, and undoubtedly fed the competitive rift . Kohut himself (1977) declared the two incompatible. Only in the 1980s, has infant research taken on a theoretical bent congenial to self psychology (Stern, 1985).

Philip Cushman (1990) puts the problem most succinctly: the empty self of today is historically and socially constructed. Object relations theory, and ego psychology to a lesser extent, presuppose a "bounded self", with the goal of therapy to fill that self with representations from the outside. Self psychology has as its purpose the strengthening or stimulation of development of the client's own inner structures (Stolorow,1992). Both processes begin with externals; at issue is to what degree the client is encouraged to them as raw material for their own personality structures or merely adopts them wholesale through gross identification (Masterson, 1985) or through force majeure (Meares & Hobson, 1977, Kernberg, 1984, Wile, 1984). While self psychology and object relations theory describe the same clients, their philosophy, purpose and treatment are at loggerheads. At heart is an unbridgeable philosophical difference over the goodness or badness of humans (Straker, 1987).

Because Kohut's theory has always been rooted in concepts of traumatic interference with development, it has survived the 1980s revulsion against psychoanalysis that came with the uproar (Masson, 1984) over Freud's rejection of the seduction theory, and the growing acknowledgement of wide-spread child abuse in our own day.

Perhaps Kohut's personal example of willingness to venture, whether to the unknown New World as a young man, to new, empathic methods of going with the clients' experience, to being willing to go with the younger generation into the future, is his greatest legacy. More than anything else, he showed us how we, too, can jettison our eternal verities (Goldberg, 1990). We too can claim the vigorous joy (and the exhilaration, and conflict, and terror, and tragedy) inherent in setting out for the 21st century with only twenty-five dollars worth of theoretical certainty in our pockets.

3. DISORDERS OF THE SELF

BRIEF HISTORY

The word 'narcissism' comes from the Greek 'Narka' which means ' to deaden.'

[Toward the end of his career, Kohut tended to concentrate on the use of the phrase 'disorders of the self' rather than on the term 'narcissism.' He likely did this because by that time his own thinking had accounted for most character pathology in terms of 'self' formulations. This left him in the position of using a category term, narcissism, to account for an entire spectrum of disorders.]

Let us trace the progress of this thinking.

It may be recalled that Freud felt narcissism was the "libidinal cathexis of the ego" (Cooper and Maxwell, 1995, p. 4).

Freud came to hold to a view of "physicalism," that the mind and the brain were the same thing. Thus, according to this view, thinking was neuronal activity and not the product of some fanciful region beyond science.

He regarded "thinking" and "mind" talk as regrettable language and not rigorous enough for science. For a thought to become conscious, he thought, it had to be linked in language.

Thus the regret: our language is more fanciful than factual. Freud set out to create a more scientifically accurate language for psychology.

So Freud regarded talk of, say, the "self" as convenient in social discourse but a term that told us nothing about psychological phenomena. Still, though there is no self, there are self-representations. According to Cooper and Maxwell (1995), Freud used the term: 'das Ich' (ego) as a shorthand term for self-representation. Thus, for Freud, narcissism was a condition that affected one's self-representations.

(Actually, it was Hartmann (1950) who distinguished between the ego (mental structure), the self (the whole person), and the self-representation (essentially one's self concept).)

Cooper and Maxwell described Freud's view of narcissism as the state of infatuation with one's own idea of oneself (p.5).

Infants, he came to feel, pass from a disorganized period of autoerotism, to narcissism, and then to object love. We solve our narcissism by creating an "ego ideal" and then striving to achieve it.

Freud's final position on narcissism held that once we are able to establish an idea of ourselves, we cast this idea in the most favorable light. "Self" is equated with everything that brings enjoyment, and "not-self" is equated with everything else.

Cooper and Maxwell (1995) claimed:

> Learning to love means giving up this illusion of personal perfection and thereby accepting the fact of one's dependence upon others. One is narcissistic to the extent that one's self-representations encompass only those things that yield pleasure. The capacity to love is built on the capacity to find the 'bad' in oneself and the 'good' in others (p. 6).

Today, there are three basic theoretical approaches to the conceptualization of narcissism. These are primarily based on the views of Klein, Kohut, and Kernberg. All three approaches stress developmental arrest. Kohut stressed this in terms of how much the infant's self had been "usurped" rather than being free to emerge in a more or less "realized state." Klein stressed the need to defend against and manage feelings of envy related to the discovery of the importance of the other. Kernberg stressed investment in the notion of a grandiose self as well as a refusal to accept the reality of separateness.

More specifically, Klein and several others in the "British school of object relations" felt narcissism and object love coexist during early infancy--indeed from the very beginning of extra uterine life. Klein's focus was on the relational character of representations of such interactions which she called "fantasies." And later Kleinian writers treated narcissism as a defense against envy. Thus, rather than suffer envy, the narcissistic person identifies with the envied object. This protects against the pain of envy but results in impoverished object relations. The "envy" notion has become a famous product of the Klein school.

Kohut's contributions are considerable, and his views have increasingly impacted the shape of modern analysis, especially Self Psychology. Kohut felt:

> It is not the object which determines whether or not an attitude is narcissistic, it is the felt quality of the relation to that object, so 'the antithesis to narcissism is not object-relation but object-love' (Kohut, 1966, p. 429).

Infants require a feeling of unity with their primary objects. This experience Kohut called 'selfobject experiences.' There are three fundamental varieties: mirroring, idealizing, and twinship.

Mirroring has to do with the reaction of an admiring audience. When we are mirrored, we tend to feel the audience is an extension of ourselves.

Idealizing involves one's immersion in another person who is felt to be greater than oneself. Thus I feel important because I am connected to another person who is important.

Twinship involves feelings of sameness with another at my own level. Thus the two of us are the same.

The establishment of successful selfobject interactions, however, is a two way street. This is important to stress. The parent must mirror the infant, but the infant must also mirror the parent. Thus the mirroring goes both ways; we are both being--in a sense--who the other person needs us to be. This leads in the direction of the special form of twinship interaction that I have called "a connection."

The same situation is a requisite for successful patient-therapist interactions. The mirroring must go both ways so that a meaningful resonance is established.

The project of adequate mirroring is initially a full time job on the part of the primary object (usually the mother). She puts her regular life on hold and devotes all her time to attending to and mirroring the infant. The path to maturity is for the parent to slowly triturate the mirroring as she slowly includes more of her regular life--that is goes back to it in small enough steps that the infant can tolerate the small incremental loss involved and thus follow. This path leads away from the artificial parent child interaction to a life in the real world.

If the parent cannot set up the self-object experience, or titrates her soothing efforts at a pace the infant cannot follow, a narcissistically wounded child will result.

> Thus the narcissistically disordered person has had insufficient or inadequate selfobject]experience, and has consequently developed an enfeebled self. Such analysands are described as using the analyst as a selfobject in a narcissistic transference which reproduces infantile narcissistic states (Cooper and Maxwell, 1995, p. 10).

As Kohut's work progressed, he became more and more focused on selfobject phenomena, their establishment and resolution, and less interested in the concept of narcissism per se.

The important Kohut-Kernberg debates highlighted Kernberg's notions that:

> ...narcissistic character pathology is not a regression to normal infantile narcissism [as suggested by Kohut]: it is caused by a libidinal investment in a pathological grandiose self consisting of an amalgam of

real self representations, ideal self-representations, and ideal object-representations
and the simultaneous repression, projection
or disavowal or negatively toned self-and
object-representations. He also stresses that
narcissistically disordered people deny difference between self and object rather than
separateness as some (especially Kleinian)
writers assert (Cooper and Maxwell, p.
11-12).

According to Kernberg, confronting this archaic grandiose self and the defense against separateness constitutes the work of treatment with such patients.

Nevertheless, regardless of the approach favored, it has been pointed out that psychoanalysis has not made the jump from visions of narcissism to testable theories. Thus the choice between ideas such as those outlined above becomes largely one of personal bias, acquaintance, one's own analyst, lover, &c.

DIAGNOSIS, TREATMENT, AND OUTCOME

The above considerations hold that narcissistic pathology has to do with a damaged relation to the primary object [which results in inadequate self-representations].

Thus the person with narcissistic pathology will tend to view others as either (1) the "depleated-devowering breast," or (2) the damaged combined parental imago.

What such a person failed to get from the primary object will be transferred with consuming intensity to the therapist, lover, child, friend, &c.

Further, the depth of narcissistic pathology is difficult to assess as such people routinely put so much investment into facade. The depth of the disturbance is, therefore, rarely exposed. (This is what Winnicott (1960) called the False Self covering the True Self.) (He also said" "It is the False Self that brings the True Self to treatment.")

Under the adept facade, the self in narcissistic individuals feels split off and dead. Kohut emphasized its grandiosity and Kernberg and Russell emphasized its aggression.

An essential element of narcissistic character--almost a defining element it itself--regardless of its manifestation, is an enormous difficulty in acknowledging dependency.

Other widely agreed-upon central traits include:

1. A grandiose sense of self-importance or uniqueness
2. A preoccupation with fantasies of unlimited success, power, brilliance, beauty, or ideal love
3. Exhibitionism, the person requires constant attention and admiration

4. Cool indifference or naked feelings of rage: 'narcissistic rage,' inferiority, shame, humiliation or emptiness in response to criticism or defeat
5. At least two of the following characteristics of disturbances in interpersonal relationships: entitlement (expectation of special favors without assuming reciprocal responsibilities), interper sonal exploitativeness, relationships that characteristically alternate between the extremes of over-idealization and devaluation, lack of em pathy and need to control (see Cooper and Max well, p. 18-19) (similar to DSM criteria).

In addition, there is a quest for body perfection and beauty, including BDD and, according to some, gender identity disorder (GID).

Such people often live in transitional space--oddly in such a way that prevents development. This is a space where no one is allowed to enter and one maintains a state of private limbo. The virtue of such an arrangement for someone with extensive narcissistic pathology is that it keeps one from accepting limits that any real or "permanent" adjustment would impose. Limits would ruin the illusion of boundless perfection or possibility. It also allows for the control of the object in the sense that one can fantasize the reactions one is getting and thus arrange them in a desired fashion.

This phenomenon is related to the "twenty dollar bill phenomenon." If I enter a store with a twenty, I could buy lots of things. I am rich in possibilities. I do not feel limited. If, however, I buy something, it is true I get the one (small) thing, but I lose all the other possibilities. All the other degrees of freedom instantly collapse--and in this sense I always lose more than I get (lose more possibilities than the one reality I get).

Faced with such a loss and consequent narcissistic wound of limitation, I cannot buy anything--thus preserving my richness of possibility. But, the problem is that until I do limit myself by buying one thing, I cannot move onto the next level--the level of true relating. In other words, I have endless possibilities, but I cannot love (cannot commit myself to human, immediate, flawed love).

What is rather sought above all other things is a sense of merger (based on the experience of mirroring and twinship), for someone to join with one's fragile core. Someone who connects and does not leave, no matter what one does. The analyst of such a person is treated as being this sought connection and thus not with object-transference, but specifically as a selfobject.

Again, the Kleinians hold that narcissism defends us against a feeling of envy. Envy would imply an acknowledgement we lack what the other has. There also must be enough of a separation between the self and the object that one can have feelings of deprivation.

For these reasons narcissistic people find the fit between the therapist and patient to be critical. The production of the patient always must be accepted and treated with respect. Analysis can only begin after this period of establishing safety and mutual resonance is established--i.e., only after the analyst successfully functions for the patient as a self object. Too quick interpretations (such as, "that's projection") are typically interpreted by narcissistic individuals as rejections or outright attacks.

The patient must feel safe and accepted enough to allow his or her real self rather than his or her façade-false self to enter the treatment context.

Slow progress is also necessary as narcissistic people have great difficulty accepting what comes from outside themselves.

All of this is to say that the transference elements with narcissistic persons is different than it is with other patients in that the therapist is not treated as a hurtful member of the patient's past, but as a missing part of the patient's self. Seinfeld (1993) called this "symbiotic relatedness." The symbiotic relatedness (transference) has three stages: idealization, ambivalence, and finally resolution.

Aggression and hostility especially must be tolerated as must distortions about the therapist based on the patient's hostile transference.

The three basic schools of treatment for narcissism differ the most in their managing of hostility and aggression.

The Klein school believes the primitive splitting seen in aggression can only be worked through by constantly exposing and interpreting the violent and sadomasochistic aspects of the transference so they can be integrated into the ego.

The Kernberg group feels that excesses of aggressive impulses be strictly limited during treatment. The establishment of rules and limits protects the safety of the therapeutic enterprise according to this approach.

Kohut and the self psychologists, on the other hand, find such impulses, comments, and behavior immature expressions of narcissism that are to be mirrored so the developmental pathways closed off during childhood can be reopened and connected.

Kohut said:

> [The critical question is]...whether or not the patient is able to develop a self-object transference when the opportunity to re-experience the selfobject of childhood is offered to him in the psychoanalytic situation. If the answer is yes, we will diagnose the patient as 'narcissistic personality disorder', if the answer is no, we will diagnose him as 'borderline'...(1984, p. 219, note 7).

For Kohut the movement in therapy is from immature selfobject relating, through more mature selfobject relating to, in the best cases, (some) separateness.

In this view narcissistic rage is the pathological but justified response of a child to injuries from which he/she could not recover him/herself. Khan's (1974) description of cumulative trauma even suggests the injuries may be small and unconscious over time.

It may be said the resistance of the narcissistic individual requires slow and deeply empathic treatment over time as the narcissistic person is attempting to avoid self-knowledge as this involves the destruction of the perfect image.

The outcome of treatment with narcissistic individuals often is to increase social adaptability though in such persons a degree of contempt for the object still remains.

The developmental process is against these patients and the danger of the pathology increases with time. There is a brief window in early middle age in which one's youth can no longer save one--and one may attempt to adjust to the reality remaining. Suicide, however, is frequent during this time.

Narcissistic individuals are able to cause incredible damage to the social structures and families to which they belong. When they have children, they cannot foster separate development. Children are routinely seen as extensions of the self.

As Levin (1993) said: "The world is pretty much run by narcissistic personality disorders...they can usually "perform (p. 242)".

MOTHER-CHILD SEPARATION

(This material is approached from a Kleinian point of view.)

Difficulties in essential separation seem to be intensified by either the absence or inadequacy of the father's effective presence--or by a paternal function within the mother (see also Stoller, 1985).

When the mother's needs come first, the baby's emotional growth can be severely impaired. Infants become stuck at the stage of separation-individuation. Narcissistic disturbances are likely to be developed, as are problems of sexual identity as well as internalization and identification with parts of the parents.

The tyrannical fantasies of children must be transformed and re-introjected in more real terms. In this process adaptation to reality can be achieved through the acceptance of psychic pain (Pozzi, p. 35).

The paternal figure here is not strong enough to interrupt the mother's narcissistic involvement with her child as well as her lack of separateness. Oedipal transformations are severely interrupted.

Freud (1917, p. 243) compared the condition of melancholia with that of mourning. He felt both were reactions to the loss of someone loved.

> ...[there is] a painful sense of dejection, a loss of interest in the outside world or an interest only in what recalls the lost object, the loss of the capacity to find another object of love, the inhibition of all activity, although in mourning activities are exclusively related to the lost object (Ibid, p. 36).

Briefly the difference is that in mourning there is object loss (anaclitic). Something "out there" that matters is now gone. The context is forever different and bereft. In melancholia, a part of the self that was invested in the lost object is now lost. Thus the loss is subjective loss (narcissistic). It is part of the self that is lost.

Mothers of children who develop separation issues and narcissistic patterns have clear difficulties in being left by their children. It is as if the child exists in a narcissistic and therefore objectless state (Rosenfeld, 1987). This is, if you will, a kind of "narcissistic object-relation." This is a relationship based on narcissistic purposes and omnipotence.

In this view, narcissism becomes a kind of defense against separateness involving the mechanism of projective identification. Here, the self and the object appear to be the same. "If two people are felt to be the same, there is no comparison, competition, envy, anger, frustration, but a flat so-called equality (Cooper and Maxwell, p. 38)."

NARCISSISTIC VULNERABILITY IN ADOLESCENCE

All history contours personality dimensions. Initially this is the mother. It is the "good enough mother" (Winnicott, 1958) who is able to provide a workable platform for the inevitable losses of maturation. It is what Bowlby (1988) called a "secure attachment."

Puberty is intrusive; it is outside conscious control. These changes are interpreted through the lenses the individual has already developed. At the same time archaic elements centering around experiencing joy and mastery are re-awakened.

Kohut (1971) stressed intensified emotions of shame. Klein (1957) and Rosenfeld (1964) stressed an envious intolerance of loss. These are the elements seen in narcissistically vulnerable people.

Flanders (1995) stressed:

If early experiences of separation or, indeed, of intimacy are too enraging or terrifying, then individuality and intimate communication are colored too intensely with emotional experiences of abandonment or violent intrusion or engulfment... (p.42)

The magic of the protection of the parents, whatever the nature of the childhood has been, necessarily decreases as the child approaches adolescence and increases in power him or herself. The parents' strongly held notions of the child's special-ness are dramatically challenged. Clearly the more rigid and defensive this idealization of childhood on the part of the parents has been, the more intrusive and disturbing the beginnings of adult and sexual life will be. The most extreme case will be that of the narcissistically idealized.

If the parents' relationship is [has been] too cruelly or hatefully conceived, it is likely that the hatred will permeate and pervert the adolescent's relation to his own body and that of his object. Brittle rigidities that have resulted from loss experiences as too traumatic, separation too frightening strong feelings too disturbing, sexuality too intrusive or violent or dirty (Grunbergher, 1979) will leave the adolescent poorly equipped to face up to the challenges of his new opportunity and defensively estranged from sexual realities (Flanders, p. 42-43).

The development of the sexually mature body typically issues in panic associated with frightening and unexpected developments. Defenses must be erected against hated sexual feelings that do damage to the adolescent's fragile sense of self-esteem. The body is often interpreted as betraying the self. Such reasoning often issues in symptoms of anorexia, bulimia, self-inflicted injury, and attempted suicide.

Narcissistically vulnerable adolescents are compelled often to magically control their development in order to make it all come out as required to maintain the narcisictally arranged sense of esteem. The darkest fear is internal and external abandonment.

NARCISSISM AND ADOLESCENCE

There is a need on the part of adolescents for mastery in a vastly changing context. Separation from previously valued caretakers is essential for the adolescent's ability to take responsibility. Almost everything is experienced as fragile.

"Adolescents are...in a peculiarly precarious and isolated position (Wilson, p. 52)." They are disconnected from all that has held them together in the past and confronted at the same time by all that is new, unfamiliar, and threatening in the future. They are consequently unavoidably driven back into themselves in order to find a balance, and take refuge in the realm of narcissistic defense.

Kohut (1977) felt adolescents tended towards idealizing or grandiose solutions. This is what Greenberg (1975) called "the omnipotent quest during adolescence."

Adolescents use others and things as selfobjects to magically carry the parts of themselves they feel are lacking. Thus the "right sneakers" may "repair" an unsure esteem, befriending the group hero, shacking up with the basketball team hero, &c.

Adolescents are "full of themselves" (Wilson, p. 53). They are innocently arrogant, know it all, invincible, and can ride alone. They are counter phobic. They take risks to the brink, drink too much, &c. They are absorbed with other people, causes, activities, and theoretical positions. In short, adolescence is a time of heightened narcissism.

Most adolescents nevertheless get by--and through--on a core of well-being they have built up from the largely positive and affirmative parental love of childhood.

Vulnerable adolescents lack such a secure inner core. Such persons are fearful and helpless in the face of what may happen to them next. They lack confidence and feel betrayed by those they have idealized.

They are inclined to withdraw from social interaction, fortifying themselves in grandiose or idealising fantasies which in turn serve to isolate them further from others. They build in effect an inner world of certainty and perfection which they struggle to protect at all costs against any incursion (Wilson, p. 54).

This withdrawal can become so extreme as to include insulation within an encapsulated inner world, completely consumed by private matters and fantasies, and embroiled in solitary activities.

Their lives become set, stuck and very lonely. They effectively hole themselves up in self-created fortresses and quite actively, often violently fend off any threat of encroachment. Their self-imposed isolation of course is not absolute; it occurs in the proximity of others who are inevitably concerned. It functions both to defy and to torment those who are around—and paradoxically to call forth the very influence it seeks to resist (Ibid, p. 55).

THE COUPLE

A central problem in all relationships concerns the times when one partner or the other is more focused on him or herself and his or her own issues than on the relationship. The capacity to tolerate this tension is critical.

In less mature interactions, the separateness of the self and the other is not recognized.

Thus failures in the relationship will tend to be characterized by either (1) an inability to establish and maintain a meaningful relationship or (2) a highly fused and essentially undifferentiated relationship (Ruszczynski, p. 65).

Bion (1957), echoing Freud, held that attraction in the couple essentially comes from an unconscious acceptance of the other's projections. Thus parts of the self are located in the other and carried by that person. This allows for processing and a gradual reclaiming of these parts in a more mature fashion. The couple, thus, daily acts out the conflicts and self issues of each person in the relationship itself.

Ruszczynski (Ibid) went so far as to claim:

> The love relationship may be said to be a form of transference relationship, with internal object relations substantially shaping the nature of the couple's interaction with each other.

Freud (1914) differentiated between intimate relationships that were what he called analytic and those he called narcissistic. The basic difference is this. In analytic relations, one's focus is on the external object (person) and on the impact of this external element on one's life. In narcissistic relations, one's focus is on the internal significance or consequence the relationship has.

In loss, if the object is lost and one's world is significantly diminished as a result, such a loss is called analytic (i.e., external loss). If the focus on the loss is regret at the personal prices that must be paid, or a destruction of a part of the self that the object was carrying, the loss is called narcissistic (internal loss).

Klein (1952) held the infant experiences in the mother a satisfying good object and a frustrating bad object. The impulses felt as a result of this are projected onto the mother and then internalized as the nature of the object introjected. As a result of these early object relations, subsequent relationships are similarly colored.

Her stress on projective identification (1946, 1955) increases understanding of how this might happen. Given the projection of parts of the self as well as the acting in accord with these projected parts on the part of the other, it is easy to see that when the subject relates to the object he/she is really related to parts of him/her self. Aspects of the other that do not fit the projections may be ignored, attacked, or withdrawn from.

The result is a relationship primarily with the self-mediated through another person.

Ruszczynski argued:

The interesting clinical question in relation to the couple is whether the committed couple relationship institutionalises the pathological psychic structure, or whether the more healthy part of the couple, even when the relationship is primarily under the dominance of paranoid-schizoid anxieties, defenses and object relations, allows for some psychic work to take place in the relationship which neither individual could manage alone (p. 68)

.

Chances are, however, the couple together--or one member of the couple--will possess more healthy personality elements which will act to modify and develop more mature interaction styles for both members than either member has experienced before (prior interaction styles were likely acted out in terms of primitive object relations).

The worst outcome, on the other hand, might be described as projective gridlock. Here, there is an inability to move beyond earlier introjects to reality testing and interactions with present partners instead of past experienced realities.

A similarly destructive problem was highlighted by Balint (1968). He argued that the connection problem between the subject and object often could be understood in terms of the subject's realization of its dependence on the object as well as the object's separateness. These realizations can lead to destructive envy leading to disintegration and/or hatred.

Heinmann (1952) argued:

> The essential difference between infantile and mature object relations is that, whereas the adult conceives of the object as existing independently of himself, for the infant it always refers in some way to himself. It exists only by value of its function for the infant (p. 142).

Actually this above described tension within an individual between a more narcissistic and more mature mode of relating is present in all individuals. We all shift between more primitive defenses having to do with fear of incorporation and hurt to more mature worries about ambivalence and real concern for the other. The narcissistic pattern is to be "trapped" in the more primitive position.

NARCISSISTIC DISPLACEMENT IN CHILDBEARING.

Healthy narcissism is fostered by the parent's use of empathy and mirroring (Kohut, 1977; Winnicott, 1967).

Pathological narcissism is fostered by the parent's unresponsiveness that leads to the child's ego-depletion.

Parental fantasies of the child and parenthood also play a central role.

Most parents have many kinds of fantasies about the unborn child and its relationship to their lives that, once the infant has been born, must gradually give way to a "flawed reality."

The pathologically damaging position is when these fantasies overshadow the reality so that the real child is "missed" by the parent in favor of the fantasized child (i.e., the selfobject).

There are several dimensions that might bring on narcissistic type disturbances associated with childbearing.

1. Prolonged failure to conceive.
2. Joint dependency in reproductivity.
3. Conception and creating life from within oneself (good and bad implications).
4. Life and death responsibility.
5. Intrauterine experience and the issue of boundaries.
6. Unconscious return of elements from one's own infancy.
7. Vicarious enjoyment of close contact and intimate care.
8. Active reenactment or "turning the tables."
9. Involving another in one's 'accumulated emotional experience.'

10. Healing opportunities for self overshadow child.

How these and similar factors are managed have important implications for "enhanced or diminished self-esteem and/or overvaluation or devaluation of the child to be (Raphael-Leff, p. 81).

Typically overly narcissistic parental notions tend to fade in light of the reality of the infant, and continue to do so with the birth of subsequent children.

Raphael-Leff, however, claimed:

> When, in spite of the passage of time, a parent cannot conceive of the baby as separate and existing independently from her or him, it becomes apparent that the baby is equated with part of the self..through extensive over-identification or projective mechanisms of fusion, invasion, possession and control, psychic boundaries between the baby and parents are negated and the infant is treated not as a person but as a personification of some aspect of the parental internal world--out there, available for all to see (p. 82).

Here, the baby is not recognized as a person in his/her own right--or special parts of the child are valued excessively, devalued excessively, and consequently wounds of the self are created.

Thus only "special" aspects of the child might be valued at the expense of the rest, there may be a specific age at which the child loses his or her appeal and is replaced by another, or symbiosis or boundary violation that may persist beyond infancy.

This is also seen when the child is treated as a being with no existence but what I give it, as a person who can have no needs/initiative of its own because it is me, as one with the same feelings as me (I am feeling hungry, so you must be fed), a zero-sum interaction (If you eat, I go hungry).

The parents' pride and narcissistic enhancement over the child can constitute a exhibitionistic gratification and the developing infant can form a representation of the parents' ideal self. The parental influence here may even go so far though selective responding to attempt to actualize the child of his or her desire (rather than responding to the real child).

The reverse of the coin is the child may be considered to be a messianic force that has come to take over and destroy the lives of the parents. When the child fails to develop in the expected direction or to follow the expected format for being a person designed by the parents, the child may be blamed in narcissistic fashion for the disappointment and flatness that enters the parents' lives.

The child may be used entirely as a reflecting selfobject (see Kohut). ("She's only two, but she's so sensitive she can read my mind.") "The baby's function is merely to feed back gratitude and admiration, boosting parents' views of themselves as ideal providers (Raphael-Leff, p. 85)."

The extreme case is when the child is treated as a replacement baby who is allowed to have no needs beyond those possessed by the earlier child.

A particularly crippling pattern is established when the parents prevent the child from experiencing mitigating counter-experiences from outside the family (i.e, the child is held as in a cult, a fundamentalist system, or [even] an analytic institute).

Unwanted or damaged aspects of the parental selves may be exported to the child who is then expected to function as a container for these split off parental aspects. The parents thus can be seen as superior and as bountiful sources of all goodness, bravely guiding and protecting the defective child.

Intergenerational patterns of narcissistic distortions are often repeated when the child, treated as parental property, inhibits both personal needs and resourcefulness... Many...ascriptions of parental narcissism are absorbed into the forming identity of the child to become unquestioned features of her or his own self-image. (Raphael-Leff, p. 85, 87).

The consequence of this is the child may feel "one day" I will get my turn and be able to be rescued, noticed, compensated, loved for my past deprivations. Or some "magical event" will come along to save me and transform my life from the bondage in which I now live. Or I will make huge achievements and then everyone--even my parents--will have to acknowledge me. Or I will "make good" the sacrifices of my parents.

The list goes sadly on....

NARCISSISM AND AGING

Growing old often involves experiences of shame, humiliation, and narcissistic injury.

Adolescents are famous for their worries over whether or not "others" will like my body. This worry re-appears, it seems, in the elderly.

The grave danger here is that interpersonal relationships may lose the investment of libido that is increasingly required to maintain the self.

People with more narcissistic structure are more at risk for serious esteem assaults during the aging process.

NARCISSISM AND BEREAVEMENT.

Common manifestations of grief in our culture include: hallucinations, somatic disorders, delusions, and narcissistic regressions with increased dependency, vulnerability, anxiety, insecurity, and extreme withdrawal symptoms.

There has been an explosion of research on attachment and loss.

In Mourning and Melancholia (1917), Freud distinguished between mourning, which is normal, and melancholia (chronic depression), which is not. The difference is that in melancholia the object loss has been lost from consciousness. Mourning, on the other hand, is entirely conscious.

As a result of this distinction he reasoned psychotherapy was inappropriate for melancholia.

Allingham (1952) claimed:

Mourning is not forgetting...it is an undoing. Every minute tie has to be untied, and something permanent and valuable recovered and assimilated from the knot. The end is gain, of course. Blessed are they that mourn, for they shall be made strong, in fact. But the process is like all human births, painful, long, and dangerous.

Further, there is always a strong sense of regression in mourning which is narcissistic and entirely normal.

Thus there are a tumult of oscillating emotions and states that must be passed through by the person in mourning. It is for this reason "stage theories" of grief are so inadequate. These imply the sequential negotiation of each stage before passing to the next. The reality is far more chaotic.

The problem with the narcissistic individual is his or her hanging on to the lost object in an attempt to preserve it out of a need for control.

The most severe experiences involve the death of (1) a parent, (2) a spouse, (3) one's child. This is so as the experience of mirroring is central to these attachment relationships.

In order to complete mourning one must separate from the lost object. To do so requires one to be able to see what parts belong to the lost object and what parts belong to oneself. One must let go of the former and retain the latter.

Attachment patterns are critical in mourning. The pattern of the attachment with the primary object (individual) influences the ability to form subsequent attachments. For example, securely attached individuals are able to relax into the dimensions of the relationship and not feel undue distress. Insecurely attached individuals, on the other hand, have difficulties in relationships.

> Insecure attachment can result in the person remaining narcissistic, because narcissism is essentially a problem of separation (Danbury, p. 104).

Ainsworth (1991) stated that: "...the first step towards establishing an affectional bond is made with a secure attachment." An affectional bond is a relatively long lasting tie in which the other is an important person "interchangeable with no other (Danbury, p. 105).

It is clear that the question of whether or not to offer psychotherapeutic help to a grieving person depends on an assessment of his or her attachment and loss history.

With the loss of a loved one, huge narcissistic wounds are opened. The loss of the mirroring object produces narcissistic rage.

> For adequate grieving to take place, the narcissistic elements in love have to be shed. Those who really love have a part of themselves dying with the deceased and have to

integrate the dead part within themselves and get into a new relationship with the dead person (Bowlby, 1980) so that reinvestment in life can take place...(Danbury, p. 106).

When working with grieving persons it is important to stress that mourning is not a steady progression toward "recovery" but a series of fluctuations over a wide range of feelings and levels of adjustment.

THERE IS NO 'NORMAL' LENGTH OF TIME FOR GRIEVING.

"There is no such thing as recovery from bereavement; one learns to live with it and through it, gradually adapting to the changed circumstances (Danbury, p. 112)."

Narcissistic individuals always seem to get hung up at the point of "what this has done to me."

If mourning is too painful to face, it may become displaced and channeled into chronic depression or a series of somatic complaints.

It is interesting that Freud stressed the withdrawal of ALL investment in the lost object, in order to be able to reinvest in a new one.

THE SEARCH FOR THE PRIMARY OBJECT.

Persons with high degrees of narcissism have a constant need to attack the therapeutic relationship. The primary symptoms seen are futility and despair. And since they cannot internalize anything, their lives seem constantly empty. The therapist will be able to feel directly the patient's avoidance of the transference, and it is the therapist who will have to carry the despair of the failure to make contact (Steiner, 1993).

Such persons have high expectations to receive and therefore constantly feel disappointed. They cannot give anything, as this would deplete them.

It may be said the "narcissistic patient pushes ruthlessly in search of a primary object. That is there is a constant search for the connection with the primary object that was not successfully achieved in actual childhood. Hence, such persons are always on a search.

The transference therefore will not be an object transference as with more neurotic patients. The analyst will not be asked to be a person but to serve a function (i.e. serve as a selfobject).

In short "they cannot tolerate any recognition of separateness between self and object. This would lead to feelings of intense anxiety about dependency (Cooper and Maxwell, p. 119, see also Rosenfeld. 1965)."

These sorts of relationships are constructed over a long period of time during disrupted object relationships during early childhood. Kahn (1963) posited a series of cumulative traumas.

The experience of the mother includes the provision of contact and warmth. The need to find a proper kind of warmth persists for narcissistic individuals. There is a constant search for "just the right degree of connectedness." The mothers of such patients have not been there to provide the right degree of physical contact.

After birth it is essentially to preserve the right amount of physical proximity.

This is why narcissistic patients are searching for warmth and perfect understanding. That is to say, the analyst must provide the patient a link with the primary object. Hence the analyst must possess a naturally warm attitude coupled with a reasonable degree of involvement--rather than the cold, authoritative, "expert," stance of the medical model.

Such patients may be seen as being in the position of children forever. They must constantly act out the scenario of merging and breaking. The danger for the analyst is that early infant holding is exhausting. He or she must realize the patient is stuck, not oppositional. When the patient is stuck, something in the analytic situation must be changed.

Narcissistic patients will resist seeing the basic fault in order to protect the primary object.

It is likely the greatest gain comes from an emotional experience that is shared than through interpretations and other "goal directed" work. Shared experience includes the mirroring transference.

But the prognosis for change in these patients is poor, regardless of the level of the therapy. Through all destructive attacks, the patient is searching for connection. Thus the search for attachment is more important than the concept of regression.

NARCISSISM AND PERVERSIONS (i.e., symptom formation).

These symptoms are the result of disruptions in the earliest years of life. Typically the damaged or absent maternal object must be replaced by a fantasy object that is felt to be "entirely under the control of the subject (Morgan, p. 137)."

For example, a toddler may suck his thumb as a replacement for the breast--and be soothed. This is an autoerotic experience that is completely under the control of the subject.

Pathological narcissism as manifested in the perversions occurs where the need to have absolute control over the object has been so great that the equivalent phantasy of the thumb, the rubber fetish, for instance, becomes idealized...There is enormous hostility against any awareness that life and goodness lie outside the self (Ibid, pp. 138-139).

To acknowledge there is a source of gratification outside the self is equal to admitting a limitation in the self.

Any recognition of separateness between self and gratification and dependency upon another for that gratification is strictly defended against at whatever cost.

In extreme cases cruelty and hate are displayed against the object in the service of avoiding awareness of envy and dependency.

The denial of the other as being the source of love and comfort leads the patient to act destructively. This destructiveness is a defense against the knowledge of the need for love. The more this knowledge has to be destroyed, the more the other has to be enslaved, marginalized and, in the final scenario [even] killed (Ibid, p. 140).

In the perversions the goal is to eradicate any knowledge of need for the other. Good aspects of others are recast as parts of the self--over which one might have complete control. These are often the sequelae of early narcissistic wounds and are in the interests of survival to the degree that this survival of the self comes before anything or anyone else. The other can thus only be seen as a vehicle in this project, not at a real person.

ADDICTION: NARCISSISTIC CONTROL OVER THE OBJECT.

The psychotic attempts to alter reality whereas the addict attempts to alter his own consciousness so as to avoid disturbing affects.

> Early adolescence is a time when excitation, tension, gratification and defensive issues relating to previous years, that is, during the psychosexual development of infancy and early childhood, return. This infantile admixture is responsible for the bizarreness and regressive character of adolescent behavior. Adolescence could be considered the second edition of childhood (Good, p. 149).

Early adolescence involves the severing (decathexis) early object ties. Development of visions and morals independent of the parental structure occurs.

Narcissism is seen at this juncture in the child who is unable to give up the gratifying parent upon whom the child has depended rather than developing his/her own resources.

For some the need to control affect in the service of preserving a narcissistic state is of utmost importance.

It is for this reason some addicts are able to grow out of their addictions by developing an ability to tolerate, at least somewhat, depressive anxieties--rather than keeping negative affects projected onto others and the surround.

Fenichel (1945) felt that persons who are able to severely weaken or give up all object libido are persons who have never esteemed object relations very highly. Such persons typically have a passive, narcissistic aim that is entirely focused on their own gratification, never in satisfying the personalities of their partners or in the specific personalities of their partners.

Some can tolerate relationships only if there is some area of their lives that is split off and hidden from the rest of the world where they can "re-enact the need for mastery over the object (Good, 152)."

In severe addicts, separation may be experienced as deadly.

Others experience an intense fear of change as change requires letting go of the familiar and a movement into the unknown (where one will lack the valued control).

Many addicts display an uncanny talent for deception. They display what Winnicott (1960) called the "false self" ("the false self brings the true self to therapy").

It is in these secret worlds that the person's narcissism is indulged and contained. These are typically hidden from everyone, even the therapist.

Fairbairn (1952) held that ambivalence is a reaction to deprivation and frustration.

In describing a patient, Good stated:

> Clearly he could not tolerate not being the center of attention. His destructive attacks manifested themselves at times when his wife's narcissism was heightened and she had less energy available for him. He felt left out when she was planning 'her' wedding and when she was pregnant with 'her' baby. He could not tolerate not being the special one (p. 154).

4. DEVELOPMENT AND TREATMENT OF THE FALSE SELF

[Originally: TRANSFERENCE DILEMMAS, PART III: THE FALSE SELF. Lecture presented for the Intermountain Private Practice Association, University of Utah Neurophysiatric Institute, April 16, 1997.]

DEVELOPMENT

To begin, I want to read a fairly involved quotation. This, in my opinion, outlines the problem fairly clearly:

A critical requirement for the child's attainment of individualized selfhood is the presence of caregivers who are reliably able to recognize, affirm, enjoy, and pridefully treasure the unique affective qualities [i.e., "real feelings"] and independent aspirations of the child. When a parent cannot recognize and affirm the child's central qualities and strivings because they conflict with the parent's own self-organization requirements, then the child's self-delineating efforts will be seriously compromised.

The derailment of the self-differentiation process occurs when central affective states associated with the emergence of individualized selfhood are consistently not responded to or are actively rejected. A fundamental psychic conflict thereby becomes enduringly established between the requirement that one's developmental course must conform to the emotional needs of the caregivers, and the inner imperative that its evolution be firmly rooted in a vitalizing affective core of one's own (Stolorow, in Wolf and Kutash, 1991, pp. ix, x).

[Sources quoted below use the pronoun "him" to refer to both males and females. It is too cumbersome to change every quotation I have used, some of which can be quite involved. Please bear with me.]

Three basic options present themselves for the child outlined above:

[1] The child may "abandon or sacrifice central feelings in order to maintain indispensable ties. This is the path of submission and chronic depression, as the child feels compelled to "become" what the parent requires and thus to subjugate any striving to develop according to his own separate design (Ibid, p. x).

What such a child does in this situation is to develop a "submerged self" (i.e., "submerged real self"). This is covered with what Winnicott (1960) called the "false self." Such an adjustment, as Alice Miller (1979) pointed out, serves the needs of the parent at whatever cost to the child's "authentic experience."

[2] The child may attempt to preserve and protect his core of individualized vitality at the expense of emotional ties by adopting a pattern of resolute defiance and rebellion. This is the path of isolation and estrangement... (Ibid).

This approach is carried out, according to Kohut (1984) in the service of "psychological survival."

[3] a life of restless, tormenting ambivalence, of being endlessly torn between inner aspirations and needed relationships that seem irreconcilably opposed. This is the path of wrenching indecision and non-commitment (Ibid).

There is, of course, a fourth option that is a combination of all above patterns into one.

Here, the primary, or "core" personality is submerged and replaced by two elements: the compliant and approved false self as well as a negative, rebellious self, whose mission it is to prevent the false self from taking over the identity completely. Further, the individual endlessly oscillates between these two poles, never able to crystallize, it would seem, a solid identity.

Such an adjustment is a kind of inevitable "product of a basically defensive adaptation to a narcissistically exploitive parent, usually the mother (Ibid.)."

Stolorow, (1991) emphasized:

Essentially, the child perceives that any expression of his own distinctness that frustrates the mother's need for him to serve her self-extension results in the loss of her love. In the hope of regaining that love, he submerges his offending feelings and aspirations-that is, his "true self"-and becomes the compliant "pseudo- self" in harmony with his mother's narcissistic needs. However, since such subjugation threatens the child with self-extinction, he [or she] develops a second pseudo-self characterized by compulsive rebellion that serves to counteract the compliance (Ibid, pp. x, xi).

The rebellion that is developed may, of course, be either overt or covert (i.e., active or passive). Such a complex pattern likely is constructed on top of originally correct perceptions about the mother-child interaction.

Why is it usually the mother?

It isn't always the mother. Still, the mother, or mother surrogate, is typically the primary symbiotic object and also who is the one who is responsible for the majority of essential infant care. She, therefore, is the person in intimate terms of whom, the developing personality establishes the basics of adjustment.

The mother in such cases (or mothering figure) reacts to her infant child's needs to express his or her own genuine feelings whatever they may be--as well as need to pursue a path of his or her own—with:

> "...disregard or by looking and feeling wounded or disconcerted. She indicates by word or gesture that he [or she, i.e., the child] ought not to feel as he does but to feel as she feels. She then punishes him for his transgression by giving him the silent treatment for being, in her view, deviant (Wolf and Kutash, 1991, 11)."

Such a mother is actually afraid she will lose the child or that her fragile adjustment will be exposed. The child's life literally becomes that of a sacrificial object.

The fathers of such persons are either incapable or unavailable to neutralize the mother's effects on the child. It is mother who runs things.

An addition to the countless personal problems created by the need to maintain a submerged self are endless problems such an approach creates with relationships. Perhaps chief among these is a fundamental inability to trust. Thus, in a very crucial way, such individuals maintain a fierce need to be alone in the sense that they simply cannot bring themselves to reveal themselves fully to another.

Tragically, such a pattern persists and becomes a characteristic of relationships outside the home as well; it, in fact, comes to be a characteristic mode of interaction that continues in adulthood.

Such a pattern with typical certainty, thus, finds a circle of friends, acquaintances, and lovers with similar adjustment problems. These people also feel (superficial) interactions are normal-or at least all that could possibly occur.

Thus, people who display such patterns have learned (falsely) that "the sham sells." When it doesn't, after all, there is something wrong with others.

People who due to different histories are quite comfortable in revealing (greater portions of) themselves will likely become frustrated, bored, or somewhat tangentially associated with those who maintain such constant "pseudo-disclosure."

Technically, what occurs here is that the submerged person projects the negative mother (i.e., the punishing mother) onto everyone and then behaves as if the rules in the present situation with others are the same as the rules in childhood.

Thus the image portrayed by such individuals is the image he or she believes others want to see. (This is for sure what was demanded in childhood.) Such an image may be over controlled and in-charge, highly creative, idiosyncratic, or even rebellious.

Thus, through the mechanism of *projective transference*, the patient "misperceives present-day figures as if they were persons in his [or her] past (Ibid. p. 68)."

In projective transference, the significant person or persons from one's past is/are projected onto present-day acquaintances who, it is thought, will certainly judge one and react to one just as past persons did.

Through the related mechanism of *intorjective transference*, the patient interprets the self as being identical to persons in his or her past and acts accordingly. A ubiquitous variant of this is that the parental "voice" is introjected, so through the mechanism of inner dialogue or the "head voice," one constantly tells oneself the same messages that significant persons delivered in the past.

The net effect of both these developments is that one is continually surrounded by one's childhood, able to live forever in that childhood environment, and employ the strategies that worked there. This interferes with living in the present context, the present reality. It is, if you will, a profound failure of individuation and thus the capacity to become a functioning and mature individual.

Needless to say such people tend to be unhappily "married and remarried and remarried (Ibid, p. 14)."

Persons with pseudo or submerged selves tend to be quite quickly drawn to examples of warmth with the hope those examples will treat them as would the longed--for supportive parents. If the warmth and affection is maintained, the individual involved will likely feel a childlike sort of bliss--for a while. But the infantile nature of such a response will slowly become clear to others that will tend to distance any but a similarly trained partner.

When two submerged persons marry, each functions, blissfully, as the projected ideal mother--for a while.

Soon, however, (and inevitably) the other transforms into the hated bad mother who denies love, devotion, and attention.

Still, submerged persons routinely appear to others as "sincere and genuine people."

Men who illustrate this pattern usually do well with women as they are quite compliant as well as wanting to be idealized love objects to women, but they soon end up unable to endure the responsive love received as this is typically seen as a demand for love and attention. Such persons tend to be personally vulnerable but publicly invincible. Such men are often morbid boasters. Severe identity uncertainties are common, though shielded, including sexual perversions. Men of this pattern tend to be demandingly dependent on a long succession of women. Secretly, in his submissiveness, however, he feels unmanly.

The severity of the disorder depends upon how much the mother allowed the child to live on his own, that is, upon what the parent demanded or imposed. (For example, was TV monitored, friends screened, &c?)

Women displaying the pseudo or submerged pattern live in chronic fear of abandonment, yet are repeatedly "stunned by failure to win the love of a mother surrogate (ibid, p. 17)." Such a person's theory is that love redeems. Loved she can love in return. But her love usually resembles an obsession. Thus she lives a life of love and loss. Such people are actually children living as adults. Quite bluntly, she is her mother's prisoner-and is always referring to her. It is quite possible, bonded to her mother's distorted views of her father, she has learned to see the problem is due to him, not her. She may intensely, therefore, fear or dislike men. Thus the men in her life are really projected mothers, and she can only display her feelings more or less openly when away from her husband.

"She is manifestly a conformist but with vast stores of anger (Ibid, p. 19)." She may be seen to be in a deep conflict whether to be charming or cruel. Nevertheless, she is always trying to get her own way, often under a cloak of submissiveness. In fact, she may be seen as an essentially phallic woman who keeps emerging to victimize others.

Further phenomena that may be traceable to the submerged pattern include: procrastination, stuttering, difficulty concentrating, gambling, ADHD, psychosomatic symptoms, among others.

Persons displaying such pseudo patterns, nevertheless, may function reasonably well in situations such as: political office, the clergy, various forms of religious fundamentalism, even in professional fields-including psychology and psychiatry!

Actually it may be said that the notion of the false self is really not the problem of *our* time; it is the problem of *all* time.

TREATMENT

Clearly liberation of the real self is the goal of treatment here. Technically one wants to be able to "effect introject dispersion (Ibid, p. 51)."

What the patient has done, as we all do to one degree or another, is to introject the nature of the relationship with the primary caregiver (i.e., the object relation). This, then, becomes the basis in terms of which all interactions, the self, and others are forevermore interpreted (albeit erroneously).

Thus one wishes as a therapist to create a different sort of environment that will allow for progression in ego development.

Clanging off of a famous statement by Freud, the goal may be summed up as: "Wo es war, soll ich werden." (Where IT was, shall I be.)

It is important to assess who or what was the pseudo development originally for? Parents? Society? Others?

If the repressed real self can finally emerge it may be able to discover who it is. This allows patient and therapist to encounter a different sort of experience from the one that the patient experienced growing up (i.e., accepting and encouraging rather than punitive and demeaning).

This is accomplished not by the therapist attacking the false or pseudo self, but upon creating the conditions in terms of which the patient feels (more or less) safe to emerge.

Thus the ideal therapist will be capable of maintaining an effectively neutral stance. The therapeutic attitude that is important is the one that can (genuinely) say: "You can do whatever you want, but this is what you are doing."

That is, a genuinely nonjudgmental environment is essentially critical.

Such patients have long learned to respond in response to perceived threat. Further, the patient will have a long history of projecting his or her pseudo or false selves onto others. Thus, such projection will definitely occur in interaction with the therapist.

Long imprisoned by his or her conformity or compulsive rebellion, the patient has become blind to his or her submission and helplessness on the one hand and/or his or her sadism and exploitive tendencies directed toward others on the other. This results in an abuse of power that is actually directed toward the real self as well as others.

Obviously to heal, the patient must be able to separate from both the parents and also from whatever bias the therapist's views of him or her may contain.

In order for this to happen, the therapist must respond to the submerged or real self rather than to the false or pseudo selves that are on public display.

Responding to the surface, or what is apparent, is to ensure the patient is able to move nowhere, having encountered another instance of his or her childhood.

When the therapist is successfully able to focus on the real submerged self rather that the apparent or displayed self the patient is allowed to experience a totally new situation. He or she must not be compliant in order to be accepted! Imagine!

One can be the truly rotten kid one actually is rather that the compliant phony that one was assigned to be (the self which, further, was liked better.)

Thus the therapist must not unwittingly function as either the primary or secondary parent (i.e., supporting or punishing).

In this sense, all recovery in psychotherapy is firmly based on nonconformity. (Nonconformity is notT rebellion, which is actually the activity of the secondary false self.)

When the treatment combination is effective, patients are able to stop hiding and begin to openly express the rage they feel toward parents.

The problem is, this rage is typically first directed toward the therapist. The therapist simply must be able to tolerate this rage as appropriate (something the parent who caused the wound clearly could not do).

If this occurs, the patient can begin to be more genuine, more plain speaking, relaxed, and uncertain than before.

The submerged real self will not dare to show itself until sustained expressions of repressed hostility have been well received.

This is true as the patient will fear that the therapist will respond negatively as the parent would have done.

Only when the self is experienced as allowed-as it has not been allowed before-will elements which dared not be expressed begin to find a voice.

Again, the therapeutic trick is precisely not to display the same pattern the parents displayed in the child's formative years.

Thus the therapist must be a different sort of creature (i.e., more developed and thus less self-focused or narcissistic than the effective parent was).

If the therapist has an agenda for the patient (either known or unknown), the therapy situation will likely duplicate the essential character of the home experience.

Thus the patient will likely feel he or she is in known surroundings (and either compliant or rebellious) or waste a lot of time getting nowhere.

SPECIFIC CONDITIONS

DEPRESSION: Problems of the false self may be initially manifest as depression. Such patients describe their lives as being "empty." Often strict fathers and guilt inducing mothers are described. These were usually compliant children whose genuine selves have long lived in terms of being alone, withdrawn, and isolated. There is often an extremely low frustration tolerance (due to intense frustration in childhood). Actually, beneath the depressed demeanor there is usually a furious child, who is terrified of his or her own anger.

PARANOID CHARACTERISTICS: These characteristics often develop when the patient as a child was forced to deny his or her own perceptions and abide by the judgments of the parents, especially the mother. A deep and abiding sense of distrust of others ensued with a constant fear of situations that might repeat the parental treatment.

OEDIPAL PROBLEMS: Here the mother typically did not view herself as being separate from the child. Again, under the compliant demeanor, such persons exhibit intense resentment and anger. A continual ambivalence between complying and rebelling tends to drain creative energy.

IDENTITY PROBLEMS: Here the individual has not been able to resolve deep seated Oedipal relationship issues with the parents and thus it has been impossible to identify with either parent. Thus such children were faced with a difficult dilemma. Either they must give up their erotic attachment to the contra-sexual parent, or sacrifice their identity. In addition, either they must give up the specific object of desire for another (i.e., "appropriate" replacement) or give up their desire for it. For example, either the daughter must give up her erotic attachment to the father or give up femininity, or give up her desire for such persons altogether-and substitute a desire for different gendered creatures or some paraphillic development instead. Underlying these problems at root is typically found an intense hatred for the mother.

BORDERLINE PROBLEMS: Here, as in borderline personality disorder, the self did not get a chance to become a coherent entity. The mother was highly inconsistent. What may have been submerged was the split sense of self (the so-called "good me" and "bad me"). In such cases, a high degree of therapeutic structure IS required to help stabilize the split ego. There is likely very little that is submerged in comparison to the split nature of the development.

The goal in treatment of each of these situations is to free the submergence first and then treat whatever emerges as a secondary consideration.

5. THE SELF AND ITS WOUNDS

When a child is consistently required/restricted to function as a selfobject by the parent (i.e., treated as who or what the parent personally experiences or needs the child to be for his or her own economy) instead of being treated as an object by the parent (i.e., as who the child actually is), the experience for the child is often traumatic in a powerfully lasting way. This trauma is typically minimized when an empathic resonance exists between the parent and the child that comprises a mutuality or, in Kohut's words, a profound sense of unity.

The problem is often quickly duplicated when persons who were traumatized as infants in this fashion come into psychotherapy. Such patients may seek an archaic form of twinship "that recreates, the infant-parent traumatizing relationship by imposing on the therapist the function that had been imposed on them as infants (Lee, p. 177)."

Until this archaic twinship is empathically understood, accepted, and adequately explored with the patient, the lasting effects of the early traumatization will not be resolved.

Further, easily the most troublesome countertransference mistake is thought to be when the therapist unwittingly duplicates the parental wound that brought the patient into treatment in the first place. Further, such a wound is actually quite easy to duplicate--for example, the therapist may routinely act as an "expert" who (aside from being problem-less him or herself) knows what is best for the patient!

Many patients who seek psychotherapy seek to establish a selfobject rather than an object transference with the analyst/therapist. That is, such people seek a therapist who will be available to function as a needed source of supplies for a damaged self-representation. Such a therapist would be able to provide an experience the patient was not able to have with his or her own parents (i.e., the "primary object").

Thus, in the selfobject transference, the patient unwittingly needs the therapist to function as a part of the patient's self rather than as a separate external being (object) in his or her own right--and for an extended enough period of time that the experience may be internalized as a introject (transmuting internalization). For example, the patient may need the therapist to empathize and resonate with what he or she is saying instead of acting the way the therapist wants based on the therapist's own impulses.

This need for selfobject functioning that came from Kohut's experience with his patients has been called the most important advance in the development and treatment of psychological life since Freud discovered the importance of the transference itself.

The basic idea is that the child needs the parent to function as a selfobject at crucial times in order to maximize development. When the parent, the therapist, or significant others consistently fail in this selfobject function, the infant, patient, or lover suffers a repeat of prior wounds.

Stolorow and Brandchaft (1987) stated:

When a parent consistently requires an archaic state of oneness with a child...then the child's strivings for more differentiated selfhood become the source of severe conflict and guilt. In such instances the child perceives that his acts of self demarcation and uniquely affective qualities are experienced by the parent as psychologically damaging, often leading to the child developing a perception of himself as "omnipotently destructive" (p. 245).

The parent has to have rather consistently failed at empathic attunement with the child in order for trauma to occur. Thus even a child who has a generally positive experience with the parent may suffer trauma if there is sufficient breach in the empathic attunement between the two.

Grotstein suggested:

There seems to be a field of mutual empathy between child and mother in which each is encouraged and mirrored by the other. That imparts a feeling of self-satisfaction to the infant. Good "mirroring" by a maternal selfobject is probably not enough to make an infant self feel good...The infant must also develop the sense of reciprocity and responsibility--the capacity for care and concern for the mother and the desire to mirror her as well (pp. 175-176).

The absence of this kind of mutuality helps produce a traumatic state.

In a healthy mother-child dyad, "mother and infant mutually influence each other beneficially (Lee, p. 180)." That is mother and child function as mutual selfobjects.

An infant's functioning is traumatic, not from the direction of the interaction, but from the lack of interaction itself. This is a dynamic form of Kohut's "absence" idea. Mutuality helps the infant energize the mother who in turn continues her investment in the infant. Under such a model, what is traumatic is an infant's prolonged functioning as a selfobject for a parent who has no capacity for mutuality, or has a significant temporary inability to respond. The infant's selfobject function for the parent becomes exhausting, burdensome, then traumatic, without a reciprocal selfobject experience with the parent (Ibid).

It is also the case that the mother's functioning as a selfobject for the infant may become burdensome, exhausting and traumatic if the infant is not able to mutually function as a selfobject in return for her.

The danger is much greater for the infant. If the mother has selfobject resources outside the parent-infant dyad, these additional resources can sustain her as she is functioning as a selfobject for the child. The child, however, has no energizing resources outside the parent-child dyad and is therefore more easily traumatized.

Lee argued:

The breakdown of mutuality makes the initial experience of "individualism," the desperate solo efforts of the infant to restore a parent's cohesiveness, traumatic. As long as there is mutuality, an infant is able to function as a selfobject for the parent without feeling exploited, enraged, or traumatized (Ibid.).

Thus it is not the functioning of the child as a selfobject that is pathogenic but when this functioning directly conflicts with his/her own needs and precludes a response to his/her own affective needs.

To the extent mutual selfobject functioning is established and maintained, both parent and infant are able to grow as well as maintain cohesion.

"Trauma consists of "unbearable affects" that result from a failure to establish alternating, mutual responding (p. 181)."

When the child functions as a reparative selfobject for the parent by mirroring or soothing the parent--or is idealized by the parent--the parent is able to function as a selfobject for the infant and a sense of mutuality will be established. This typically happens when the parent lacks other selfobject opportunities and resources. The amount of trauma experienced by the child in this situation will depend on the degree of mutuality involved in the parent-infant dyad.

"Selfobject functions of blame, abuse, and identity, imposed by a parent, generally leave little room for mutuality, unless they are brief and intermittent (Ibid, p. 182)."

On the other hand: "Patients who function as selfobjects of verbal or physical abuse as children are generally hostile, obnoxious persons as adults, full of hatred, and involved in destructive behavior (Ibid, p. 183)." Such people are often forced into treatment when parents, part-

ners, or employers are no longer able to tolerate their behavior. Even so, such patients often experience treatment
as nothing more than verbal abuse.

When the parent imposes identity on the child, "a parent imposes a mantle of unfulfilled parental goals and
ambitions on a child (Ibid.)."

Lee stressed:

> One problem with the imposed selfobject
> of identity concept is that children may
> thrive under such a mantle, while others,
> who have been "pushed" incessantly by
> parents, are traumatized by it. If mutuality
> occurs, then the infant will accept a great
> deal that is imposed. In a similar way,
> blaming, verbal abuse, or even physical
> abuse may not traumatize if there is no sus-
> tained breakdown in mutuality. Such a
> view is similar to the popular notion that
> parents can be demanding as long as they
> are also giving (p. 181).

Actually blame, abuse, impositions of identity and task
all tend to fuse together in practice. It is the lack of mutuality in attunement that is the critical element in creating trauma.

The famous case of Mr. Z underlines Kohut's shift from
an essentially ego-psychology base to his rudimentary

understandings of narcissism that became the foundation of self psychology. Mr. Z was treated as an idealized selfobject by his mother. Her own archaic merger needs prevented him from developing a sense of his own abilities as she routinely usurped the child's abilities into her own.

TWINSHIP TRANSFERENCE

The examples presented by Kohut of twinship depict a child who feels he/she is a twin to the parent. The child "feels a sense of sameness by entering and sharing a parent's world (Lee, p. 183)."

Typically, the twinship transference includes mirroring.

The opposite of this is a child who has been subjugated into a selfobject position by a parent. Later, such children as patients require the therapist to enter and share their world--and they will not bond with a therapist/analyst who cannot/will not. The therapist/analyst's capacity for mutuality is always tested before emotional ties are allowed to form.

If patients were blamed as children, they find something with which to blame the therapist; if abused, they verbally abuse the therapist; if a mantle was traumatically im-

posed on them, they impose demandson how
the therapy proceeds (Ibid.).

In other words, the therapeutic dyad involves a role reversal. The patient treats the therapist as the parent once treated the patient. The assumed reason for this is to provide for the therapist an experience similar to the patient's and allow for the understanding necessary to form the twinship interaction.

To form a healing bond, the therapist/analyst employs mirroring and idealizing responses where there were none before. This is the experience for which the patient has been longing since being a child. It is, if you will, the missing link. With this link in place, the developmental process that was interrupted in the patient's own childhood is allowed to complete itself under more healthy conditions.

This "second outcome," if you will can then function as a "present day resonance" which is an option to the patient's archaic introjects and thus allows the patient to have a different "reference point" for interpreting experience. For example, if the parent did not hear, and the therapist/analyst did hear, the patient's world is different now because it includes the experience of being heard. Being heard is as ordinary and expected as not being heard once was. The patient's self concept can be "one who can be heard" instead of "one who can't be heard."

Based on this sort of experience, the patient can seek for people in the world who hear him/her. This builds a selfobject base in the present that includes the experience of being heard.

The result is nothing less than a different sense of self in a different sense of the world. An entirely new dimension has been opened.

6. DEVELOPMENTAL LEVELS

Character structure is ascertained by considering two different and interacting dimensions: developmental level, and defensive style within that level.

Thus the developmental level assesses the degree of individuation. the pathological level (psychotic, borderline, narcissistic, neurotic/dysfunctional/"normal"). The defensive style describes the type of character involved (obsessive, depressive, schizoid, &c.)

Nancy McWilliams described a friend of hers as holding that the vast study of psychology was unnecessary as he held there were only two categories for people: (1) nuts, and (2) not nuts. She replied that there were actually only two categories for psychologists too: (1) How nuts? and (2) Nuts in what particular way?

Three basic assumptions of Freud have held throughout the history of psychoanalytical thinking. These are:

(1) Current psychological preoccupations reflect infantile precursors.

(2) Interactions in our earliest years set up the
    template for how we later assimilate
    experience by (unconsciously) using
    categories that were present in childhood.
(3) Identifying a person's developmental level
    is a critical part of understanding the person.

Developmental level is strongly reflected in a person's self-other differentiation and type of pathology under pressure.

The therapist must create the conditions for the development of a working alliance with the patient. Many of the issues which are in the way of successful functioning will appear within the context of the working alliance.

When I was trained, there was thought to be a difference between what was called a "symptom neurosis" and a "character neurosis." The basic distinction was between what might be called an untoward or "overreaction" to a specific circumstance versus a long standing characteristic of typical behavior.

In recent years, these two categories have tended to blend together and have increasingly been seen to affect each other. Kohut's famous statement that the problems analysts had been treating no longer existed due to complex cultural shifts illustrates the virtual disappearance of the "neurosis" category from contemporary clinical concern.

Though "neurotic" reactions do occur, increasingly they are seen to operate in the context of an adjustment pattern that is problematical.

Borderline personality occupies a middle ground between neurotic/dysfunctional/normal adjustment level and psychosis.

Such people rarely report delusions and hallucinations and yet they rarely display the relative stability of a character problem at the neurotic/dysfunctional/normal range. When regressions occur, such people may exhibit transient psychotic or psychotic-like episodes.

McWilliams (Ibid.) stated:

> People in a psychotic state seemed fixated at a fused, preseparation level in which they could not differentiate between what was inside and what was outside themselves; people in a borderline condition were construed as fixated in dyadic struggles between total enmeshment, which they feared would obliterate their identity, and total isolation, which they equated with traumatic abandonment; and people with neurotic difficulties were understood as having accomplished separation and individuation but as having run into conflicts between, for example, things they wished for and things they feared, the prototype for which was the oedipal drama (pp. 51-52).

This distinction is fairly current in psychoanalytic thinking with the exception that many schemas have included narcissistic personality between borderline and neurotic functioning levels. The narcissistic person has been able to develop a coherent sense of self, but the self has not been able to interact with the world in any but the most truncated fashion.

Thus persons with a vulnerability to psychosis are seen as psychologically fixated at the issues of the early symbiotic phase. Persons with borderline personality organization are understood in terms of their preoccupation with separation-individuation themes, those with narcissistic structure are seen as struggling with the results of "cold, empathy less parenting." Those with neurotic/dysfunctional/"normal" (NDN) structure are usually construed in more oedipal terms.

NDN persons are currently seen as able to function at a high level of capacity despite some emotional suffering. As a rule, these people primarily rely on the more mature and second-order defenses. Primitive defenses are used less prominently than in more severe pathologies. The presence of primitive defenses does not rule out the presence of NDN adjustment level, but the absence of mature defenses does.

Higher order functioning also includes a more integrated sense of identity, and behavior shows some consistency. The inner experience is of a continuity of self through time. There is a solid connection to reality.

"Typically, the therapist feels no compelling emotional pressure to be complicit in seeing life through a distorted lens (McWilliams, pp. 54-55)."

NDN people exhibit the capacity to engage in what Sterba (1934) called the "therapeutic split" between the observing and experiencing parts of the self.

NDN people typically are capable of establishing a solid working alliance which is the prime indicator of a solid observing ego.

REFERENCES *

Abelin, E. L. The Role of the Father in the Separation-Individuation Process. In Mc Devitt, J.B., and Settlage, C.F. (Eds.) Separation-Individuation. International Universities Press, 1971.

Adler, G. Borderline Psychopathology and its Treatment. Aronson, 1985.

Ainsworth, M. Attachment: Retrospect and Prospect. In Parkes, C. M., Stevenson-Hinde, J. (Eds.) The Place of Attachment in Human Behavior. Tavistock, 1982

Ashbach, C. The Burden of the Other. Lecture. SLVA, 2001.

Aichhorn, A. Wayward Youth. Northwestern, 1984.

Ainsworth, M. D. S., Blehar, M. C., Waters, E., and Wall, S. N. Patterns of Attachment: A Psychological Study of the Strange Situation. Psychology Press, 2015.

Akhtar, S. Broken Structures: Severe Personality Disorders and their Treatment. Aronson, 1992.

Aron, L. The Internalized Primal Scene. In Diman, M. and Goldner, V. Gender in Psychoanalytic Space. Other, 2002.

Atwood, G. and Stolorow, R. Structures of Subjectivity. Analytic Press, 1984.

Bachofen, J.J. Myth, Religion, and Mother Right. Princeton/Bollingen, 1967.

Balint, M. The Basic Fault: Therapeutic Aspects of Regression. Northwestern, 1992.

Bartholomew, K. "Avoidance of Intimacy: an Attachment Perspective," Journal of Social and Personal Relationships," 1990, 7-2, pp. 147-178.

Beck, A. T. and Weishaar, M. Cognitive Therapy. In Freeman, et. al. (Eds.) Comprehensive Handbook of Cognitive Therapy. Plenum, 1989.

Begg, E. Myth and Today's Consciousness. Coventure, 1984.

Beier, E.G. The Silent Language of Psychotherapy. Aldine, 1966.

Benhabib, S. and Cornell, D. (Eds.) Feminism as Critique. Minnesota, 1987.

Benjamin, J. The Bonds of Love, Pantheon, 1988.

Benjamin, J. Like Subjects, Love Objects: Essays on Recognition and Sexual Difference. Yale, 1995.

Benjamin, L. Lecture. University of Utah Neuropsychiatric Institute, 1997.

Bernstein, J.S. The Decline of Rites of Passage in our Culture: The Impact on Masculine Individuation. In Mahdi, L.C., Foster, S., and Little, M. (Eds.) Betwixt and Between: Patterns of Masculine and Feminine Initiation. Open Court, 1987, pp. 135-158.

Bion, W. R. Second Thoughts. Aronson, 1967.

Blankenhorn, D. Fatherless America: Confronting Our Most Urgent Social Problem. Harper, 1996.

Bly, R. Iron John. Addison-Wesley, 1990.

Bretall, R. (Ed.) A Kierkegaard Anthology. Modern Library, 1946.

Brown, S.L. Family Therapy and the Borderline Patient. In Grotstein, J.S., Solomon, M.F., Lang, J.A. (Eds.) Borderline Patient: Emerging Concepts in Diagnosis, Psychodynamics, and Treatment. Vol 2. Analytic Press, 1987.

Bollas, C. The Shadow of the Object: Psychoanalysis of the Unthought Known. Columbia 1987.

Bourlet, M. Nouvelle Revue d'Ethnopsychiatrie, No. 1. La Pensee Savage, 1983.

Bowlby, J. A Secure Base: Clinical Applications of Attachment Theory. Hogarth, 11969/1980.

Bowlby, J. A Secure Base: Parent-Child Attachment and Healthy Human Development. Basic, 1988.

Burkert, W. Greek Religion: Archaic and Classical. Wiley-Blackwell, 1991.

Cahan, D. Hermann von Helmholtz and the Foundations of Nineteenth-Century Science. California, 1994.

Campbell, J. and Moyers B. The Power of Myth. Anchor, 1991.

Campbell, J. The Hero with a Thousand Faces. Princeton/Bollengen, 1949/1972.

Campbell, J. Transformations of Myth Through Time. Harper, 1990.

Campbell, J. The Inner Reaches of Outer Space: Metaphor as Myth and Religion. A. van der Marck, 1985.

Campbell, J. The Hero's Journey. Harper, 1987.

Camus, A. The Plague. Modern Library, 1962.

Cavell, S. Must We Mean What We Say? Cambridge, 1969/2002.

Chan, W. (Trans.) The Way of Lao Tzu. Bobbs-Merrill, 1963.

Chasseguet-Smirgel, J. (Ed.) Female Sexuality. Michigan, 1970.

Chessick, R. Psychology of the Self and the Treatment of Narcissism. Aronson, 1993, 1985.

Chodorow, N. J. Feminism and Psychoanalytic Theory. Yale, 1989.

Connor, P. T. George Battaille and the Mysticism of Sin. Johns Hopkins, 2000.

Cooper, J.C. Chinese Alchemy, Sterling, 1990.

Cooper, J. and Maxwell, N. (Eds.) Narcissistic Wounds. Aronson, 1995.

Copleston, F. A History of Philosophy, Vol. 1-7 II, Doubleday, 1962.

Corneau, G. Absent Fathers, Lost Sons. Shambala, 1991.

Crane, H. The Complete Poems of Hart Crane. Doubleday, 1958.

Demeter. http://greekgodsandgoddesses.net/goddesses/demeter/

Diman, M. and Goldner V. (Eds.) Gender in Psychoanalytic Space. Other Press, 2002.

Dinnerstein, D. The Mermaid and the Minotaur. Harper, 1976.

Dionysus. http://greekgodsandgoddesses.net/gods/dionysus/

Dostoyevsky, F. The Brothers Karamazov. The Modern Library, 1996.

Edgecumbe, R. and Burgner, M. The Phallic-Narcissistic Phase: The Differentiation Between Preoedipal and Oedipal Aspects of Development. In The Psychoanalytic Study of the Child, Vol. 30, 1975.

Edinger, E. The Mystery of the Coniunctio, Inner City, 1994.

Edinger, E. Anatomy of the Psyche. Open Court, 1985.

Eliade, M. Myth and Reality, Harper, 1963.

Eliade, M. The Sacred and the Profane, Harcourt, 1957.

Eliade, M. The Forge and the Crudible, Chicago, 1956.

Eliot, T.S. Fragment of an Agon. http://www.atherden.com/Eliot/fragment.html

Ericsson, E.H. Identity and the Life-Cycle: Selected Papers. In Psychological Issues, Vol. 1, 1959.

Euripides, The Bacchae. Trans. Cacoyannis, M. Meridian, 1987.

Evans, A. The God of Ecstasy: Sex-Roles and the Madness of Dionysos. St. Martins, 1988.

Fabricius, J. Alchemy. Diamond, 1976.

Fairbairn, W.R.D. Psychoanalytic Studies of the Personality: The Object Relations Theory of Personality. Rutledge, 1952.

Fast, I. Gender Identity: A Differential Model. Analytic Press, 1984.

Ferencz, S. Stages in the Development of a Sense of Reality. In First Contributions to Psycho-Analysis. Brunner/Mazel, 1913/1980.

Flax, J. Thinking Fragments: Psychoanalysis, Feminism, and Postmodernism in the Contemporary West. California, 1990.

Foucault, M. The Order of Things: An Archeology of the Human Sciences. Vintage, 1994.

Foucault, M. Madness and Civilization: A History of Insanity in the Age of Reason. Vintage, 1988.

Freeman, K. Ancilla to the Pre-Socratic Philosophers, Harvard, 1962.

Freud, A. The Ego and the Mechanisms of Defense. International Universities Press, 1936.

Freud, S. The Dynamics of Transference. In The Standard Edition of the Complete Works of Sigmund Freud. Strachy, J (Ed.) Hogarth, 1912/1958, pp. 97-108.

Freud, S. The Freud Reader. Gay, P. (ed.) Norton, 1995.

Fonagy, P. Attachment Theory and Psychoanalysis. Other Press, 2001.

Fonagy, P. and Target, M. Psychoanalytic Theories: Perspectives from Developmental Psychopathology. Whurr, 2003.

Foucault, M. The Order of Things. Vintage, 1970/1994.

Foucault, M. Discipline and Punish: The Birth of the Prison. Vintage, 1995.

Fuller, B.A.G. and McMurrin, S.M. A History of Philosophy. Holt, 1955.

Gabbard, G.O. An Overview of Countertransference with Borderline Patients. J Psychother Pract Res. Vol 2, 1993.

Gabbard, G. O. Psychodynamic Psychiatry. Third Edition. APA Press, 2000.

Gabbard, G.O. Long-Term Psychodynamic Psychotherapy. APA Press, 2004.

Gabbard, G.O. and Wilkinson, S. M. Management of Countertransference with Borderline Patients. APA Press, 1994.

Gill, J.D. The Letters of Juliet to the Knight in Rusty Armor. Create Space, 2014.

Gilligan, C. In a Different Voice: Psychological Theory and Women's Development. Harvard, 1982.

Giovacchini, P. L. A Narrative Textbook of Psychoanalysis. Aronson, 1987.

Gitelson, M. On Ego Distortion. In International Journal of Psycho-Analysis, Vol 39, 1958.

Grinker, R. R. Jr., Werble, B., and Drye, R.C. The Borderline Syndrome: A Behavioral Study of Ego-Functions. Basic, 1968.

Gunderson, J.G. Borderline Personality Disorder. APA Press, 1984.

Grossman, W. L. Discussion of Freud and Female Sexuality. Int. Journal of Psychoanalysis. Vol 57, 1976.

Gunderson, J.G., Kerr, J., Englund, D.W. The Families of Borderlines: A Comparative Study. Arch Gen Psychiatry, Vol. 37, 1980

Gustafson, F. R. Fathers, Sons, and Brotherhood. In Mahdi, L.C., Foster, S., and Little, M. (Eds.)
Betwixt and Between: Patterns of Masculine and Feminine Initiation. Open Court, 1987, pp. 159-174.

Hahn, W. K. Shame: Countertransference Identifications in Individual Psychotherapy. Psychotherapy, Vol. 37, No. 1, 2000.

Hamilton, E. Mythology. New American Library, 1942.

Harlow, H.F. Learning to Love. Jones and Bartlett, 1971.

Harnack, A. Outlines of the History of Dogma. Beacon. 1957.

Hartmann H. Comments on the Psychoanalytic Theory of the Ego (1950). In Essays on Ego Psychology: Selected Problems in Psychoanalytic Theory. International Universities Press, 1964.

Hatch, E. The Influence of Greek Ideas on Christianity. Harper, 1957.

Heimann, P. On the Necessity for the Analyst to be Natural with his Patient. http://www.psychoanalysis.org.uk/heimann.htm 1978

Heimann, P. Certain Functions of Introjection and Projection in Early Infancy. In Klein, M., Heimann, P., Isaacs, S., Riviere, J. (Eds.) Developments in Psychoanalysis. Masefield, 1952.

Heimann, P. Counter-transference. British Journal of Medical Psychology. Vol 33, 1960.

Henderson, J.L. Thresholds of Initiation. Wesleyan, 1967.

Henderson, J.L. and Oakes, M. The Wisdom of the Serpent. Princeton/Bollengen, 1990.

Henrichs, A. Changing Dionysiac Identities. In Meyer, B.F. and Sanders, E. P. Jewish and Christian Self Definition. Vol 3. Fortress Press, 1982.

Hill, G.S. Masculine and Feminine: The Natural Flow of Opposites in the Psyche. Shambala, 2001.

Hillman, J. The Soul's Code: In Search of Character and Calling. Random House, 1996.

Hinshelwood, R.D. Countertransference and the Therapeutic Relationship: Recent Kleinian Developments in Technique. http::/www.psychematters.com/papers/hinshelwood.htm

Holmes, J. John Bowlby and Attachment Theory. Routledge, 1993.

Honos-Webb, Laura and Stiles, William. "Reformulation of Assimilation Analysis in Terms of Voices," Psychotherapy, 1998, 35-1, pp. 23-33.

Horney, K. Feminine Psychology. Norton, 1967.

Horowitz, L. Group Psychotherapy of the Borderline Patient. In Hartocollis, P.L. (Ed.) Borderline Personality Disorders: The Conbcept, the Syndrome, the Patient. International Universities Press, 1997.

Horowitz, M.J. Stress Response Syndromes. Aronson, 1992.

Iron John. (Summary.) https://en.wikipedia.org/wiki/Iron_John

Jacobson, E. The Self and the Object World. International Universities Press, 1964.

Jung, C. G. and Kerenyi, C. Essays on a Science of Mythology: The Myth of the Divine Child and the Mysteries of Eleusis. Princeton, 1969.

Kahn, M. M. R. The Privacy of the Self. Hogarth, 1974.

Kahn, M. M. R. The Restoration of the Self. International Universities Press, 1977.

Kavanaugh, P. B. Postmodernism, Psychoanalysis, and Philosophy: A *World of Difference* for the Future of Psychoanalytic Education.   http://www.academyanalyticart-s.org/kava3.html

Keller, R.   Reflections on Gender and Science.   Yale. 1985.

Kerenyi, C. and Jung, C.G.   Essays on a Science of Mythology: The Myth of the Divine Child and the Mysteries of Eleusis.   Princeton/Bollengen, 1949/1978.

Kerenyi, C.   Eleusis: Archetypal Image of Mother and Daughter.   Princeton, 1967.

Kerenyi, K.   Hermes: Guide of Souls.   Spring Publications, 1976.

Kernberg, O.F.   Borderline Personality Organization.   J Am Psychoanal Assoc.   Vol 15, 1967.

Kernberg, O. F.   Borderline Conditions and Pathological Narcissism. Aronson,   1975.

Kernberg, O. F.   Transference and Countertransference in the Treatment of Borderline Patients.   In Object Relations Theory and Clinical Psychoanalysis.   Aronson, (1975) 1976.

Kessler, E.   Flannery O' Connor and the Language of the Apocalypse.   Princeton, 1986.

Kierkegaard, S.   Fear and Trembling and the Sickness unto Death.   Doubleday, 1954.

Kitto, H.D.F. The Greeks. Penguin, 1991.

Kleeman, J. A Boy Discovers His Penis. In The Psychoanalytic Study of the Child. International Universities Press, Vol 20. 1965

Klein, M. Notes on Some Schizoid Mechanisms. Int. Journal of Psycho-analysis, Vol. 27, 1946.

Kohut, H. The Analysis of the Self. International, 1971.

Kohut, H. The Search for the Self. International, 1978.

Kohut, H. How Does Analysis Cure? Chicago, 1984.

Kohut, H. http://www.sfu.ca/~psimpson/kohutppr1.htm#to)

Kohlberg, L. The Philosophy of Moral Development. Harper, 1981.

Kaufmann, W. (Ed.) The Portable Nietzsche. Penguine, 1954.

Lacan, J. The Four Fundamental Concepts of Psycho-Analysis. Norton, 1981.

Langman, P. "White Culture, Jewish Culture, and the Origins of Psychotherapy." In Psychotherapy, 1997, pp. 207-218.

Lasch, C. Haven in a Heartless World: The Family Besieged. Basic, 1977.

Lichtenstein, H. Identity and Sexuality. In: The Dilemma of Human Identity. Aronson, 1977.

Lineman, M. M., Armstrong, H.E., Suarez, A. et. al. Cognitive-Behavioral Treatment of Chronically Parasuicidal Borderline Patients. Arch Gen Psychiatry, Vol 48, 1991.

Lessing, D. Prisons We Choose to Live Inside. CBC Enterprises, 1986.

Levin, J.D.L. Slings and Arrows: Narcissistic Injury and its Treatment. Aronson, 1993.

Little, A.M.G. Myth and Society in Attic Drama. Octogon, 1967.

Leeward, H. Papers on Psychoanalysis. Yale, 1980.

Mahdi, L.C., Foster, S., and Little, M. (Eds.) Betwixt and Between: Patterns of Masculine and Feminine Initiation. Open Court, 1987.

Mahler, M. S., Pine, F., and Bergman, A. The Psychological Birth of the Human Infant. Basic. 1975.

Malcolm, N. Ludwig Wittgenstein: A Memoir. Oxford, 1970.

Maltsberger, J.T. Countertransference in the Treatment of the Suicidal Borderline Patient. In Gabbard, G.O. (Ed.) Countertransference Issues in Psychiatric Treatment. APA Press, 1999.

Marcuse, H. Eros and Civilization. Vintage, 1968.

Masterson, J.F. and Klein, R. Psychotherapy of the Disorders of the Self. Brunner/Mazel, 1989.

Masterson, J.F. and Rinsley, D. B. The Borderline Syndrome: The Role of the Mother in the Genesis and Psychic Structure of the Borderline Personality. Intl j Psychoanal. Vol. 56, 1975.

McWilliams, N. Psychoanalytic Diagnosis: Understanding Personality Structures in the Clinical Process. Guilford, 1994.

McWilliams, N. Psychoanalytic Case Formulation. Guilford, 1999.

Menninger, K. The Vital Balance: The Life Process in Mental Health and Illness. Viking, 1963.

Miller, A. Thou Shalt Not be Aware. New American, 1984.

Miller, A. The Drama of the Gifted Child. New York, 1983.

Miller, A. For Your Own Good. New York, 1983.

Miller, A. Thou Shalt Not be Aware: Society's Betrayal of the Child. New American Library, 1984.

Millon, T. Disorders of Personality: DSM-III, Axis II. Wiley, 1981.

Mitchell, S.A. Influence and Autonomy in Psycho-analysis. Analytic Press, 1977.

Mitchell, S. A. Relational Concepts in Psychoanalysis. Harvard, 1988.

Mitchell, S.A. Can Love Last? The Fate of Romance Over Time. Norton, 2002.

Mollen, P. The Fragile Self. Aronson, 1993.

Money, J. Lovemaps. Irvington, 1986.

Money, J. and Ehrhardt, A. Man and Woman, Boy and Girl. Johns Hopkins, 1972.

Monick, E. Castration and Male Rage: The Phallic Wound. Inner City, 1991.

Neumann, E. The Origins and History of Conscious-ness. Princeton, 1954.

Neumann, E. Depth Psychology and a New Ethic. Shambala, 1990.

Neumann, E. The Great Mother. Princeton, 1991.

Neumann, E. The Child. Shambala, 1990.

Neumann, E. The Fear of the Feminine. Princeton/ Bollingen, 1994.

Nicea. http://www.religionfacts.com/council-of-nicea

Nietzsche, F. The Philosophy of Nietzsche. The Modern Library, 1954.

O'Connor, F. "A Circle in the Fire," in 3 by Flannery O' Connor. The New American Library, 1960.

Ogden, T.H. The Concept of Internal Object Relations. In International Journal of Psycho-Analysis, Vol. 64, 1983.

Ogden, T. H. The Primitive Edge of Experience. Aronson, 1989.

Ogden, T. H. The Matrix of the Mind: Object Relations and the Psychoanalytic Dialogue. Aronson, 1990.

Ogden, T.H. The Analytic Third: An Overview. http:// www. psyche matters.com/papers/ogden.htm 2001.

Osherson, S. Finding our Fathers: The Unfinished Business of Manhood. Free Press, 1986.

Ottaviani, J. and Meconis, D. Wire Mothers: Harry Harlow and the Science of Love. G.T. Labs, 2007.

Pagels, E. The Gnostic Gospels. Vintage, 1981.

Pagels, E. Adam, Eve, and the Serpent. Vintage, 1988.

Pagels, E. Beyond Belief: The Secret Gospel of Thomas. Random House, 2003.

Perkins, J. The Forbidden Self. Shambala, 1993.

Pine, F. Drive, Ego, Object, and Self: A Synthesis of Clinical Work. Basic, 1990.

Rappoport, A. The Patient's Search for Safety: The Organizing Principle in Psychotherapy. In Psychotherapy, Vol 34, 1997.

Reage, P. Story of O. Blue Moon, 1993.

Reichenbach, H. Rise of Scientific Philosophy. California, 1951.

Rilke, R. M. Trans. Leishman, J.B. and Spender, S. Duino Elegies. Norton, 1939.

Robinson, J.M. The Nag Hammadi Library. Harper, 1977.

Rodgers, I.R., Widiger, T.A., Krupp,A. Aspects of Depression Associated with Borderline Personality Disorder. Am J Psychiatry, Vol. 152, 1995.

Rosenfeld, H. Impasse and Interpretation. Rutledge, 1987.

Ross, N. On the Significance of Infantile Sexuality. In Toksoz, B.K. and Socarides, C. W. On Sexuality: Psychoanalytic Observations. International Universities Press, 1979.

Sander, L. Polarity, Paradox, and the Organizing Process in Development. In Call, J.D., Galenson, E., and Tyson, R. L. (Eds.) Frontiers of Infant Psychiatry. Vol. 1. Basic, 1983.

Scharff, J.S. Projective and Introjective Identification and the Use of the Therapist's Self. Aronson, 1992.

Schure, E. From Sphinx to Christ: an Occult History. Kessinger Publishing, 1996.

Schwartz-Salant, N. Narcissism and Character Transformation: The Psychology of Narcissistic Character Disorders. Inner City, 1982.

Scott, W. Hermetica: The Ancient Greek and Latin Writings which Contain Religious or Philosophic Teachings Ascribed to Hermes Trismegistus. Shambala, 1993.

Segal, C. Dionysian Poetics and Euripides' Bacchae. Princeton, 1982.

Segal, H. A Psychoanalytic Approach to the Treatment of Schizophrenia. In Lader, M. (Ed.) Studies in Schizophrenia. Headley, 1975.

Spark. http://www.sparknotes.com/drama/bacchae/summary.html

Steiner, J. Psychic Retreats. Routledge, 1993.

Seinfeld, J. The Bad Object Handling Negative Therapeutic Reactions in Psychotherapy. Aronson, 1993.

Stevenson, J. and Meares, R. An Outcome Study of
Psychotherapy for Patients with Borderline Personality
Disorder. Am J Psychiatry. Vol 149, 1992.

Socarides, C. W. A Unitary Theory of Sexual Perversions. In Toksoz, B.K. and Socarides, C. W. On Sexuality: Psychoanalytic Observations. International Universities Press, 1979.

Stoller, R. J. Observing the Erotic Imagination. Yale,
1985.

Stoller, R. J. Presentations of Gender. Yale, 1985.

Stolorow, R. D. Toward a Functional Definition of
Narcissism. International Journal of Psycho-Analysis,
Vol. 56, 1975.

Stolorow, R.D. and Lachmann, F. M. Psychoanalysis of
Developmental Arrest. International Universities Press,
1980.

Stolorow, R. D., Brandchaft, B., and Atwood, G. Psychoanalytic Treatment: An Intersubjective Approach.
Analytic Press, 1987.

Stolorow, R.D., Orange, D. M., and Atwood, G.E.

Thinking and Working Contextually: Toward a Philosophy of Psychoanalytic Practice. http://www.selfpsycology.org/neutrality/thinking.htm

Strozier, C. Heinz Kohut: The Making of a Psychoanalyst. Other Press, 2004.

Strupp, H. "Some Salient Lessons from Research and Practice," Psychotherapy, 1996, 33-1, pp. 135-138.

Strupp, H. "Research, Practice, and Managed Care." in Psychotherapy, Vol 34, No. 1, 1997.

Suter, R. Interpreting Wittgenstein. Temple, 1989.

Talbot, N. L. Women Sexually Abused as Children: The Centrality of Shame Issues and Treatment Implications. In Psychotherapy, Vol. 33, No.1, 1996.

Taplin, O. Greek Fire: The Influence of Ancient Greece on the Modern World. Atheneum, 1990.

Taylor, T. Eleusinian and Bacchic Mysteries: A Dissertation. Third Edition. Wizards Bookshelf, 1980.

Thilly, F. and Wood, L. A History of Philosophy. Holt, 1957.

Waelder, R. Theory of Psychoanalysis. International Universities Press, 1960.

Waldinger, R.J., and Frank, A.F. Clinicians Experiences in Combining Medication and Psychotherapy in the

Treatment of Borderline Patients. Hospital and Community Psychiatry. Vol. 40, 1989.

Warmington, E. and Rouse, P. (Ed.). Great Dialogues of Plato. Mentor, 1956.

Weinhold, J.B. and Weinhold, B.K. Breaking Free of the CO Dependency Trap. Stillpoint, 1989.

Wells, M. and Glickauf-Hughes, C.. "A Psychodynamic-Object Relations Model for Differential Diagnosis, Psychotherapy Bulletin, 1993, 28-3, pp. 41-48.

Wickes, F. G. The Inner World of Childhood. Sigo, 1988.

Wickes, F.G. The Inner World of Choice. Sigo, 1988.

Winnicott, D.W. The Child, The Family, and the Outside World. Penguin, 1964.

Winnicott, D. W. Playing and Reality. Basic, 1971

Winnicott, D. W. Through Paediatrics to Psycho-Analysis: Collected Papers. Brunner/Mazel, 1992.

Winnicott, D. W. Ego Distortion in Terms of True and False Self. In The Maturational Processes and the Facilitating Environment. Hogarth, (1960) 1976.

Winnicott, D.W. Mirror Role of the Mother and Family in Child Development. In Playing and Reality. Tavistock/Penguine, (1967) 1980.

Wittgenstein, L. Philosophical Investigations. Macmillan, 1953.

Wittgenstein, L. Tractates Logico-Pholosophicus. Rutledge, 1921/2001.

Wolf, E. Treating the Self. Guilford, 1988.

Wolf, E.S. Mutually Mutative Moments in the Psychoanalytic Experience.   http://www.selfpsychology.org/papers/wolf_1999.htm   1999.

Wolf, A., and Kutash, I   Psychotherapy of the Submerged Personality. Aronson, 1991.

Woodman, M. From Concrete to Consciousness: The Emergence of the Feminine. In Mahdi, L.C., Foster, S., and Little, M. (Eds.) Betwixt and Between: Patterns of Masculine and Feminine Initiation. Open Court, 1987, pp.201-222.

Yeats, W.B. The Second Coming. In Ellmann, R. and O'Clair (Eds.) The Norton Anthology of Modern Poerty. Norton, 1973.

Yorke, C. Openness and Rigidity. http://www.psychoanalysis.org.uk/yorke.htm

Zanarini, M.C., Gunderson, JH., Frankenburg, F.R., et. al. Discriminating Borderline Personality Disorder from other Axis II Disorders. In Am J. Psychiatry, Vol. 147, 1990.

Zanarini, M. C., Williams, A.A., Lewis, R.E. et. al. Reported Pathological Childhood Experiences Associated with the Development of Borderline Personality Disorder. Am J Psychiatry. Vol 154, 1997.

Zimmer, H. and Campbell, J. The King and the Corpse: Tales of the Soul's Conquest of Evil. Princeton/Bollengen, 1971.

* NOTE:

References are listed as well as remaining papers and notes have allowed. These lectures were prepared for presentation at the time and not for publication. Despite considerable effort, it is the case that in the twenty years since the early lectures were presented several references have been lost. The author regrets this omission.

ABOUT THE AUTHOR

J.D. Gill is a clinical psychologist at the University of Utah. She is an Adjunct Associate Professor of Psychology, a Clinical Professor of Counseling Psychology, and an Adjunct Associate Professor of Psychiatry in the University of Utah School of Medicine. Dr. Gill maintains a busy practice at the University of Utah.

Dr. Gill has degrees in English Literature, Philosophy, Psychology, and two post docs in psychoanalytic psychotherapy. She studied in the Writing Program at the University of Utah. She has been a practicing psychologist for over forty years and has presented over five hundred seminars, lectures, workshops, and papers. A world traveler, Dr. Gill has actively sought to experience multiple viewpoints and perspectives.